To Know Him
is to
Love Him

Getting to Know God

by
Nicole Ann Mardian

CONTENTS

FOREWORD

It occurred to me recently that I had been spending the last half-century walking with God and that I had no recollection of a time when I did not know him. It was a sobering realization. Since childhood, I had been explaining God to others and found that most people have a benign curiosity, some have no idea what he was like and are too busy to look into it, and a handful of people I have encountered do not believe he exists.

As I have spent decades learning about and personally experiencing who God is, as well as explaining him to others, I realized that it all boils down to one simple thing: who he says he is. Thus, I felt compelled to humbly share who God is by selecting twelve aspects of his distinctly revealed character and delving deeply into each one. I chose to write this book in the format of a personal or group study, therefore each chapter provides Bible verses to read, study questions to answer, Bible verses to memorize, and additional recommended reading. The goal is to get to know God better and to dispel misconceptions, misinformation, and misunderstandings that can shroud who he is. At the end of this book, you will know twelve profound character traits about God and have something historically and experientially concrete to talk about, ponder over, and study further.

To Know Him is to Love Him is an arrow that is intended to point to God's revealed Word, The Bible. As we say in Armenian, The Bible is the *Asdvadz Ashoonch*, the very *"breath of God."* It is the record of how God breathed life into creation and human history, and how he introduced himself to us. Once you have completed this book you will know twelve elements of God's character, however, it is my desire for you to spend a lifetime delving into the Bible, where God's voice will speak to you clearly and distinctly and beckon you to respond.

Embarking upon a journey where I endeavor to introduce God to you is a daunting one. I always enjoy the challenge of a steep up-hill hike, but such trips take much preparation and encouragement to reach the destination. Therefore, I give my deepest thanks to one of my greatest gifts that God has given me: my family. First, I thank my husband, Eric, whose walk with God is an ever-present encouragement to me and whose constructive criticism is well taken. Next, I wish to thank my mother, Pat Bedikian, for her hours spent reading and editing, and her prolific use of red ink. I also thank my children, Alexia and Andre', who have been a ceaseless encouragement to me and a reminder that knowing and loving God is one thing that can be passed down to the next generation. My final thanks are extended to my grandchildren, Weston and Willow. As young children who are already learning about who God is, they joyfully proclaim his name, his power, and his love and willingly respond to him without the slightest inhibition. They already have come to know God early in life and love Him.

Deuteronomy 7:9, *"Know therefore that the Lord your God is God, the faithful God who keeps covenant and steadfast love with those who love him and keep his commandments, to a thousand generations"*

INTRODUCTION

Dena, my coworker, sauntered purposefully into my office back in the 1980s. She had a serious look on her face, and I thought perhaps she wanted me to drop what I was doing and quickly get a graphics project done for someone. She was training me to take her place while she moved on to another job opportunity.

I sensed that Dena was drawn to me. It was easy to befriend her in the chaotic, male-dominated office. Women stuck together here for survival, for confidence boosts, and for overall support in our fast-paced office environment. Dena appeared to others--and to me--young, confident, and forward-thinking. Strangely, she became another person when she was with me. Dena closed the door abruptly, which she knew locked from the inside (after all, this used to be her office). She grabbed a nearby chair and scooted it up near mine and sat down. Then Dawn stared right into my eyes and dropped the bombshell!

"I know you're a Christian!" She stated it in a rather bluntly as if she was quietly telling someone they had a piece of food stuck in between their two front teeth. I began thinking that perhaps I had said or done something in front of others in the office that was alarming or unprofessional. In an office setting it was generally considered "taboo" to appear religious or a "person of faith." Clearly, I had been found out! I just sat there and stared back at her with a weak and unsure smile on my face. When I am nervous, I smile a lot. I imagined everyone in my Marketing Department was now queuing up outside my door as a wrathful mob brandishing flaming torches and pitchforks and would now smash open the door and take me away. On the exterior, I was as cool as a cucumber, though. I thought I was pretty much my own equally young, confident, forward-thinking self, just like Dena. I had sensed early on that she saw something "different" in me that drew her easily into a friendship. We were very much alike on the surface. Underneath, we were very, very different.

"I can tell you're a Christian, Nicole," she reiterated. She still didn't smile; she barely moved a muscle in her fair-skinned face. I just smiled again, because I was momentarily speechless. Dena proceeded to spill her entire life story to me, and some of it wasn't pretty. Some of it was quite alarming, actually, and other things were fairly benign. One hour later, with one of the international sales guys banging on the locked door of my office trying to get in and bug me about another project, I learned everything Dena wanted me, for some reason, to know about her. I didn't see this coming.

Well, being a person of few words, at least at that particular moment, I said, *"Yes, I'm definitely a Christian, Dena."* A little uncomfortable, I continued, *"Thank you for being so honest with me. I didn't know this stuff about you. I'm glad you told me."* It was pretty serious stuff, ugly things, from her childhood, teenage years, unspoken family things, and all of it had become a churning pit in her stomach that she wanted to share with me. Strangely, it reminded me of someone picking up a plate of jumbled spaghetti and just dumping on my head. I wasn't sure how to scrape it all up and do something with it.

She chimed in, *"You're different, I can tell. I felt I could tell you all of this. What do you think?"* It was an awful lot of stuff from the past that explained why a very young twenty-something woman was somewhat aloof, wooden, and overly confident with others around her, yet kept to herself. She had always seemed to be aged beyond her years, and not in a good way. Now I knew why.

I quipped back to her gently, *"Well, I'm pretty humbled that you told me all of this,"* but in my mind, I was thinking that perhaps she wanted to know details about why I was "different," because I was a Christian. I deduced that she saw something —or someone—different in me, something different perhaps than others in her life. She apparently observed—even sensed —that I was strangely set apart and other than the norm in the office. I thought maybe I was just a curiosity, or maybe a rock-like person she could lean on and dump a boatload of bad memories on for comfort.

"I want what you have," she said softly. *"Tell me about it."* She just sat there and looked deeply into my eyes and waited expectantly.

I was floored. If the massive typesetting machine wasn't in the way, I would have keeled over and face planted onto the display of letters and ink arranged neatly across the metal typesetting plate that filled about 1/4 of the room. I took a deep breath like I usually did when I had conversations like this with others. I proceeded to tell her who my God was, what the Bible tells me God is like, and what he has done for me personally. I tried to explain how God's "self" is God the Father, God the Son, and God the Holy Spirit. Sometimes I explained him to others with the analogy of an egg: there is the shell, the egg white, and the egg yolk, yet the entire entity is the egg, yet all parts are distinct and different. I explained that God was always with me and gave me peace, strength, and courage, no matter what the situation. In a nutshell, I emphasized how great, loving, caring, and forgiving God is.

She looked contemplative, intrigued, and satisfied with my answer. From that point onward, our friendship moved to an entirely new level.

* * *

Fast forward to the late 1990s, my husband and I and our two kids met some new neighbors who had moved in next door with two young children. All of them had first names that started with the letter "J," and their last name began with the letter "J." We loved all the "J's" and tried to memorize all of their names quickly in a perky little song. We loved this new family because they were a breath of friendly fresh air after the rude family next door had moved away. That family had behaved abominably and then hopped into their car every Sunday morning and went to church. There had never lived out even a whisper of God's love, neighborliness, or kindness, ever. They reflected the world rather than the amazing God they professed to know. At least the new family that moved in had an interest in being friendly neighbors. We cherished their kind and genuine overtures to us. They were easy to get to know.

The new "J" family was, like ours, a close and loving family. They were a family that wanted to get to know their neighbors beyond just a casual wave and then a press of a button with the garage door closing quickly behind them. They were not a family of any kind of faith or particular religious affiliation whatsoever. They were simply kind, friendly, and approachable because it was part of their personality as a family. Before we could invite them over for dinner, they invited us. And that is where they had an opportunity to know us, and the fact that we endeavored to be a caring, friendly, conscientious Christian family that really, really tried to practice, "*Love your neighbor as yourself.*" (Lev. 19:18, NIV) And, mind you, this wasn't an easy neighborhood to practice this.

As neighbors, we learned first about the "J" family, and we demonstrated our faith in God through neighborliness, friendship, help with projects, and hospitality. We made it a point to show this in our neighborhood through our lives, our friendship, and our day-to-day observable behaviors. These were the things we knew our neighbors would see over the course of their own daily lives, and over the 16 years that we lived in this neighborhood. Neighbors have eyes, and they watch you carefully. We made an effort in our daily, visible lives to reflect the attributes of the God we loved, followed, and served. We tried to make a habit of simply being "*Doers of the Word, and not merely hearers who delude themselves,*" (James 1:22). We knew what that looked like because the previous neighbors had never modeled the God they professed to follow.

One night, about a year later, right after I finished cleaning up the kitchen from dinner, there was an unexpected knock at the front door of my home. It was Jamie, my neighbor. My husband opened the door and saw Jamie, our neighbor, standing there with a serious look on her face. Eric encouraged her to come inside, and I threw the dishtowel somewhere on the counter and motioned for Jamie to sit down on the couch with us. I had no earthly idea what was going on, but Jamie took on an ethereal look on her face as my coworker, Dena, had back in the 1980s the day she burst unexpectedly into my office and spilled the beans. I was going to need a broom and dustpan in a moment because more beans were about to spill.

Jamie just looked at Eric and me with tears in her eyes, and said, *"I want what you have. I want the faith you have. Please share God with me and tell me everything about him. What you have is real."* My heart leaped nearly out of my mouth, and I had a vision of falling face-first on that massive ink coated typesetting machine in my office many years before, when Dena came into my office and nearly said the same thing to me. I thought, *Lord, I literally can't believe this is happening, and this time you're sending someone to knock on my door! This woman is pointedly asking to know you, Lord! Good heavens, you make this so easy!*

Out loud, however, I was a bit taken aback and simply said, *"We're so happy you're here! Well, Let's pray, Jamie. And, let's talk."* That night we simply shared who God is and what he had done for us and others throughout history in sending a savior to reconcile us, declare us righteous, and provide a perfect sacrifice--one final sacrifice--that would repair the broken relationship between us and God. And we told her that God had done all the work; we could do nothing to merit this favor or earn this unconditional love. We assured her that we are all sinners--yes, even Eric and me--and that we were so thankful for God's promised Son's sacrifice on our behalf; he had paid a steep price—unto death—for our sin.

I realized later on that moment that there was a pattern emerging here. People were seeing my family and I live a life that rested on the attributes of God. They saw the joy, the peace, the strength, and the endurance that others lacked. They saw us as a mirror reflecting God's character until they felt they were almost seeing him face to face. This pattern suggested to me that God opened others' eyes to see the genuineness of his love, joy, peace, patience, kindness, goodness, faithfulness, gentleness, and self-control, that heavenly orchard of fruit, God's *Fruits of the Spirit*, that he bestows upon his followers in this ugly world. People were apparently hungry for it! They didn't want me; they wanted my God.

* * *

Over the last fifty years, I have rested on God's real, tangible, and visible attributes, and I have learned to trust them implicitly. I have had God conversations with friends and family who are atheists, agnostics, Bahai, Muslim, Mormon, and Jehovah's Witnesses, to name a few. God wants to be the subject of discussion; he makes sure that I tell my story, even if rattles other's cages. I can only share what I have experienced personally and what history unequivocally records. I can share other people's God-experiences whose lives are visibly different, set apart, and life-changing to others, because of what God has done in their lives.

As we move forward now on a trek through the vast landscape of God's multi-faceted character, I will decrease and he will increase, because this is a book about God and who he has revealed himself to be. He has made himself visible in all created things, within the pages of history, and within the lives of real people. He has desired from the beginning of time to be knowable and accessible.

If you already know God, you will perhaps learn something new or something deeper about his true character and divine nature. If you are seeking to know the God of the universe who created all of us and who revealed himself into human history as the one and only author of it all, you will learn twelve distinct aspects of his character. You will find this book to be a factual, personal, and historical trek through several millennia of recorded history where you will see God's hand at work, not only in the creation, but in the lives of real people.

This book is designed in an easy self- or group-study format. Each chapter ends with study questions, Bible verses for further reading, reflection, discussion, a personal action plan, memory verses, and an outstanding selection of recommended reading by well-known Biblical scholars and authors. Each of the twelve chapters will humbly provide you with a factual journey through Biblical history, brief biographies, and personal experiences that clearly illustrate God's distinct personality and character. He has been actively and intentionally revealing himself throughout history to ensure that he is known.

So, let's put on our spiritual hiking gear, open our eyes and ears, and walk together through a rock-solid path where we can get to know the one and only God that there is. He wants to be known. He desires a relationship. God wants to know you and he wants to know me.

The more I have come to know him the more I love him. It is my hope that you, too, will fall in love with the God who *is* love itself.

Chapter One

AN UNEXPECTED GIFT – GOD'S GRACE

Ephesians 2:8-9 *"For by grace you have been saved through faith. And this is not your own doing; it is the gift of God, not a result of works, so that no one may boast.*

Deep in the heart of each of us is an innate knowledge that someone intelligent and separate from us has orchestrated everything from the vast fabric of the universe to the awe-inspiring intricacies of the human body to the wonderous precision and order of the sub-atomic realm. Our hearts yearn for significance and hunger for understanding of the world around us because human life is the only living thing in this universe with a soul. Because we have a soul, we fundamentally know that a purpose exists for us, and that someone has imputed that to us. Though our doting dog or indifferent cat may cozy up to us for a meal or a gentle pat on the head, they do not desire to know their origin, nor do they search for their purpose and who authored it in the first place. Likewise, our house plants may bend to the light and use energy from the sun in the process of photosynthesis, but our leafy green friends do not have a soul or an intellect, either. They cannot and do not desire to know their creator, nor do they have the intellect to do anything other than what their pre-programmed genetics compel them to do.

People are quite different than anything in the created plant or animal kingdom, and we innately know it. We all know that there is someone out there greater than ourselves, and if we can't find him or her, then we declare ourselves sovereign and the author of our own destinies. The irony of it all is that we will pick up multiple self-help books a year and attempt to learn the true purpose of our lives from another person just like us. Why do we do this? We do this because it is easier to search for our purpose inside of ourselves. It is the fastest short-cut offering the least effort, much like water that flows through paths that provide the least resistance. The self is simply an easier god to develop and to serve than the one who created the complex world around us.

Throughout history, people have always known that there is a creator. Every person bears the stamp of that creator within every single person's soul, conscious intellect, and cells. Some-what like a piece of fine Limoges china in my cabinet which is imprinted with the specific identifying image of its maker, every person has a knowledge deeply embossed within their heart, soul, and mind that there is a God who made them. Our souls are engraved with the very "image" of God because he intentionally designed us that way and left his mark so we know our maker exists. Interestingly enough, every culture, every tribe, and every tiny people group in the most remote corner of the globe knows that there is a creator. The stories may vary, but the premise is the same.

We can either get to know the God who created this limitless universe, or we can create our own. Either way, the soul needs to be satisfied that it has acknowledged a creator because it knows there is one. In the Bible, the Book of Romans, chapter 1, verses 19-23 explains this clearly:

(19) "For what can be known about God is plain to them, because God has shown it to them.
(20) For his invisible attributes, namely, his eternal power and divine nature, have been clearly perceived, ever since the creation of the world, in the things that have been made so they are without excuse.
(21) For although they knew God, they did not honor him as God or give thanks to him, but they became futile in their thinking, and their foolish hearts were darkened.
(22) Claiming to be wise, they became fools,
(23) and exchanged the glory of the immortal God for images resembling mortal man and birds and animals and creeping things."

The ancient world preferred to worship a wide pantheon of gods, all manmade of hand-hewn stone and metal, or they looked up and deemed the sun, moon, and stars—even fire--to be their god. But these are created things therefore they cannot simultaneously be the Creator. Simply put, God's creation is not him, and he is not the creation. Therefore, neither a plant, an animal, a force of the universe, a celestial body, nor an explosion, can be the Creator. These things do bear witness to a creative and intelligent author, but they are not him.

Thus, we begin in this chapter a journey toward understanding the God of all creation. It makes sense that our trek begins with his revealed and recorded story. As a basic definition, history records people, events, and circumstances that have occurred. God chose to step into history so that he could be a part of his own creation. He wanted people to get to know him. He wanted people to write down as well as orally communicate to the next generation who he is, what he is like, and what he has done. The sixty-six books of historical, literary, and poetic writings which comprise the Bible are a written historical record of God and his relationship with his creation. Over the last several thousand years God has openly revealed himself throughout human history; the Biblical narrative records this. Ancient history was recorded by oral tradition and passed down to children, grandchildren, and on and on. As spoken languages began to evolve into written form, people began to permanently record events on stone, wet clay, papyrus, and other material that could be carved, stamped, painted, or inscribed. This is how knowledge was recorded, preserved, and transferred from generation to generation.

The foundation of this study is the Biblical record and what it says. It is supported and affirmed historically, archaeologically, and personally by people throughout history who have come to know the only God that there is. This chapter begins a journey where you will get to know the Creator, the God who revealed himself in human history, so that you can know him.

He likes things recorded orally and in written form, and he wants to be remembered. He wants you to know him and to remember him. He wants a relationship with you because he has made you in his very image, and he has implanted in your heart the knowledge that he exists. God, the author of everything, naturally wants his creation to get to know him.

Let's begin with the basics. Does God have a name? In the ancient world names were important and carefully chosen to reflect particular virtues or aspects of that person's life to come. In the Old Testament books of the Bible, the name "*El*" is god's name, as well as its many derivatives. It means "mighty," and "strong." Attached to his name, *El*, are other aspects of God's character such as *El Shaddai* (God Almighty), or *El Ohim* (God Creator, Mighty and Strong). Also, ancient Israelites wrote God's name as "*YHWH*" (four Hebrew letters pronounced *Yahweh*, though the name was so holy it wasn't spoken). Another pronunciation of that holy name is *Jehovah*. God is often called in the ancient world "*Yahweh-Rapha*" (The Lord Who Heals), "*Yahweh-Nisi*" (The Lord Our Banner), or *Yahweh-Jireh* (The Lord Will Provide), as well as many other *Yahweh*-based names that specifically illustrate a part of God's character that the people of ancient Israel experienced directly and personally as they came to know God and walk with him through history.

Next, we will define God's grace, because in our day and age we think of this word quite differently. We often ascribe grace to a polite, poised, or elegant person. God's grace is something else altogether. It is his unmerited and unearned favor toward mankind. In Hebrew, grace is the word "חֵן" (pronounced *khen*). It comes from a root word meaning "kindness, mercy, and favor." That is the word used throughout the Old

Testament books of the Bible to describe God's grace. In the New Testament books of the Bible it is the Greek word *"charis,"* which forms the basis of the word "charity," or being "charitable." God's grace is marked by kindness, goodness, and forgiveness. These are all elements of his personality and nature. He gives charity and favor to people, even though we have cannot do anything to earn it.

In our culture today, we are taught that we deserve everything and are entitled to whatever we deem are our personal needs and wants. It may come as a shock that we don't deserve God's grace. The Biblical record explains this clearly. At the beginning of creation, the first two people were in a perfect place that offered them everything they could ever need or want. You have likely heard of them: Adam and Eve. They were made in God's "image," unlike anything else in creation. They were given a heart, a soul, and a will of their own so they could have a relationship with God. Their will enabled them to think critically and to make judgments, choices, and decisions in life. Amid perfection, they exercised their judgment and chose to question and disobey God's goodness, his power, and his provision. They wanted more.

Their hearts swelled with pride and discontentment because they wanted to be like God. Trusting and obeying him wasn't enough. A perfect world handed to them was not enough. They decided that disobeying the one main rule God gave them, which was to refrain from eating the fruit from the "tree of knowledge of good and evil" (Genesis 2:17), was worth the attempt. They pridefully and arrogantly made a conscious choice to disobey the one specific thing they were forbidden to do. At that moment, the first two people broke the perfect state of their relationship with God. Like a mirror broken in a thousand pieces, Adam and Eve couldn't put it together again, and they no longer reflected God's perfection. Instead, they hid, they lied, and they dug a deeper hole for themselves.

If we examine ourselves honestly, we must admit that this same innate propensity to want more, be more, and have more is in all of us. We have been convinced that we are owed more than we have, we are entitled to everything that this world has to offer, and that we have been deprived of what we truly need. When we choose to arrive at this realization, the first thing we do is take things into our own hands and seize what we want. We are no different than the first two people; their sin and disobedience tainted all of us. You might say that it's genetically wired into our DNA to be just like Adam and Eve. A day doesn't go by where we do not exercise pride, arrogance, bad judgment, and disobedience to someone, some authority, or some law. We never cease hungering for more, whether it be recognition, power, success, or money. The original sin of Adam and Eve has affected each of us. It is an uphill battle to be good, and we've lost the battle.

This fundamental reality is an abiding and unchanging truth since the first two people on this earth. We need to establish this fact now; it is the backdrop of all human history. We all enter into this world inheriting this depraved state of being, and that has consequences. We cannot please God in this state of being right from the beginning. There is a chasm between us and the Creator which we are unable to repair, despite our best efforts. From the beginning of human history, once Adam and Eve committed the first sin, God began his gracious plan to fix what we have ruined. Romans 3:23 says, *"All have sinned and fall short of the glory of God."* This simply states that everyone is imperfect and falls short of what God is like. He is perfect, we aren't. We fall short of perfection and that's where we stay until God reaches out and his grace moves into action. Now, let's continue.

Two Types of God's Grace

Thus far, we have explored the origin of the human will and soul, and the history of man's separation from God, the Creator of this universe. Grace, God's unearned favor toward mankind, is the foundation for his plan to bridge the gap between us and him. Grace provides reconciliation and acceptance that is undeserved. It is in the realm of the grace giver to decide on whom he will bestow it. We cannot buy God's grace, we cannot cajole him into giving it, and we cannot be good enough to ever earn it. It is a gift. That should come as a blessed relief. For many this comes as an unpleasant surprise. We are used to working for what we have, and we desire to take the credit for things earned. Gifts are considered a holiday pleasantry for some and recipients will accept them with a general sense of deserving them. For others, gifts are offered as a cultural statement of respect and received with appreciation because respect is considered to be earned and rewards are deserved. God's grace is a gift to those who cannot, will not, and never will earn it. It is solely based on God's desire to give it. It is not based on the recipient whatsoever.

Another aspect of God's grace is that it is extended to people in several forms. A general type of grace that God extends to all of us is "*common grace.*" This is undeserved blessing and favor offered to the entire world. Psalm 145:9 assures us that, *"The Lord is good to all, and his mercy is over all that he has made."*

Expanding upon that, Matthew 5:45 tells us, *"For he makes his sun rise on the evil and on the good, and sends rain on the just and on the unjust."* That is blessing and abundance that just happens to fall upon all of us, even though we may not attribute it to God and certainly not because we earned it or even deserve it. It is his will and good pleasure to offer the entire sinful world an array of gifts that come from his gracious, loving, and forgiving heart.

Contrasted with that is God's more specific and transformative *"saving grace."* This is a different type of grace altogether. In Ephesians 2:8-9 we can find an excellent description of God's saving grace: *"For by grace you have been saved through faith. And this is not your own doing; it is the gift of God, not a result of works, so that no one may boast."* In a nutshell, this is grace that some of us respond to, receive, and obtain from God personally, even though we have done absolutely nothing to earn it. It is a type of grace that, if we reject it, we will not enjoy it or its eternal benefits. Saving grace is a gift that simply requires a response. Some of us want it, some of us don't, and some of us are exploring our options. God's grace involves our recognition of our need for it, our responsive receipt of it, and God's regeneration of our hearts and minds to desire his grace and reconciliation in the first place.

The Apostle Paul, who God personally selected in the first century to spread his message of forgiveness, reconciliation, and salvation, wrote in Romans 6:23: *"The wages of sin is death, but the free gift of God is eternal life in Christ Jesus our Lord."* Paul defines the compensation that we earn on this earth as a "wage." Because we are all sinful, the wage that we ultimately earn is death and separation from God. However, the free gift of God is offered, bought, and paid for by a gracious God who put his Son's own life on the line for us. God's plan of grace is for his own Son (a part of God's three-part being, God the Father, God the Son, and God the Holy Spirit) to take our sin upon his shoulders and conquer it once and for all. In response to this completely finished act, all God asks is that we respond to that with gratitude and accept what he has done for us. The gift of saving grace is that he paid the price for our sin, and then he walks with us throughout our life making us into a "new creation" (2 Corinthians 5:17). His Holy Spirit actively and permanently lives within us, and he promises an eternal existence with him when this short earthly life is over. All of this comes from him, the Giver. We are asked for nothing in return but faith, trust, and obedience. Paul learned this first hand and was forever changed by it. We will delve into this momentarily.

God's saving grace transforms our heart, our mind, and our soul when we respond to it, yet his regenerative process begins first, somewhat like putting a key in the ignition and turning on the engine so that we can move forward with him. His saving grace is an unearned, transformative, and unde-served gift. One has to open their hands to receive a gift. When God desires to bestow his saving grace upon us, he provides a gift of faith, something we can't conjure up on our own, so that we can extend our arms and our hearts to receive his gift of grace. Once that gift of unearned favor is placed in our hands and into our hearts, no one can take that gift away, ever. He wants us to embrace that unearned grace, be filled with gratitude for it, be changed by it, and pass on the good news of that gift of grace and all of its life-changing implica-tions to others. Gifts are meant to be appreciated, enjoyed, and shared. The Gospel (which means "good news)" was and is God's message about his free and unearned gift of grace, reconciliation, and forgiveness from sin which some joyously accept, and others consciously reject.

In summary, common grace and saving grace are both gifts. They are not a payment for work done, nor are they brownie points earned for various niceties that you have said or done in the past twenty-four hours. If we have to work for something, we earn an expected and mutually agreed-upon compensation for it, a wage. Someone is obligated to pay you for labor performed. There is no unearned favor, gift, or blessing in that case. There is no employment contract between us and God where, if we perform, then he is obligated to pay us back. God is a selfless gift giver and desires to provide everything we need if only we would reach back and accept what he has to offer. We are far from perfect (as much as we think we're quite likable), and we fall short of God's glory and perfection. We're dead in the water until he fishes us out. It is akin to our sinful state drowning us and rendering us wholly unsavable by ourselves. God has tossed a life preserver toward us. That is grace.

Have you ever fallen in the water, felt like you couldn't keep on treading and keeping your mouth and nose above the waterline, and then someone came and pulled you out and saved you? God is that *someone* extending his hand and pulling you out, wrapping you in a nice, warm towel of his loving care, drying you off, and putting on a new suit of clothes for you to walk around in permanently. Once saved by him, the natural response is unspeakable gratitude and a desire to tell others about how you were saved. God's grace is like that. It transforms us, puts us in a new suit of clothes, and it sets us firmly on dry land where we can walk forward a changed person, with more changes to come. And, we have done none of it ourselves!

Out of such an experience with God's grace comes not only gratitude toward him, but love, respect, and obedience. That is why God spent most of human history pointing a very discernible finger toward his Son, Jesus Christ, his promised gift to sinful mankind. From the beginning of creation and throughout ancient history, God promised, described in detail, and explained who his Savior would be. He would be coming to save sinking, depraved souls, which all of us are. God's grace would be given sacrificially and selflessly to people so that we could be restored into relationship with him and be cleaned up from the inside out. It would be a massive self-sacrifice that was both painful and necessary, yet he chose to do it when he did not have to. The choice was his.

What God wants us to do is simply reach out and respond to his grace and his Savior, Jesus Christ. After responding to his grace, he will alter our heart, soul, mind, and life until we desire to bear witness of who God is and what he has done for us. We will want this good news spread far and wide until others respond to God, as well. That is precisely what the apostle Paul and Christ's followers did. They responded to God's grace and his gift of faith, and they were transformed by it. Only then did Paul and the other believers have the ability to share God's grace with others and turn the polytheistic 1st-century pagan world of false gods upside down. God's plan of gracious, undeserved salvation spread like warm, aromatic oil throughout the world where it continues to flow today to the farthest corners.

Now that we have a solid overview of God's grace, we can move ahead to examining the lives of specific people whose lives are living illustrations of God's grace in action.

Portraits of God's Grace

One of the most stunningly described personal encounters with God in history was that of Saul (also known as Paul), as recorded in the Book of Acts, in the New Testament portion of the Biblical record. Saul/Paul is a remarkable example of someone receiving God's undeserved grace and becoming massively transformed by it. Saul was a Roman citizen, born in Tarsus (which is in modern-day Turkey) in 6 A.D. His parents were Jewish and sent him to study the Torah (the first five books of the Bible) in Jerusalem. Saul became a *Pharisee*, which was a Jewish high priest. He was well educated, knew ancient Israel's history and law well, and was highly regarded in his position. Saul also willingly engaged in cruel persecution of followers of Jesus throughout Jerusalem and Judea (modern-day Israel). He was legally authorized to arrest anyone who followed Jesus Christ. What can we deduce from Saul's upbringing and status? He knew the Old Testament Biblical record very well, and he hated Christians (i.e., followers of God's promised Savior, Jesus). Saul was not deserving of God's grace by any observable means whatsoever.

In the year 33-36 A.D. Saul took a walk on a Damascus road (in modern-day Syria). He wasn't expecting much to happen other than to reach his destination. A voice came out of nowhere and Saul's life changed forever.[1] This account was descriptively recorded in Acts 9. It is important to look at this historical narrative from verse 1 through verse 22:

(1) But Saul, still breathing threats and murder against the disciples of the Lord, went to the high priest

(2) and asked him for letters to the synagogues at Damascus, so that if he found any belonging to the Way, men or women, he might bring them bound to Jerusalem.

(3) Now as he went on his way, he approached Damascus, and suddenly a light from heaven shone around him.

(4) And falling to the ground, he heard a voice saying to him, "Saul, Saul, why are you persecuting me?"

(5) And he said, "Who are you, Lord?" And he said, "I am Jesus, whom you are persecuting."

(6) "But rise and enter the city, and you will be told what you are to do."

(7) The men who were traveling with him stood speechless, hearing the voice but seeing no one.

(8) Saul rose from the ground, and although his eyes were opened, he saw nothing. So they led him by the hand and brought him into Damascus.

(9) And for three days he was without sight, and neither ate nor drank.

(10) Now there was a disciple at Damascus named Ananias. The Lord said to him in a vision, "Ananias." And he said, "Here I am, Lord."

(11) And the Lord said to him, "Rise and go to the street called Straight, and at the house of Judas look for a man of Tarsus named Saul, for behold, he is praying,

(12) and he has seen in a vision a man named Ananias come in and lay his hands on him so that he might regain his sight."

(13) But Ananias answered, "Lord, I have heard from many about this man, how much evil he has done to your saints at Jerusalem."

(14) "And here he has authority from the chief priests to bind all who call on your name."

(15) But the Lord said to him, "Go, for he is a chosen instrument of mine to carry my name before the Gentiles and kings and the children of Israel."

(16) "For I will show him how much he must suffer for the sake of my name."

(17) So Ananias departed and entered the house. And laying his hands on him he said, "Brother Saul, the Lord Jesus who appeared to you on the road by which you came has sent me so that you may regain your sight and be filled with the Holy Spirit."

(18) And immediately something like scales fell from his eyes, and he regained his sight. Then he rose and was baptized;

(19) and taking food, he was strengthened. For some days he was with the disciples at Damascus.

(20) And immediately he proclaimed Jesus in the synagogues, saying, "He is the Son of God."

(21) And all who heard him were amazed and said, "Is not this the man who made havoc in Jerusalem of those who called upon this name? And has he not come here for this purpose, to bring them bound before the chief priests?"

(22) But Saul increased all the more in strength, and confounded the Jews who lived in Damascus by proving that Jesus was the Christ.

What you have witnessed in this passage of the Biblical historical record in the Book of Acts is a Christian hater and killer who is transformed by the grace of God. Did Paul initiate or facilitate this massive transformation? No. Did he work to earn God's favor, forgiveness, and commissioning to share the Savior, Jesus Christ, with others? No. The crucified and risen Savior, the Son of God, was reaching out to Saul audibly, graciously, forgivingly, and overtly. Saul had done nothing to merit this life-changing encounter with God and his risen Son, Jesus Christ. Nothing. We are no less or more worthy of God's grace, forgiveness, and reconciliation than Saul. God's grace and forgiveness is simply a manifestation of his divine character. It is his outstretched hand to Saul—and to us—that provides the conduit through which flows God's love, power, forgiveness, and complete reconciliation.

God desires to transform us through his grace; it gives us access to him. If you have not yet responded to God and the direct access that he has given you to his outstretched hand of love, grace, and forgiveness, be assured that you are no worse and no better than Saul. There is no crime too serious that separates you from God's gift of saving and transformative grace. There are no good deeds that you can perform to earn his favor, either. He waits patiently for your heart and hands to open wide and accept his free gift of reconciliation, forgiveness, and transformation. He initiates the process of coming into a relationship with him; he wants you to respond to him.

Grace Transforms Us

God's grace begins regenerating our hearts out of a state of literally being "dead in sin." Once he gives us the gift of faith and we have the ability to respond to that grace, God will begin the life-long transformative process of cleaning house within our heart, mind, and soul. His broom is big, and he will sweep out everything hidden deep within us that must be exposed.[2] Why does his grace initiate this cleaning process? He does this because he desires for you and me to face the ugliness that lies within us, like all of the filthy stuff that lies under our rugs and in between our sofa cushions, things that we would rather not see in ourselves. When he shows us what we truly are, his gracious heart will initiate within us a desire to repent (meaning to apologize earnestly, genuinely, and remorsefully), for all that we have done that is unacceptable to him. He will embark upon a lifelong path of transformation in our lives by beginning with exposing the ugly things, so we can get them out on the table and see what sin looks like. It isn't pretty. He hates sin, and he can't be in a relationship with those who choose sin over salvation from it. God intensely hates sin and will not tolerate it. He cannot share his perfect eternal home, heaven, with anyone who is sinful. That's just the way things work, I'm afraid. He is a perfect, gracious, and holy Creator; he makes the rules.

What he wants is for you and me to be a mirror reflecting to others what he is doing inside our heart, mind, and soul, and throughout every area of our lives. The proof is always in the pudding. His work within us will create infectious gratitude, joy, and peace that every human heart desires yet cannot manufacture on its own. We must reflect God's transformative presence in our speech, in our public and private behavior, on the road, in the workplace, within our families and relationships, everywhere. God's undeserved grace needs to be a warm blanket we share with others so they know he exists. Our transformation is living proof of God's grace, and it will encourage others to desire a relationship with God, as well. Practicing, modeling, and living out grace takes practice throughout one's lifetime, but a good starting point is now. After all, we are pilgrims in progress; our journey isn't just a day's easy walk. We are not perfect spouses, siblings, neighbors, parents, or employees. But the desire to practice grace until it becomes a reflex should be our response to God's gift of grace to us. Jesus Christ, God's promised Savior who came, who conquered once and for all sin, modeled grace for us perfectly, because he was God in the flesh, face to face, up close and personal. Our necessary response must be to follow his model.

Let's delve into the Book of Luke, chapter 7:36-48 (ESV) where we see the story of grace that Jesus Christ models to one woman who had lived a life of wrong choices:

> (36) "One of the Pharisees asked him to eat with him, and he went into the Pharisee's house and reclined at the table.
> (37) And behold, a woman of the city, who was a sinner, when she learned that he was reclining at the table in the Pharisee's house, brought an alabaster flask of ointment,
> (38) and standing behind him at his feet, weeping, she began to wet his feet with her tears and wiped them with the hair of her head and kissed his feet and anointed them with the ointment.
> (39) Now when the Pharisee who had invited him saw this, he said to himself, 'If this man were a prophet, he would have known who and what sort of woman this is who is touching him, for she is a sinner.'
> (40) And Jesus answering said to him, 'Simon, I have something to say to you.' And he answered, 'Say it, Teacher.'
> (41) 'A certain moneylender had two debtors. One owed five hundred denarii, and the other fifty.

*(42) When they could not pay, he canceled the debt of both.
Now which of them will love him more?'
(43) Simon answered, 'The one, I suppose, for whom he
canceled the larger debt.' And he said to him, 'You have judged
rightly.'
(44) Then turning toward the woman he said to Simon, 'Do
you see this woman? I entered your house; you gave me no
water for my feet, but she has wet my feet with her tears and
wiped them with her hair.
(45) You gave me no kiss, but from the time I came in she has
not ceased to kiss my feet.
(46) You did not anoint my head with oil, but she has
anointed my feet with ointment.
(47) Therefore I tell you, her sins, which are many, are
forgiven—for she loved much. But he who is forgiven little
loves little.'
(48) And he said to her, 'Your sins are forgiven.'*[x]

What would the world look like if we regarded others with
visibly imperfect lives as a friend? It is admittedly not our first
inclination to spend time getting to know someone who
doesn't live a life of good choices. Most of us will instinctively
cross to the other side of the street rather than engage with a
homeless person, a wayward teen, or another person we deem
a misfit or undesirable. If we sought out others who were
down and out and sat down and spoke to them for a while, we
may just find out they are no different than we are. Extending
grace, a non-judgmental heart, and a few kindly spoken words
can change someone's life. Jesus modeled this for us because
he wanted his followers to do the same.

* * *

Making It Real

God's unearned favor toward us should be reflecting to others a beautiful orchard of spiritual fruits in our lives: love, joy, peace, patience, kindness, goodness, faithfulness, gentleness, and self-control (Galatians 5:22-23). As we walk with God through his life-long transformative process, these are the manifestations to ourselves and others around us that we are truly walking with the one true God. If you are currently in a relationship with God, then it is incumbent upon you to reflect the grace of God in your life visibly, tangibly, and lovingly to others. Keeping his hand, his power, and his transformation in your life hidden and unseen is doing others—and God—a disservice. God graciously sent his Son, Jesus Christ, as a visible part of his very being, so that he could model his character to us, and save us from sin and permanent separation from him. His purpose was clear, his grace and love visible, and he was a perfect mirror reflecting the one true God to others. Likewise, we should be mirroring God and his Son, Jesus Christ, in all aspects of our lives. We should be doing this not for our self-aggrandizement, but to glorify God and share him with others with a gracious, humble, and winsome spirit exuding joy and gratitude for what God and his Son have done for us. In a nutshell, God's undeserved grace should have transformed us; we need to act like it.

If you are currently in a relationship with God, here are some tough questions that I will pose: When was the last time you clothed someone in forgiveness when you heard that they slandered you or gossiped about you behind your back? When a neighbor has repeatedly been rude or combative, have you taken a deep breath and reached out a hand in friendship? At the grocery store this past week, when someone slammed your cart rudely because you were in their way, was a gracious response the first instinct? With your kids, have you incessantly demanded perfect behavior at all times without a shred of grace extended in the understanding that they, too, are as fallen as you are?

Elyse M. Fitzpatrick and Jessica Thompson, authors of *Give Them Grace*, offer up a simple word of encouragement as we discuss the issue of making God real to others: "*The primary theme is to be Jesus Christ and the work He has already done.*"[3] To show others Jesus and God's gift of him to a dying, depraved world of hopeless souls, you simply have to *be* Jesus to them. No amount of laws, do's and don'ts, pious admonitions, etc. are going to make someone hunger for a gracious, loving, and self-sacrificing God. No one wants to really be us; they want to know the God who is shining through us. Once someone desires to know him, we must walk the journey with them in discipling them into a deeper relationship with God.

German theologian, Dietrich Bonhoeffer, explains the divine foundation of grace with a caveat that mankind, in our sinful state, can inadvertently "cheapen" it, if we don't recognize the cost that God paid for us to receive his grace through Jesus Christ. God's grace is far more profound than ours, because it is perfect and righteous whereas ours can be tainted by sloth, selfish motives, and other vestiges of sin within us. Bonhoeffer says: "*Cheap grace is grace without discipleship, grace without the cross, grace without Jesus Christ, living and incarnate.*"[4] The ultimate and perfect model of God's grace for us is Jesus Christ. What Bonhoeffer means is, God's favor toward all mankind is vastly undeserved, yet he gives it freely through sacrificing his own Son for us to pay the price for our sin. God did every-thing for us. Sharing with someone God's grace without mentioning the finished work of Christ and without walking side by side with someone in their walk with God, disciple-ship, is not grace at all. It is a lazy, cheap, and distorted rendi-tion of real grace.

What does this have to do with showing grace to others? What it means is that we have to break out of our comfort zones and not only model grace to others, we have to engage, whenever possible, in the long-term follow-up work: *disciple-ship*. This costs us our time, convenience, money, energy, and a host of other things we consider important daily. We can't model just God's grace for a day and then walk away from someone. That is *cheap* grace. When we share God and his Son, Jesus Christ, with others, we must stay engaged with them over the long haul, continuously teaching them to look to Christ alone for their salvation, forgiveness, and transfor-mation. We cannot turn another's eyes away from the cross and toward us instead; we are no one's savior. The foundation of the world's history is God's grace. It must be carefully explained, openly discussed, and carefully modeled by following Jesus' example.

Our goal is to reflect the grace and love of God and his Son Jesus Christ to every person we meet. God will use us as tools to draw others to himself. This is where the rubber meets the road. We have to invest long-term in people's lives, showing endless grace and self-sacrifice as we walk with someone down the road to the cross. Only there can all of us meet God and receive him and his gifts of grace, love, and redemption. Are you a long-distance runner for Christ who is willing to walk the distance with someone until they desire to know God, and then continue treading alongside them as they embark upon a life-changing journey?

I will leave you with a thought-provoking devotional from Charles H. Spurgeon that describes God's grace beautifully. In a collection of his sermons, *Morning and Evening: A Contemporary Version of a Devotional Classic based on the NIV*, Spurgeon offers us this portrait of God's grace to chew on in his morning devotional entitled, "Be strong in the grace that is in Christ Jesus, 2 Timothy 2:1":

"Christ has grace without measure in Himself, but He has not retained it for Himself. As the reservoir empties itself into the pipes, so has Christ emptied out His grace for His people. 'From the fullness of His grace we have all received one blessing after another.' (John 1:16). He seems only to have (grace) in order to dispense it to us. He stands like the fountain, always flowing, but only running in order to supply the empty pitchers and the thirsty lips which draw close to it. Like a tree, He bears sweet fruit, not to hang on boughs, but to be gathered by those who need.
Grace, whether its work is to pardon, to purify, to preserve, to strengthen, to enlighten, to quicken, or to restore, is always to be had from Him freely and without price; nor is there one form of the work of grace which He has not given upon His people. As the blood of the body, though flowing from the heart, belongs equally to every member, so the influences of grace are the inheritance of every saint united to the Lamb; and herein there is a sweet communion between Christ and His church, inasmuch as they both receive the same grace. Christ is the head upon which the oil is first poured; but the same oil runs to the very skirts of the garments, so that the

meanest saint has an unction of the same costly moisture as that which fell upon the head. This is true communion when the sap of grace flows from the stem to the branch, when it is perceived that the stem itself is sustained by the very nourishment which feeds the branch.

As we daily receive grace from Jesus (God) and more constantly recognize it as coming from Him, we shall behold Him in communion with us, and enjoy the felicity of communion with Him. Let's make daily use of our riches, and always have recourse to Him as to our own Lord in covenant, taking from Him the supply of all we need with as much boldness as taking money out of our wallets."[5]

God's grace freely flows from himself through his Son, Jesus Christ, to us. It is the basis of our lives, the history of mankind from the very beginning, and it is open to all who want to receive it. God plays no favorites. All are equally beckoned to come to God's outstretched arms of forgiveness, reconciliation, and healing. He initiates the process; you'll know it when his hand begins regenerating your heart. The meeting place is the cross, where God's promised Son would pay for our sin with his own life. A life lived in recognition of what God has done for us is marked by radical, life-changing gratitude. If we know God, we must live with the gratitude-driven desire to pass on his undeserved gift of grace that simply keeps on giving, on and on and on, throughout history.

* * *

Study Questions

1. In Hebrew, grace is the word "חֵן" (pronounced *khen*).

It comes from a root word meaning "kindness, mercy, and favor." That is the word used throughout the Old Testament books of the Bible for describing God's grace. In the New Testament books of the Bible it is the Greek word *"charis,"* which forms the basis of the word "charity," or being "charitable." Do you see areas of your life where God's grace is obvious to you? Are there areas where you struggle with God being a "gracious" God?

2. What people in the Bible can you identify who received God's grace in a real and tangible way? What can you learn from their stories? (The Apostle Paul, for example, in Acts 9)

3. Read Luke 7:36-48. What does this Biblical passage reveal about God's grace?

4. Why can we never earn God's grace and why doesn't anyone deserve it?

5. How can you practice grace to others in your neighborhood, school, workplace, church, etc.?

6. God's common grace and specific (saving) grace are different. What types of common grace do you see around you? How would you describe common grace —and what examples would you give--to someone who has never heard of this term?

7. In Acts 9, what surprises you about God (and Jesus Christ) seeking Saul/Paul, interacting with him, changing him from his previous life, and commissioning him to go out and spread the truth?

8. How did you define and understand the concept of grace before you learned about God's type of grace?

Additional Bible verses on God's grace

Do: Discuss and ponder over these verses, and pray for God to illuminate each one. (For additional context, read the entire Biblical chapter in which each of these verses appears.)

2 Timothy 2:1 - *"Be strong in the grace that is in Christ Jesus,*

Romans 4:4–8 - *"Now to the one who works, his wages are not counted as a gift but as his due. And to the one who does not work but believes in him who justifies the ungodly, his faith is counted as righteousness, just as David also speaks of the blessing of the one to whom God counts righteousness apart from works: 'Blessed are those whose lawless deeds are forgiven, and whose sins are covered; blessed is the man against whom the Lord will not count his sin.' "*

Romans 3:20-24 - *"For by works of the law no human being will be justified in his sight, since through the law comes knowledge of sin. But now the righteousness of God has been manifested apart from the law, although the Law and the Prophets bear witness to it — the righteousness of God through faith in Jesus Christ for all who believe. For there is no distinction: for all have sinned and fall short of the glory of God, and are justified by his grace as a gift, through the redemption that is in Christ Jesus."*

Acts 20:32 - *"And now I commend you to God and to the word of his grace, which is able to build you up and to give you the inheritance among all those who are sanctified."*

Ephesians 2:8-9 - *"For by grace you have been saved through faith. And this is not your own doing; it is the gift of God, not a result of works, so that no one may boast."*

Matthew 22:36-40 - *(36) "Teacher, which is the great commandment in the Law?' (37) And he said to him, 'You shall love the Lord your God with all your heart and with all your soul and with all your mind. (38) This is the great and first commandment. (39) And a second is like it: You shall love your neighbor as yourself. (40) On these two commandments depend all the Law and the Prophets.'"*

John 1:16 - *"For from his fullness we have all received, grace upon grace."*

2 Corinthians 12:9 - *"But he said to me (God), 'My grace is sufficient for you, for my power is made perfect in weakness.' Therefore I will boast all the more gladly of my weaknesses, so that the power of Christ may rest upon me."*

Jeremiah 31:2-3 - *"Thus says the LORD: 'The people who survived the sword found grace in the wilderness; when Israel sought for rest, the LORD appeared to him from far away. I have loved you with an everlasting love; therefore I have continued my faithfulness to you.'"*

1 Peter 5:10 - *"And after you have suffered a little while, the God of all grace, who has called you to his eternal glory in Christ, will himself restore, confirm, strengthen, and establish you."*

Memory Verse:

Ephesians 2:8-9 - *"For by grace you have been saved through faith. And this is not your own doing; it is the gift of God, not a result of works, so that no one may boast."*

Action Plan - Following are some areas where I struggle with understanding God's grace:

1.

2.

3.

Suggested Reading:

1. *Grace: More Than We Deserve, Greater Than We Imagine*, Max Lucado, Feb 18, 2014
2. *Desiring God, Revised Edition: Meditations of a Christian Hedonist*, John Piper, Jan 18, 2011
3. *The Cost of Discipleship, Dietrich Bonhoeffer,* September 1, 1995
4. *John Newton (Foreword by Philip Yancey): From Disgrace to Amazing Grace,* Jonathan Aitken & Philip Yancey, Jun 15, 2007

Notes.

Chapter Two

SUNSETS AND SONGS – GOD'S COMPASSION

James 5:11 "Behold, we consider those blessed who remained steadfast. You have heard of the steadfastness of Job, and you have seen the purpose of the Lord, how the Lord is compassionate and merciful."

Who has not asked the question: *"If God is so loving and compassionate, why does he let this happen?"* The atheist who believes there is no divine entity or creator, the devout believer in God, and all those who fall somewhere in between have posed this question in the deepest recesses of their hearts and minds. We need only look at the depressing news of the day, gaze at the homeless soul walking the street, or see a deformed child gently pushed by loving parents in a wheelchair, and our hearts tighten with an understandable question: "Why?" We're human after all, and we want answers.

Stated plainly, God's compassion is not like ours. It is uniquely marked by omniscience (foreknowledge—what will happen in the future—and complete knowledge of all things). That foreknowledge informs God's sympathy and concern for someone's suffering. He can see ahead to what his plans are for an individual, and this sometimes leads him to choose for one's suffering and difficulties to remain. He chooses to take action by using suffering to bring about good for the individual and for others. His compassion is a purposeful demonstration of love, sympathy, and concern for the recipient with an eternal view of each person's life.

Our compassion is mostly prompted by reactive sympathy and a desire to alleviate suffering. To us, compassion is sympathy in action prompted by our desire to make suffering and discomfort go away. Though it embodies an admirable element of kindness and concern, it only sees the here and now, the physical and the tangible. God's compassion is marked by a desire to work difficult circumstances into something good for someone and to walk side-by-side with them through it. There is a higher and more eternal motive behind God's compassion; he sometimes allows challenges, suffering, and difficulty to remain in a person's life so that he can mold them into something far better and bless others through it, as well.

God's compassion has a purpose

The late 19th Century was a time of great spiritual reawakening in America, following a brutal Civil War era that pit fellow Americans against each other and left nearly 850,000 dead. Many Americans were drawn to tent revivals booming with traveling preachers sharing a loving and compassionate God with a hungry public that sought to recover from war, division, and death. An awakening of yearning for a closer walk with God swept across the country.[1]

In 1820, a girl was born who would shape the course of Christian worship for the next two centuries up through today. Born Francis Jane Crosby, "Fanny" Crosby was an amazing young woman who was rendered blind in infancy by a charlatan doctor administering a devastating poultice to her infected little eyes. Blinded by this doctor's misguided medical attention, Fanny's life was changed forever. It would be a walk by faith, not by sight. Though she went forth throughout life in visual darkness, she was guided by a marvelous light.

Fanny grew into a strong believer and follower of God, though she would never see with her own eyes his majestic creation, a vivid sunset, a drop of glistening dew on a blade of grass, nor see the eyes of another open in faith and sparkle at new-found knowledge that God is a God of compassion and can indeed be known. Yet, Fanny would influence the nameless traveler, the hopeless widow, the wayward teenager, and several U.S. Presidents as a bright light reflecting God's hand in every moment of her life. Fanny loved God fervently and spoke of his love and compassion to all who would listen. Her way of impacting lives was specific, unique, and God-ordained.

Fanny leaned upon God's compassion, a deeply felt concern that is intensely personal to a holy God and life-changing to us. As Jerry Bridges, author of *Respectable Sins: The Sins We Tolerate in Ourselves*, tells us simply, "*I am His personal concern.*"[2]

And, throughout a life of sightlessness, Fanny Crosby embraced and basked in God's personal concern and uniquely purposeful compassion for her. She praised God for her blindness, for she could "see" how God had used her through her sightlessness. When a young preacher, moved by pity for her blindness, spoke with Fanny, their conversation was inspiring and unexpected. The preacher said, "*I think it is a great pity that the Master did not give you sight when he showered so many other gifts upon you.*" The man referred to Fanny's "gifts" as her growing fame in hymn writing. Fanny simply replied, "*Do you know that if at birth I had been able to make one petition, it would have been that I was born blind?*" *Because when I get to heaven, the first face that shall ever gladden my sight will be that of my Savior.*" [3]

Eight thousand hymns later, many of which we sing today in America's churches, God's attribute of deep and abiding compassion is evident in Fanny's life, in her hymns, and in her deep-seated compassion for others who struggled to know God. Her well-known hymns move the hearts of God's people today as much as they did over one hundred and fifty years ago. Some of her most well-known songs are: "*Blessed Assurance,*" "*All the Way My Savior Leads Me,*" "*To God Be the Glory,*" "*Pass Me Not, O Gentle Savior,*" "*Safe in the Arms of Jesus,*" "*Rescue the Perishing,*" and "*Jesus Keep Me Near the Cross,*" to name just a few. Her hymns are vivid paintings in song, touched with tender brushstrokes of love for God. In her lyrics, there are no subtle or overt colors of self-pity, resentment, or weariness of how God has worked in her life. Her songs depict clear scenes of trust and understanding of who God is and what he is like, things that her eyes had not seen but her heart knew intimately.

. . .

Understanding God's type of compassion

So, where is God's compassion in this, you say? As the young preacher commented to Fanny about what a pity it was that *"The Master did not give you sight when he showered so many other gifts upon you,"* it was understandable to ask why God would allow a quack to render Fanny sightless at six weeks of age. Does that sound like a compassionate God? Some would question whether God's compassion for Fanny was absent, or perhaps harsh and heartless. The young man who conversed with Fanny had missed the point: God's gifts to Fanny were heightened by her blindness, not the other way around. God, in his foreknowledge, saw all that Fanny would do, all 8000+ hymns she would write, and his compassionate choice was to let her be a blessing to hundreds of thousands (if not more) people throughout the ages.

The average person, though, will question pain, suffering, and tragedy and ask why a supposedly compassionate God would allow such things to occur. We define compassion as sympathy—sometimes empathy—combined with a heartfelt connection to the one suffering. Some will take it further and act upon it by attempting to alter, eliminate, or alleviate another's harsh circumstances. God's compassion takes the long-term view.

Let's see what God says about compassion in the Bible. God said the following to the Israelites in Exodus 33:19 (Note: Moses wrote Genesis, Exodus, Leviticus, Numbers, and Deuteronomy):

"And the Lord said, 'I will cause all my goodness to pass in front of you, and I will proclaim my name, the Lord, in your presence. I will

have mercy on whom I will have mercy, and I will have compassion on whom I will have compassion." (Exodus 33:19)

It is important to understand the word mercy and compassion and the Hebrew words that were used by Moses to describe what God said to him in describing his divinely compassionate and merciful self. The word used is רָחַם (*râcham*). This word denotes both mercy and compassion, and it is the very first appearance of this word in the Bible. God specifically calls himself *râcham*.[4] Interestingly enough, the word also means "bowels" or from the very depths of God's being. Additionally, the word carries with it a connotation of deep love and tender affection. It is a multi-faceted word intended to depict God's type of compassion.

God's perfect will chooses to render compassion and mercy on whom he chooses; this is his sovereign right. This includes how he chooses to do it, and when he chooses to do it. God offers *râcham* to his people because he chooses to do so. He has the eternal view of everything and everyone (we'll discuss his attribute of omniscience in another chapter of this study). He states unequivocally that he chooses upon whom, as well as when, where, and how he will exercise his compassion and mercy, his *râcham*. Being a righteous and holy God, his choice is always perfect, for he sees the beginning, the middle, and the end of all things, and he chooses to work everything together for good for his people. Romans 8:28 serves as a timely reminder: *"And we know that for those who love God all things work together for good, for those who are called according to his purpose."* Simply stated, those who love God will be recipients of his uniquely purposeful, merciful, and deeply-felt compassion.

Let's face it, Fanny Crosby could have been the recipient of God's compassion in the form of his choosing to heal her blindness, as she was not born with that impairment. This would cross most people's minds, mine included. However, we must accept that God chooses to define *râcham* compassion by how he exercises it, by his omniscience, and by his innate goodness. In Fanny's case, God chose not to show his perfect compassion by actually healing her. In his foreknowledge and omniscience, God knew that Fanny would be more of a blessing to others if she remained blind. He knew it would make her bloom like the most beautiful rose, and that she would willingly model God's sweet fragrance to others. This is God's deeply tender and loving compassion planted into Fanny's life with an express purpose. His compassion is specific, intentional, and always loving.

God chooses how, when, where, and to whom he shows compassion; it is his omniscient, sovereign, and omnipotent right to do so. Furthermore, when we follow him, we are recipients of his compassion and mercy at all times. And as his people who are *"called according to his purpose"* (Romans 8:28), we are assured that he has our back despite what befalls us and despite what we choose or do not choose to do. When we recognize that, as totally depraved sinners one and all, we should all receive God's judgment for sin, we begin the process of understanding his longsuffering, patient, and tender compassion. When we know him, it becomes clearer that, because of his unique compassion and mercy, he willingly chose to provide the world a perfect Savior who bore our sins and provided a path to reconciliation with God. This is deeply tender compassion with an eternal purpose.

In Psalm 103:1-14 we see David's heartfelt musings about God's unique form of perfect compassion infused with tender fatherly love and intentional forgiveness:

> (1) *Praise the Lord, my soul; all my inmost being, praise his holy name.*
>
> (2) *Praise the Lord, my soul, and forget not all his benefits—*
>
> (3) *who forgives all your sins and heals all your diseases,*
>
> (4) *who redeems your life from the pit and crowns you with love and compassion,*
>
> (5) *who satisfies your desires with good things so that your youth is renewed like the eagles.*
>
> (6) *The Lord works righteousness and justice for all the oppressed.*
>
> (7) *He made known his ways to Moses, his deeds to the people of Israel:*
>
> (8) *The Lord is compassionate and gracious, slow to anger, abounding in love.*
>
> (9) *He will not always accuse, nor will he harbor his anger forever;*
>
> (10) *he does not treat us as our sins deserve or repay us according to our iniquities.*
>
> (11) *For as high as the heavens are above the earth, so great is his love for those who fear him;*
>
> (12) *as far as the east is from the west, so far has he removed our transgressions from us.*
>
> (13) *As a father has compassion on his children, so the Lord has compassion on those who fear him;*
>
> (14) *for he knows how we are formed, he remembers that we are dust.*

This Psalm, borne out of David's suffering, pursuit, and abuse at the hands of King Saul and his men, groans with pain coupled with deep faith in his compassionate God. David saw God as he is: a father who loves deeply, forgives fully, and mercifully withholds judgment and punishment deserved. Psalm 103 illuminates the tender heart of God that, in his compassion, allows his people to suffer—often for a long time--that he might work his perfect love and will through them. Underlying that is God's gentle hand rewarding *"those who fear him"* with forgiveness and withholding a harsher judgment that all of us fully and completely deserve, for he chooses to *"not treat us as our sins deserve or repay us according to our iniquities" (see verse 10 above)*.

In David's dire circumstances, described in The Book of Psalms, we also can draw strength from his suffering and his trust in God's greater plans. Though David and Fanny Crosby lived several thousand years apart, they both knew the very same unchanging God. Through weakness, suffering, and perseverance, God's compassion upon them ultimately shined through them so brilliantly that they would change many lives. God's intentional compassion coupled with his goodness and sovereignty infused David—and Fanny Crosby—with otherworldly patience, peace, joy, and power to withstand anything.

This type of compassion with a purpose may, to some, seem cruel and even cavalier. I struggled with Fanny Crosby's unfortunate blindness that God could have chosen to heal. Fanny's life—like David's—was not easy. She endured years of loneliness and challenge in learning to live away from her mother and attend a school for the blind far away from all that was familiar to her. Through her visually dark world, her heart ignited into a beautiful sun radiating her walk with God. This infused her soul with inspiration to begin writing hymns. She also became deeply involved in the lives of many people in the 19th Century who yearned to know God. From the average person to several U.S. presidents, Fanny brought many to true faith in her compassionate God. Her blindness, perseverance, and her hymns became a beacon of God's light to a world hungry for him.

In Fanny's hymns, she gushes forth with tender words of pure adoration of God, attesting to her true understanding and faith in his *râcham* compassion for her. Let's delve into Fanny's heart and see how God's compassion affected her personally, as that is the basis for every one of her eight thousand hymns. In *"Pass Me Not, O Gentle Savior,"* we see her response to God's mercy, compassion, and love in her life:

> *Pass me not, O gentle Savior,*
> *Hear my humble cry;*
> *While on others Thou art calling,*
> *Do not pass me by.*
> *Refrain: Savior, Savior,*
> *Hear my humble cry,*
> *While on others Thou art calling,*
> *Do not pass me by.*
> *Let me at Thy throne of mercy*
> *Find a sweet relief;*
> *Kneeling there in deep contrition,*
> *Help my unbelief.*
> *Trusting only in Thy merit,*
> *Would I seek Thy face;*
> *Heal my wounded, broken spirit,*

Save me by Thy grace.
Thou the spring of all my comfort,
More than life to me,
Whom have I on earth beside Thee,
Whom in Heav'n but Thee.

In this well-known hymn, Fanny writes of God as gentle, merciful, a giver of sweet relief, a healer, a Savior, a spring that brings comfort, and one who is gracious. Though blind, she sees all that God is. Though weak, she sings a song of humble praise. She writes of someone she knows very well, and yet she need not see him with human eyes. He is real, tangible and present with her. In her physically sightless life, she had spiritual 20-20 vision and sang of profound conclusions about God's compassion. Through weakness, God's power through her—and to his people--is magnified. Through God's merciful and compassionate care for Fanny—and for his people--we receive healing, comfort, and hope. God's tender and purposeful compassion infused Fanny Crosby's heart with flowing rivers of praise and descriptive hymns that flooded the world around her with God's love for a lost world.

* * *

We have established that God has revealed himself to be deeply compassionate and tender and that he exercises this in a way that he chooses. He does this because he is gracious and has plans for us that are far better than our own. We may not always like, understand, or prefer the type of compassion God exercises with us or with others. More often than not, we prefer things to be fair, equitable, painless, and perfect; we grumble when circumstances digress from the easy path because we rarely, if ever, will choose that. Suffering and weakness are often how God renders us dependent upon him and keeps the lines of communication with him open. His compassion is fashioned much like a horse's bit and bridle which keep it close to its master. How else can we have a concern for others without first knowing that God is in control and that we are his personal concern and he prefers to hold the reigns of our lives?

We ask God why he allows us to suffer because we are uncomfortable with suffering, struggling, or having seemingly insurmountable challenges. Suffering is uncomfortable and unpleasant. Worse, others' suffering is inconvenient because it makes us feel uncomfortable, as if we are obligated to do something about it. We may even lament about our struggles and pain yet curiously muse about another's suffering and wonder whether they've brought it upon themselves. In the case of someone like Fanny Crosby, our curious minds will inquire as to why God could not have allowed her to skip the suffering and tragedy. Yet, as we can see, God allows weakness and suffering to be his tool for blessing others. Fanny declared that she would not have traded this for the world.

Fanny Crosby's Hymn, *"Near the Cross,"* offers us a thoughtful glimpse into her heart, and how she viewed God's love, mercy, and compassion, despite suffering blindness. The lyrics are instructive:

> *(1) Jesus, keep me near the cross,*
> *there a precious fountain,*
> *free to all, a healing stream,*
> *flows from Calvary's mountain.*

Chorus:
In the cross, in the cross,
be my glory ever;
'til my raptured soul shall find,
rest beyond the river.
(2) Near the cross, a trembling soul,
love and mercy found me;
there the bright and morning star
sheds its beams around me.

(3) Near the cross! O Lamb of God,
bring its scenes before me;
help me walk from day to day,
with its shadows over me.

(4) Near the cross I'll watch and wait,
hoping, trusting ever,
'til I reach the golden strand,
just beyond the river.

The key to her hymn is quite subtle, for in the chorus we find her words reveal where she lives her life every waking moment: "*In the cross,*" and "*near the cross.*" Keeping in and near God and his promised Savior and Son, Jesus Christ, at all times, she encourages us to look only to God and what he has selflessly and compassionately chosen to do in paying the price for our sin. It is only in him that we find an endless fountain of healing, mercy and compassion, love, and hope. Fanny sings, "*trembling soul, love and mercy found me,*" ..."*Near the cross! O Lamb of God, bring its scenes* (of the cross) *before me; help me walk from day to day, with its shadows over* me," and *"Near the cross I'll watch and wait, hoping, trusting ever..."* She lived her life in lockstep with God's will for her and accepted humbly his purposeful compassion in her life.

Trusting in God's ultimate compassion--his giving of his very own Son as a perfect substitutionary sacrifice for our sinful selves--we can draw true and lasting hope, peace, rest, patience, love, and mercy that God offers his people. If we are suffering, whether it be physically, emotionally, spiritually, or in any other way, we can draw strength from a God who cares about us at every moment and is the only fountain of compassion that can give us power in our pain, humility in our suffering, and love for others in our intense weakness. Fanny had it right, and she put it into song in the most descriptive detail. Though she could not use her eyes to see rivers, sunsets, and fountains, God used a brush of purposeful compassion to paint those scenes in her heart where she could see and experience them with the eyes of her soul.

Elements of God's Compassion

God's compassion is relational, covenantal, and familial and is described as a parent showing this to a child. In Exodus 34:6, it says, *"The Lord, the Lord, the compassionate and gracious God."* God's compassion coupled with his grace is foundational to him choosing to maintain his covenant with his people. Psalm 78:38 declares, *"Yet he, being compassionate, atoned for their iniquity and did not destroy them; he restrained his anger often and did not stir up all his wrath."* God's compassion results in his forgiveness, self-control, restraint, nurturing, and purposefully going the extra mile for his people. His entire plan of redemption of man is based upon his eternal unchanging compassion for people.

Take heart, because God's compassion is patient, and it is colored with immense restraint and boundless forgiveness. It is who he *is*. It is why all thirty-nine Books of the Old Testament Biblical records are replete with foreshadows of God's compassion for mankind; every one of them clearly shows God's finger pointing toward the promise of a perfect Savior who would offer himself up for us as the ultimate act of compassion. Each of the twenty-seven Books of the New Testament record the culmination of the Old Testament record. God keeps his promises, and he has not kept his plans a secret; they are received, recorded, and freely offered for everyone to see, to read, and the respond to.

Miles Van Pelt, in his article on the subject of God's compassion, entitled, "The Old Testament God of Compassion and Mercy," describes it this way:

> "*The Old and New Testaments are united in their affirmation that the God of the Bible is merciful and compassionate. It would not be inappropriate to characterize the entire Bible as a book that journals God's mercy and compassion. In the Old Testament, mercy, or its English synonym, compassion, constitutes a fundamental attribute of the divine character, a reality highlighted in Exodus 32–34 and the account of the golden calf. The nation of Israel had been miraculously delivered from slavery in Egypt. They were soon camped at the foot of Mt. Sinai. There, they had heard the very words of God as they thundered from the smoking mountain (Ex. 20:22). Central to God's covenantal communication with Israel at this time was that they were prohibited absolutely from repre-*

senting him with images of gold or silver (Ex. 20:4, 23). It is
almost shocking, therefore, to discover that some forty days
later Israel does the very thing that God has forbidden (Ex.
32:1–6)! This single act of disobedience constitutes the
breaking of the Sinai covenant, the penalty for which is death
(Ex. 32:10)." [5]

In Exodus 32 and 33, Moses makes fervent intercession for the Israelites because they have broken God's commandments. What does God do in response? He exercises his compassion, forgiveness, and monumental self-control in not bestowing much-deserved wrath upon the Israelites. Exodus 34:6–7 records what God says about himself audibly and descriptively to Moses: *"The Lord passed before him and proclaimed, 'The Lord, the Lord, a God merciful and gracious, slow to anger, and abounding in steadfast love and faithfulness, keeping steadfast love for thousands, forgiving iniquity and transgression and sin.'"* This is God speaking of himself. He is introducing and defining himself to Moses— and to all of us—because he wants his people to know who he is.

God's Compassion Through Christ

Now we will move to the New Testament books of the Biblical record. Here, the writers used the Greek word, *"splanchnizomai"* to describe compassion, and they used this particular word twelve times throughout the New Testament books. On one occasion, in the Book of Luke, it is used to describe the "Good Samaritan's" compassion for the injured man lying on the side of the road (Luke 10:33). The other eleven uses of this same Greek word refers to *God's* compassion. For example, in two parables, Jesus uses this same verb to describe God's compassion in saving and forgiving sinners (see Matt. 18:27 and also Luke 15:20). The other appearances of this particular Greek verb are used to describe Jesus' compassion that led him to heal and to perform various miracles.

It is crucial to look at how Christ modeled compassion to his followers. We can take great comfort and strength from the following verses:

> *Matthew 9:36, "When he saw the crowds, he had compassion for them, because they were harassed and helpless, like sheep without a shepherd."*
> *Matthew 14:14, "When he went ashore he saw a great crowd, and he had compassion on them and healed their sick."*
> *Luke 7:13, "And when the Lord saw her, he had compassion on her and said to her, 'Do not weep.'"*

Beginning with Matthew Chapter 9, we see Jesus at work healing a paralytic, calling up Matthew to become his follower and dealing with nit-picky Pharisees (High Priests). This chapter also includes Jesus' multiple healings of various people and his travels through various cities teaching at the synagogues. In this context we come to Matthew 9:36 where Jesus draws a crowd of onlookers, many seeking healing. They have seen it, heard of it, and they want it; they're desperate for his compassion and its miraculous healing results.

Amid great suffering, desperation, and need that Jesus sees in the eyes of this crowd of followers, his compassion bubbles up like a fountain. Matthew describes Jesus' role as a caring and compassionate shepherd in Matthew 9:37-38: *"When He (Jesus)*

saw the crowds, He had compassion for them, because they were
harassed and helpless, like sheep without a shepherd... Then he said to
His disciples, 'The harvest is plentiful, but the laborers are few. (vs.
38) Therefore pray earnestly to the Lord of the harvest to send out
laborers into his harvest." What Christ was modeling for his
disciples and us is that, though he was busy teaching, preach-
ing, butting heads with naysayers, and healing people, he
intentionally paused from his work, noticed the needs around
him, demonstrated tender compassion, and then instructed
his disciples to do the same.

Jesus models for us that we must cease the busyness and the
excessive commitments we have crammed into our day and
make a conscious effort to see the needs in others. Rather
than being passive observers, he wants us to do something.
Jesus was extremely busy doing his Father's work, but, *"When*
He saw the crowds, He had compassion for them." (Mat. 9:37) And
then he proceeded, in Matthew 10:1, to light a fire under his
disciples' feet by charging them with action: *"Jesus called his*
twelve disciples to him and gave them authority to drive out impure
spirits and to heal every disease and sickness." Jesus' compassion for
the poor, the sick, the despondent, and the hopeless are manifested to the world through his caring acts of healing and
miracles. Jesus is modeling *splanchnizomai.* He is showing us
what God-like compassion looks like.

Next, let's look at Luke 10:25-37, paying particular attention to
verses 29 - 37. Here we find the parable of the Good
Samaritan:

> *(25) And behold, a lawyer stood up to put him to the test,*
> *saying, "Teacher, what shall I do to inherit eternal life?"*

(26) He said to him, "What is written in the Law? How do you read it?"

(27) And he answered, "You shall love the Lord your God with all your heart and with all your soul and with all your strength and with all your mind, and your neighbor as yourself."

(28) And he said to him, "You have answered correctly; do this, and you will live."

(29) But he, desiring to justify himself, said to Jesus, "And who is my neighbor?"

(30) Jesus replied, "A man was going down from Jerusalem to Jericho, and he fell among robbers, who stripped him and beat him and departed, leaving him half dead.

(31) Now by chance a priest was going down that road, and when he saw him he passed by on the other side.

(32) So likewise a Levite, when he came to the place and saw him, passed by on the other side.

(33) But a Samaritan, as he journeyed, came to where he was, and when he saw him, he had compassion.

(34) He went to him and bound up his wounds, pouring on oil and wine. Then he set him on his own animal and brought him to an inn and took care of him.

(35) And the next day he took out two denarii (a day's wages for a laborer then), and gave them to the innkeeper, saying, 'Take care of him, and whatever more you spend, I will repay you when I come back.'

(36) Which of these three, do you think, proved to be a neighbor to the man who fell among the robbers?"

(37) He said, "The one who showed him mercy." And Jesus said to him, "You go, and do likewise."

Jesus modeled compassion and taught it through this parable to make himself crystal clear. Compassion, he is showing us, is not comfortable, it is not timely, and it is not convenient. It is time-consuming, sacrificial, costly, and often ill-timed. Earlier in the passage, where the young lawyer asks Jesus how he can inherit eternal life, Jesus' admonition is to embrace and to practice his Father's compassion, and to show care and love for another. Anyone we come across in our sphere of life is our "neighbor." Dropping what we are doing, identifying a need, and responding to it fully (even if it costs you time, money, and inconvenience) is God's type of compassion.

Making it Real

We have explored how God and his Son, Jesus Christ, define, demonstrate, and embody compassion. Now, let's bring this close to home. I warn you, what I'm going to say is uncomfortable! Today, we are all far too busy. We frequently, almost obsessively check at our "to-do" list on our phones and realize our calendar is booked solid; we don't have time for spontaneous compassion. We don't even have time to sit down as a family and have an evening meal together, much less have time or interest in making one for someone else when the need arises. We live under the tyranny of the "urgent." We serve ourselves first; there is frequently no time or desire to unshackle ourselves from our own urgent needs and notice what can be done for others.

When we receive an email that a family needs help with meals (perhaps because someone is ill or just had a child), do we quickly delete the email before guilt sets in and we assume that someone else is going to sign up, so we don't really have to? When someone is stuck on the shoulder of the road with a flat tire, do we look in the opposite direction and pretend we don't see them because we need to get to our destination and don't have time to stop? Yes, we've all done it. I've done it. Our compassion is often handcuffed by our "urgent" matters we must attend to. The tyranny of the "urgent" renders us indifferent. It is a cruel taskmaster.

True compassion is the deeply woven fabric of God's very being, which is precisely why, if we belong to him, we have to mirror it, practice it, cultivate a feel for it deep in our bones, and repeatedly act upon it until it becomes a habit. It is not, however, a reaction or an obligation; it is a response that reflects the very heart of God. It is living out his attributes when they do not exist naturally within ourselves. When we understand God's compassionate self, see how he has revealed it to others, and subsequently how he embodies it in his provision to the world a suffering and compassionate Savior, only then can we desire for him to place his type of compassion within us. Without God's divine hand imputing that attribute to us, we cannot truly possess it, much less cultivate it. God will provide the proving ground, the testing sites, and the opportunities for his people to practice and bear witness of his beautiful, perfect, and majestic character to others. Are we up to his challenge, so that others can see a compassionate God's hand in our own lives?

God poses this fundamental question to each of us: Do we want to see the world--and ourselves--through his compassionate eyes? Are we then willing to be *"doers of the Word"* (James 1:22) and practice a radical, uncomfortable, and inconvenient compassion that can turn another person's world upside down?

* * *

Study Questions:

1. How does the world today define "compassion" and how does it differ with God's type of compassion?

2. In what ways do you struggle with acting compassionately toward another? Is it unforgiveness, disinterest, busyness, or perhaps indifference?

3. When you see others suffering—or you are suffering—do you struggle to understand God's purposeful compassion? Do you attribute this to impatience? Mistrust of God's goodness? Disbelieving God's omnipotence (power)?

4. Read Luke 10:25-37. Where do you see yourself in this parable? What are the things in your life that might make you turn away from someone in need?

5. In what ways does Jesus model compassion to us in his life, teaching, and death for us on the cross?

6. Is there a difference between God's mercy and God's compassion? How does the Biblical record define and record God's mercy and compassion?

7. Do you want to cultivate more compassion for others in your life, and what issues do you have that are standing in the way today? What things in your life fall into the "tyranny of the urgent" and what does God want you to do about it?

Additional Bible verses on God's compassion

Do: Discuss and ponder over these verses, and pray for God to illuminate each one. (For additional context, read the entire Biblical chapter in which each of these verses appears.)

2 Kings 13:23 - *"But the Lord was gracious to them and had compassion on them, and he turned toward them, because of his covenant with Abraham, Isaac, and Jacob, and would not destroy them, nor has he cast them from his presence until now."*

Psalm 103:13 - *"As a father shows compassion to his children, so the Lord shows compassion to those who fear him."*

Matthew 9:36 - *"When he saw the crowds, he had compassion for them, because they were harassed and helpless, like sheep without a shepherd."*

Romans 9:15 - *"For he says to Moses, 'I will have mercy on whom I have mercy, and I will have compassion on whom I have compassion.'"*

Colossians 3:12 - *"Put on then, as God's chosen ones, holy and beloved, compassionate hearts, kindness, humility, meekness, and patience."*

Memory Verse

Exodus 22:27 - *"...And if he cries to me, I will hear, for I am compassionate."*

Action Plan - Following are some areas where I lack compassion and need God's help in being a *"doer of God's Word"*:

1.

2.

3.

Suggested Readings and Resources:

1. *Knowing God*, J. I. Packer, July 24, 1993
2. *Her Heart Can See: The Life and Hymns of Fanny J. Crosby*, (Library of Religious Biography (LRB), May 12, 2002.

Notes:

Chapter Three

FORESIGHT IS 20-20 VISION – GOD'S OMNISCIENCE

Romans 8:29 *"For those whom He foreknew, He also predestined to become conformed to the image of His Son, so that He would be the firstborn among many brethren."*

1 John 3:20 *"...God is greater than our heart, and he knows everything."*

When we consider the limitless size of the universe, the incredible complexity of the human body, the intricately formed child within a mother's womb, the mighty oak growing from the smallest acorn, or the vastness of the universe, let's admit that we all contemplate where everything came from, including ourselves. I would venture to say that even the most ardent atheist declared themselves as such because they pondered this question and decided they had no answer, and therefore declared God nonexistent. It's far easier that way; it's better not to have to think about a creator. That would imply a bit of accountability. Who wants accountability to a higher power anymore?

Rene' Descartes, the 16th Century-born French philosopher, mulled over the innate difference between living things and non-living things and concluded, "*I think, therefore I am.*" Some people exist, even if they don't think much at all; we all know some who fall into that category. We exist in all our inexplicable complexity not because we think, but because we have been created (and we have been created to think). Consider the premise that you and I exist in all of our amazing human complexity because someone else designed us. Though we cannot think ourselves into existence, someone did. Everything in this universe did not spring from a vacuum, a void, or a very large random explosion; chaos and nothingness do not create. Someone with an intellect and the power to act upon that had to create who we are, as well as the vast universe around us. Some call this *intelligent design*. The key term is "*intelligent*," which belies knowledge and the ability to think creatively and analytically. Even Albert Einstein proclaimed that his Theory of General Relativity absolutely convinced him that there is a God, (though he struggled with the concept that this intelligent designer was a "personal god").

We can infer from the observable universe's behavior that there is some "beginning." In and of itself, that carries profound implications. The fact is, the strongest telescopes observe that everything in the universe is moving away from us. There is an observable beginning to what exists right now; everything is moving away from some central point of creation. At the atomic level, looking through a powerful microscope, one can see the intricacies of the unseen universe that is all around us, yet not visible with the naked eye. Even on a molecular level, there is order, mathematical specificity, purposeful function, and intentional design. This suggests the omniscience of someone behind it all. What we will discuss in this chapter is the concept of an omniscient (all-knowing) God who authored everything and everyone and who knows everything. This is quite an undertaking. Let's jump right in.

Please note that this is not a scientific treatise on creationism versus evolution, nor is it a single-sided conversation about intelligent design. I use the Biblical record to shed light on God's intellect and omniscience. Why do I use the Bible rather than the works of great philosophers, scientists, or theologians to shed light on the omniscience of God? Because the Biblical record of sixty-six books written over several thousand years is a historical biography of God, you might say. This is the God who created the vast universe that you see all around you and who intervened into human history to reach out his hand to us in creation, forgiveness, and reconciliation. This is a God who wanted people to know him, love him, believe him, and rest in his power, provision, and promises.

So, put aside any other gods you've been mulling over lately, even the god of yourself. In the Biblical record, we will discuss how he both declares and demonstrates that he is a God who knows much more, is much more, and has done much more than you may realize or can fully grasp. He asked many specific people in the ancient world to write down what he said, what he did, what he promised, and what he accomplished. By doing this, the Biblical record specifically and intentionally illustrates to the world who God is. He planned it that way. He had his reasons.

. . .

Defining and Discussing Omniscience

First, let's start with some basic definitions. Webster's Dictionary defines *omniscience* as "possessing unlimited knowledge, an attribute peculiar to God." This isn't a bad start, as it does use the term *"unlimited"* as well as defines omniscience as an attribute that is unique to God. Omniscient knowledge is unlimited, not of this world, and covers past, present, and future, as well as things both seen and unseen by man's five senses. It is knowledge not limited to human experience, expectations, space, or time. It is a type of knowledge that belongs only to the Creator, to God alone. Omniscience cannot be ascribed to any human being, to man-made gods, or any inanimate object. We may have come across those who are convinced they are omniscient. Folks like this are merely arrogant, prideful, and often know very little. We say in Texas that folks like that are "All cattle and no hat." You get the picture.

The Biblical record delves into the profound depths of God's omniscience, for God's unlimited knowledge not only creates, but it intentionally pierces into the very heart, soul, and mind of man and knows what is within. That is knowledge more powerful than any fine measuring instrument can measure. It is a type of knowledge outside of space and time with a sharp arrow tip that punctures through tissue and matter and has an up-close view and a deep understanding of motive, emotion, and thoughts. It is both an intuitive knowledge of the unseen, an understanding of hidden implications, and a complete and perfect cognizance of all things irrespective of space and time.

The prophet Isaiah (who lived in the 8th century B.C.) explained God's knowledge this way: *"Have you not known?*

Have you not heard, that the everlasting God, the Lord, the Creator of the ends of the earth, faints not, neither is weary? There is no searching of his understanding." (Isaiah 40:28) God is all-knowing in a limitless way that is not subject to time, emotion, or physical limitations. And, he exists continuously, as does his knowledge of past, present, and future. The Book of 1 Chronicles, written between 425 and 450 B.C., tells us in chapter 8, verse 9: *"...for the Lord searches all hearts, and understands all the imaginations of the thoughts..."* God created the human soul and heart, therefore it is not surprising that he omnisciently sees what is inside.

The apostle Paul, in the Book of Romans 11:33-36 says, *"O the depth of the riches of both the wisdom and knowledge of God! How unsearchable are his judgments, and his ways past finding out."* Paul describes God's knowledge as rich, wise, unsearchable, and intelligent. This is a God who exercises wisdom, knowledge, and justice. He exercises omniscient intellect, he makes judgments about people and circumstances, and his "ways" are beyond human knowledge. Our mere five senses cannot fully comprehend the depth, breadth, and implications of God's knowledge. The exciting thing, however, is that God allows us to experience it in some fashion and to personally glimpse some of its implications for our own lives.

Because God made us, he knows the depths of our hidden thoughts, motives, and feelings. No one else can do that, though we may try to discern motives and analyze emotions with the help of licensed professionals. God knows his creation very, very well, even down to the cerebral and emotional level. He is the all-knowing author of each of us; God the Creator knows the inner workings of that which he creates. He knows our past, present, and our future in all of its intricate detail, including the choices we will make—or not make--based on his knowledge of our heart, our mind, and our soul. He alone has the front row seat on the stage of each of our lives, seeing, hearing, and anticipating all that occurs and all that will occur. His knowledge involves complete foresight, perfect insight, all-knowing hindsight, and wisdom that belongs only to he who is the divine playwright. We do not and never will have that kind of knowledge, nor will anyone or anything else. Our human knowledge is limited, minuscule, and silly when compared with the limitless omniscience of God. And, that's a good thing. Humility comes from knowing there is someone else who knows more than you.

In this present day and age, we tritely say that "*knowledge is power*," when speaking of things in the human realm. We must understand that God *is* supremely powerful, his knowledge is perfect, and it exists outside of space and time. King Solomon, a venerated wise king of ancient Israel explained things simply when he wrote many of the tidbits of wisdom which comprise the Book of Proverbs. In Proverbs 1:7 he declares, *"The fear of God is the beginning of knowledge; fools despise wisdom and instruction."* Humanly speaking, our knowledge is nothing; knowing, revering, and fearing God is how King Solomon defined true human knowledge. A God who possesses limitless knowledge outside of space and time is a God worth knowing. It provides you and me a humbling context within which to understand God and ourselves and see that there is a vast difference between us. This denotes respect and a good healthy fear of a powerful all-knowing God. This, in turn, engenders within us a natural humility and deference to a God who we learn is endlessly wiser than we are.

There have been many people preceding us in the continuous thread of human history who have come to know the one and only God that there is. In the ancient world, God revealed himself to his creation from the very beginning, because he is a gracious and compassionate God who wants a relationship with people and bothered to create everything, including us, so that we could experience him. Ancient Biblical history records the life of a particular young man who was the youngest of several brothers and spent his long days tending sheep, protecting them from predators, and playing with slingshots. You may know his biography well or at least have heard portions of his life story. His name was David.

David: Shepherd, Soldier, and King

David, the shepherd boy who killed the giant Philistine, Goliath, in approximately 1020 BC, would later become king of the united Israelite kingdoms of Judah and Israel in 1000 BC. The Old Testament Book of 1 Samuel, Chapter 17, descriptively records David's life as a young Israelite shepherd boy at a time when his country was at war with nearby Philistines. The historical record in the Book of 1 Samuel covers a well-known confrontation between David, a young man with a sling and five stones, and Goliath, an actual giant and a seasoned warrior. With God present and providing superhuman accuracy, David used a simple hand-made sling, a well-aimed swing, and with one stone he brought down an experienced soldier by smacking him with a stone right between the eyes.

Later, David's renown for prowess in battle engendered in King Saul (he is not to be confused with the Apostle Paul/Saul in the 1ˢᵗ century A.D.), insane jealousy of David. No king likes public accolades for others; they want adulation from their subjects themselves. King Saul went from friend of David to foe in two seconds. Pride does that in people. This resulted in David having to quickly flee and hide for many years from King Saul's men who relentlessly pursued him and were instructed to slay David. While spending many miserable years as a fugitive, David suffered greatly, but he also took the time to call out to God, giving us one of the most beloved books of the Bible, the Psalms. David was not the only author of the Psalms (there are several), but he was a significant contributor. Also, David was the father of King Solomon, one of the wisest men in the ancient world. David's great-grandmother was Ruth, from which we derive the Old Testament Book of Ruth.

Psalm 139, written by David, describes for us how much he loved, revered, and recognized God's omniscience and *omnipresence* (omnipresence means God's presence everywhere simultaneously). You'll notice in this passage David's poetic detail, reverent descriptiveness, and humble awe of God's omniscient character:

> *(1) "O Lord, You have searched me and known me.*
> *(2) You know when I sit down and when I rise up; you understand my thought from afar.*
> *(3) You scrutinize my path and my lying down, and are intimately acquainted with all my ways.*
> *(4) Even before there is a word on my tongue, behold,*
> *O Lord, You know it all.*
> *(5) You have enclosed me behind and before, and laid Your hand upon me.*

(6) Such knowledge is too wonderful for me; it is too high, I cannot attain to it.

(7) Where can I go from Your Spirit? Or where can I flee from Your presence?

(8) If I ascend to heaven, You are there; If I make my bed in Sheol, behold, You are there.

(9) If I take the wings of the dawn, if I dwell in the remotest part of the sea,

(10) Even there Your hand will lead me, and Your right hand will lay hold of me.

(11) If I say, "Surely the darkness will overwhelm me, and the light around me will be night,"

(12) Even the darkness is not dark to You, And the night is as bright as the day. Darkness and light are alike to You.

(13) For You formed my inward parts; You wove me in my mother's womb.

(14) I will give thanks to You, for I am fearfully and wonderfully made; wonderful are Your works, and my soul knows it very well.

(15) My frame was not hidden from You, when I was made in secret, and skillfully wrought in the depths of the earth;

(16) Your eyes have seen my unformed substance; and in Your book were all written the days that were ordained for me, when as yet there was not one of them.

(17) How precious also are Your thoughts to me, O God! How vast is the sum of them!

(18) If I should count them, they would outnumber the sand. When I awake, I am still with You.....

(We now move forward to verses 23 and 24)

(23) Search me, O God, and know my heart; try me and know my anxious thoughts;
(24) And see if there be any hurtful way in me, and lead me in the everlasting way."

In some of our darkest times, we seek and yearn for God because we all innately know that he exists, and we know that we need him. Even those who do not believe God exists will cry out to him in times of great peril because he intentionally placed an innate knowledge in all of us that he is there. As the soldier's saying goes, *"There are no atheists in foxholes."* In times of great peril, our visceral and undeniable knowledge of God comes forth. In David's misery, terror, and incessant pursuit by King Saul's men, Psalm 139 reveals how David fervently sought God and cried out to him praising God's supreme knowledge, his eternal and all-encompassing presence, his creation of all things, his perfect light in the darkness, his power over space and time, and his kindness. David cites God's knowledge of him before he was born and an intimate awareness of his innermost thoughts and desires. He descriptively praises God's omniscience, omnipotence, and omnipresence. David grasped that God was personally and deeply involved in every detail of his creation and his life. David believed this because he had experienced God's presence firsthand and knew it to be real and reliable.

David, who God called the *"apple of His eye"* (Psalms 17:8) was no saint after he was anointed as king of Israel and Judah in 1000 B.C., about twenty years after killing Goliath. David behaved like a bad apple, rather than the sweet apple of God's eye, as he drifted into covetousness and insatiable lust for another man's wife. Knowing that God is omniscient and omnipresent and can see directly into David's heart, thoughts, and motives, it comes as a bit of surprise that David stealthily indulges in a lust-induced series of adulterous and murderous events. Knowing that God is there, yet feeling compelled to satisfy one's wants immediately, is nothing more than good old-fashioned pride and envy--sin. Sin creates in all of us selective blindness to God's omniscience and his omnipresence, much like a toddler who plays hide-and-seek by hiding their face behind the sofa, with the rest of their body fully visible, yet they think they can't be seen.

The Biblical narrative in 2 Samuel (written at a point in time between 913 B.C. and 722 B.C.) provides us a birds-eye view into man's sinful tendencies and simultaneously highlights God's character. Unfolding in 2 Samuel 11 is a premeditated series of terrible and intentional choices that David made. God ensured that history recorded this because it is a life lesson that we can all learn from:

> *(1) "In the spring of the year, the time when kings go out to battle, David sent Joab, and his servants with him, and all Israel. And they ravaged the Ammonites and besieged Rabbah. But David remained at Jerusalem.*
> *(2) It happened, late one afternoon, when David arose from his couch and was walking on the roof of the king's house, that he saw from the roof a woman bathing; and the woman was very beautiful.*
> *(3) And David sent and inquired about the woman. And one said, "Is not this Bathsheba, the daughter of Eliam, the wife of Uriah the Hittite?"*
> *(4) So David sent messengers and took her, and she came to*

him, and he lay with her. (Now she had been purifying herself
from her uncleanness.) Then she returned to her house.

(5) And the woman conceived, and she sent and told David, 'I
am pregnant.'

(6) So David sent word to Joab, 'Send me Uriah the Hittite.'
And Joab sent Uriah to David.

(7) When Uriah came to him, David asked how Joab was
doing and how the people were doing and how the war was
going.

(8) Then David said to Uriah, 'Go down to your house
and wash your feet.' And Uriah went out of the king's house,
and there followed him a present from the king.

(9) But Uriah slept at the door of the king's house with all the
servants of his lord and did not go down to his house.

(10) When they told David, 'Uriah did not go down to his
house,' David said to Uriah, 'Have you not come from a jour-
ney? Why did you not go down to your house?'

(11) Uriah said to David, 'The ark and Israel and Judah
dwell in booths, and my lord Joab and the servants of my lord
are camping in the open field. Shall I then go to my house, to
eat and to drink and to lie with my wife? As you live, and as
your soul lives, I will not do this thing.'

(12) Then David said to Uriah, 'Remain here today also, and
tomorrow I will send you back.' So Uriah remained in
Jerusalem that day and the next.

(13) And David invited him, and he ate in his presence and
drank, so that he made him drunk. And in the evening he
went out to lie on his couch with the servants of his lord, but
he did not go down to his house.

(14) In the morning David wrote a letter to Joab and sent it
by the hand of Uriah.

(15) In the letter, he wrote, 'Set Uriah in the forefront of the

hardest fighting, and then draw back from him, that he may
be struck down, and die.'
(16) And as Joab was besieging the city, he assigned Uriah to
the place where he knew there were valiant men.
(17) And the men of the city came out and fought with Joab,
and some of the servants of David among the people fell.
Uriah the Hittite also died.
(18) Then Joab sent and told David all the news about the
fighting.
(19) And he instructed the messenger, 'When you have finished
telling all the news about the fighting to the king,
(20) then, if the king's anger rises, and if he says to you, 'Why
did you go so near the city to fight? Did you not know that
they would shoot from the wall?
(21) Who killed Abimelech the son of Jerubbesheth? Did not a
woman cast an upper millstone on him from the wall, so that
he died at Thebez? Why did you go so near the wall?' then you
shall say, 'Your servant Uriah the Hittite is dead also.'
(22) So the messenger went and came and told David all that
Joab had sent him to tell.
(23) The messenger said to David, 'The men gained an advan-
tage over us and came out against us in the field, but we drove
them back to the entrance of the gate.
(24) Then the archers shot at your servants from the wall.
Some of the king's servants are dead, and your servant Uriah
the Hittite is dead also.'
(25) David said to the messenger, 'Thus shall you say to Joab,
'Do not let this matter displease you, for the sword devours
now one and now another. Strengthen your attack against the
city and overthrow it.' And encourage him.'
(26) When the wife of Uriah heard that Uriah her husband
was dead, she lamented over her husband.

(27) And when the mourning was over, David sent and
brought her to his house, and she became his wife and bore
him a son. But the thing that David had done displeased
the Lord."

In God's foreknowledge, he knew David would do all of this before it took place. Remember, God knows the heart and its hidden emotions and motives, as well as all the thoughts that we had, have, and will have. His omniscience cannot be surprised or caught off guard by what occurs. God knew all along what David would choose to do. God also knew the level of remorse and repentance within David's heart and allowed him to exercise it publicly. 2 Samuel 12:1 records the next step in the story: "*The Lord sent Nathan (a prophet) to David.*" God tells this well-known and respected prophet of Ancient Israel, Nathan, what David has done. Now, look further at 2 Samuel 12:9-14 to see how God reminds David of his divine omniscience and the futility of hiding from him. He uses Nathan to dredge up a confession of guilt. Nathan says to David in 2 Samuel 12:

(9) "Why have you despised the word of the Lord, to do what
is evil in his sight? You have struck down Uriah the Hittite
with the sword and have taken his wife to be your wife and
have killed him with the sword of the Ammonites.
(10) Now therefore the sword shall never depart from your
house, because you have despised me and have taken the wife
of Uriah the Hittite to be your wife.
(11) Thus says the Lord, 'Behold, I will raise up evil against
you out of your own house. And I will take your wives before

your eyes and give them to your neighbor, and he shall lie with
your wives in the sight of this sun.
(12) For you did it secretly, but I will do this thing before all
Israel and before the sun.'
(13) David said to Nathan, 'I have sinned against the Lord.'
And Nathan said to David, 'The Lord also has put away your
sin; you shall not die.
(14) Nevertheless, because by this deed you have utter-
ly scorned the Lord, the child who is born to you shall die.'"

Many will question that, if God is omniscient, why does he let people do bad things? Why does God love someone adulterous, murderous, scheming, and lying, like King David? Our gut reaction is to think that we would never do something as egregious as the things that David did. The key is that we are no better than David. Sin is sin, period. God knew David would commit these atrocious acts, many of them irreversible. In God's foreknowledge, he knew precisely what David was going to do before he saw beautiful Bathsheba taking a rooftop sponge bath and all David's bad choices began. The profound truth illustrated in David's life is that God loves the sinner. It sounds like a cliché', but it's true. God demonstrates how his omniscience is punctuated by grace, love, compassion, and forgiveness so that we can learn from it and appreciate the profound power of his undeserved grace.

The remarkable thing about God's omniscience is that he already knows that we can never extricate ourselves from our propensity to make bad choices. Sin is a congenital *defect*, so to speak, which every one of us is born with, thanks to the original sin of Adam and Eve. Amazingly, God chooses to love us despite ourselves. In his foreknowledge and omniscience, he knows specifically what every one of us is going to do before we do it. Knowing that he sees who we are and what we do, God chooses to bathe us in grace, and forgiveness and love us anyway. All he asks of us in return is repentance, faith, and trust in him. The problem is, we just can't seem to muster up the repentance, faith, and trust that we should give back to a perfect God. He knew that, so he lovingly provided a way out of our self-made misery.

Forbidden Fruits and Rotten Hearts

The Book of Genesis, the authorship of which is attributed to Moses, records the beginning of creation when God made the universe in six days and then rested on the seventh day. In Genesis 2, it is recorded that God made the universe, the earth, water, skies, land, plants, animals, and finally Adam, the first man, and soon thereafter, Eve, the first woman. We will begin delving into the narrative of the first two people and the Garden of Eden, a perfect place, where there was, as yet, no sin or bad motives of the heart—not yet, at least. Genesis 2:15 -17 records:

> (15) *"The Lord God took the man and put him in the garden of Eden to work it and keep it.*
> (16) *And the Lord God commanded the man, saying, 'You may surely eat of every tree of the garden,*
> (17) *but of the tree of the knowledge of good and evil you shall not eat, for in the day that you eat of it you shall surely die'."*

In paradise, a place of God-made perfection, there were rules. Rules are stipulations of behavior and boundaries. Rules have consequences if broken. One measly rule was proclaimed by God: *'You may surely eat of every tree of the garden, but of the tree of the knowledge of good and evil you shall not eat, for in the day that you eat of it you shall surely die'.*" For an indeterminate amount of time, Adam and Eve complied with that rule until someone entered their neighborhood and provided an alternative to that one rule and an opportunity to exercise their intellect and their will and challenge their relationship with the Creator. Let's look at Genesis 3 to see what unfolds:

(1) "Now the serpent was more crafty than any other beast of the field that the Lord God had made. He said to the woman, 'Did God actually say, 'You shall not eat of any tree in the garden'?'

(2) And the woman said to the serpent, 'We may eat of the fruit of the trees in the garden,

(3) but God said, 'You shall not eat of the fruit of the tree that is in the midst of the garden, neither shall you touch it, lest you die.'

(4) But the serpent said to the woman, 'You will not surely die.

(5) For God knows that when you eat of it your eyes will be opened, and you will be like God, knowing good and evil.'

(6) So when the woman saw that the tree was good for food, and that it was a delight to the eyes, and that the tree was to be desired to make one wise, she took of its fruit and ate, and she also gave some to her husband who was with her, and he ate.

(7) Then the eyes of both were opened, and they knew that they were naked. And they sewed fig leaves together and made themselves loincloths."

God, knew who that serpent was and what it was intending to do. Remember, God knows the motives, thoughts, and feelings of everyone, and he knows everything that will happen. In this passage the serpent is no mere snake; this is Satan, also known as the "evil one," the "devil," "serpent," "the accuser," the "deceiver," and the "angel of light." Satan was an insurrectionist angel, a disloyal member of God's heavenly host of angelic servants. At some point, Satan decided to lead one-third of the heavenly host of angels into rebellion against God. The serpent was looking for more beings to bring down with him. The first people on this earth were meeting up with evil for the very first time.

There is no one in this world at any given time in history or today who denies that evil exists. Some will discount the concept of evil embodied in a being (such as Satan/Lucifer/the Devil). Doing this gives peace to some, because they do not need to worry further about being accountable to anyone for bad behavior, nor do they have any boundaries on their behavior at all. Some will diminish evil and gently redefine it as simply breaking someone else's rules of right and wrong, or more esoterically, the breaking of some "higher law" that all civilized people agree upon.

However, if someone believes there is no evil, they cannot tell a cannibal tribe from Borneo that it is wrong to eat their enemies. They cannot condemn the Turks for massacring over one million Armenians in the first genocide of the 20th century. They cannot charge Hitler and his Nazi followers with the genocide of millions of Jews in World War II. Interestingly enough, Hitler knew that the world was reticent to condemn the evil of the first "holocaust" of the 20th Century, the genocide of the Armenians by the Turks from 1915 to 1923. Thus, he uttered his infamous statement: *"Who remembers the Armenians?"* as he strategically and methodically planned the second holocaust of the 20th Century, the genocide of the Jews. When we deny that sin and evil exist, we allow it to run rampant. As Winston Churchill noted, *"The only thing necessary for the triumph of evil is that good men do nothing."*

Evil exists; you are going to have to face that now, as we continue this discussion of God's omniscience. We must always name our enemies and face them. God knows evil exists, yet he did not create it. Evil is the precursor of pride, arrogance, disobedience, and rebellion against God; strangely, it is also the result. Evil only begets evil. Because God is omniscient, he is in complete control of it.

At the beginning of creation, God made everything perfectly and declared it *"good."* When Adam and Eve first encountered evil, they knew it was something quite different; it was the antithesis to God. They could see, hear, and taste that evil was some entirely new thing. It wasn't "good;" it was intriguing. Something new always is. Forbidden fruit always looks tastier, even when it smells sweetly rotten.

Let's delve into the Biblical text in Genesis 3 to explore the subtleties of evil and its ramifications in the context of God's omniscience. Verse 1 says, *"Now the serpent was more crafty than*

any other beast of the field that the Lord God had made." The word
"crafty" is the Hebrew word for "cunning". The serpent's evil
intentions wove a titillating and carefully worded dialogue
with Eve, with the intent of inciting insurrection and rebellion against God and the one rule he asked his first two
people to live by. Observe how Eve misquotes what God had
specifically said to her and Adam:

> *(2) And the woman said to the serpent, 'We may eat of the*
> *fruit of the trees in the garden,*
> *(3) but God said, 'You shall not eat of the fruit of the tree that*
> *is in the midst of the garden, neither shall you touch it, lest you*
> *die.'*

God watched Eve deliberately alter his original words and say
"*neither shall you touch it.*" In the Biblical record, God had
never said "*don't touch it.*" A hint of rebellion began to slither
into Eve's heart and her words as she misquoted God's clear
and simple directive. She momentarily chose to forget that
her omniscient God was watching, and listening. In Genesis
2:16 -17 God specifically had said:

> *(16) And the Lord God commanded the man, saying, 'You*
> *may surely eat of every tree of the garden,*
> *(17) but of the tree of the knowledge of good and evil you shall*
> *not eat, for in the day that you eat of it you shall surely die'."*

Eve began the self-deception game as God watched the conversation continue to unfold between her and the serpent. By intentionally misquoting God's words, Eve was already doubting and skirting around God's omniscience, power, and his rules. Evil was beginning to entice her to test the boundaries of choice and motive even more. The serpent knew she was already wavering, and he goaded her on and responded in verses 4-5:

(4) But the serpent said to the woman, 'You will not surely die.
(5) For God knows that when you eat of it your eyes will be opened, and you will be like God, knowing good and evil.'

The serpent began to bring Eve down the road of rebellion just a bit further. He began to deny God's very omniscience, power, and character by calling God a liar. Worse, Satan proclaimed that God had selfish, power-hungry motives and that he did not wish for Adam or Eve to *"be like God, knowing good and evil."* Satan knew there is such a thing as *"evil,"* because he *is* evil; he is the catalyst behind all evil in this world. He also knew that God is good and that God is omniscient. But he had Eve right where he wanted her, doubting and desiring more than what God gives, and doubting that God's character is truly sovereign, omniscient, omnipotent, omnipresent, and good.

The serpent patiently watched as Eve's will buckled under temptation, and her eyes gazed longingly on the forbidden fruit:

(6) So when the woman saw that the tree was good for food, and that it was a delight to the eyes, and that the tree was to be desired to make one wise, she took of its fruit and ate, and she also gave some to her husband who was with her, and he ate.

Now, both the first man and the first woman exercised their will, motives, and intellect, and they chose to sin, thereby dirtying the perfect world they were given. They incurred some excruciating consequences because God is the author of justice. Genesis 3:8-13 records what consequences came from disobeying God. From the beginning, in the Garden of Eden, God searched Adam's and Eve's hearts as he called out to them in the garden and asked them where they were (he knew very well where they were) after they had disobeyed him and ate of the only tree he had told them not to eat from. God watched his first two people choose to doubt him and desire to become as omniscient and powerful as he is. They had chosen evil over good.

In his omniscient knowledge, however, God knew what Adam and Eve would choose to do before they did it. He decided to right that wrong because God's character embodies grace and forgiveness. But again, he is a just God and must address the issue of sin. He hates sin. He will not ever tolerate it. Because of his perfect justness, he chose to mete out consequences and at the same time provide reconciliation. He didn't have to do that; he chose to. Genesis 3:13-15 lays out the consequences and a promise:

(13) "Then the Lord God said to the woman, 'What is this that you have done?' The woman said, 'The serpent deceived me, and I ate.'
(14) The Lord God said to the serpent, 'Because you have done this, cursed are you above all livestock and above all beasts of the field; on your belly you shall go, and dust you shall eat all the days of your life.
(15) I will put enmity between you and the woman, and between your offspring and her offspring; he shall bruise your head, and you shall bruise his heel.'"

In these three pivotal verses, we see that a radical act of sin earned a necessary and just response from God involving very significant consequences (Genesis 3:16-24). Yet, God is so loving, so forgiving, and so gracious, that he immediately follows his punishing response with a powerful promise to *"bruise"* (injure and defeat) evil. Eve's *"offspring"* in verse 15 alludes to a promised descendent who would overcome evil and provide perfect reconciliation with God. That *"offspring"* came thousands of years later, as promised, down to the very last prophetic detail, in the person of Jesus Christ, God's very own Son.

My purpose in exploring Genesis 3 is to highlight God's all-knowing character which, coupled with his omnipresence, power, grace, and love, offers an outstretched hand of reconciliation to a sinful world. God knew all along what people's hearts would choose. In Adam and Eve's case, they could have chosen to remain in perfect relationship with God, appreciate his bounty and provision, love him, trust him, and obey him. Unfortunately, they freely and willingly succumbed to choosing pride, mistrust, disobedience, and rebellion. In his omniscience, God knew this would be their choice. Only a loving and all-knowing heavenly father can choose to love unlovable people like this, much less provide them a healing solution that restores their relationship with him.

There is no manmade god, much less the god of the self, that would choose to do this. No hand-hewn statue, no mere man or cult leader, and no mantra-chanting group consciousness can defeat sin and evil. False gods cannot make promises and fulfill them 100% of the time, they cannot create perfection and then restore it when it is damaged, and they cannot fix brokenness and evil. False gods (including the god of the self) cannot possess knowledge outside of space and time. They cannot exercise perfect foreknowledge and know all things past, present and future, including the hidden thoughts, feelings, and motives of the heart. Only God can do this.

Mended Hearts Inscribed with a Story

Romans 8:29, written by the Apostle Paul, describes the omniscience of God: *"For those whom He foreknew, He also predestined to become conformed to the image of His Son, so that He would be the firstborn among many brethren."* God knows, and always has known, who will respond to his love, forgiveness, and reconciliation throughout human history. He knows what good and bad choices each of us will make. He is aware of who will accept his reconciliation and forgiveness and who will ignore it. His omniscience provides him that bird's-eye view of the past, present, and future.

Let's look together at Ephesians 1:1-14, where Paul fully introduces to the new 1st century Christians in Ephesus (modern-day Turkey) the profound omniscience of God:

(1) "Paul, an apostle of Christ Jesus by the will of God, to God's holy people in Ephesus, the faithful in Christ Jesus:
(2) Grace and peace to you from God our Father and the Lord Jesus Christ. Praise for Spiritual Blessings in Christ.
(3) Praise be to the God and Father of our Lord Jesus Christ, who has blessed us in the heavenly realms with every spiritual blessing in Christ.
(4) For he chose us in him before the creation of the world to be holy and blameless in his sight. In love
(5) he predestined us for adoption to sonship through Jesus Christ, in accordance with his pleasure and will
(6) to the praise of his glorious grace, which he has freely given us in the One he loves.
(7) In him we have redemption through his blood, the forgiveness of sins, in accordance with the riches of God's grace
(8) that he lavished on us. With all wisdom and understanding,
(9) he made known to us the mystery of his will according to his good pleasure, which he purposed in Christ,
(10) to be put into effect when the times reach their fulfillment

—to bring unity to all things in heaven and on earth under Christ.

(11) In him we were also chosen, having been predestined according to the plan of him who works out everything in conformity with the purpose of his will,

(12) in order that we, who were the first to put our hope in Christ, might be for the praise of his glory.

(13) And you also were included in Christ when you heard the message of truth, the gospel of your salvation. When you believed, you were marked in him with a seal, the promised Holy Spirit,

(14) who is a deposit guaranteeing our inheritance until the redemption of those who are God's possession—to the praise of his glory."

Chapter 1 of the Book of Ephesians is full of descriptive elements of God's all-knowing character and how it shapes his plans from the very beginning of time when sin first occurred in the Garden of Eden with Adam and Eve. God, his Savior-Son Jesus Christ, and God's Holy Spirit were creating and planning everything from the beginning; they existed before the beginning of time. Ephesians 1:5 proclaims clearly that *"he predestined us for adoption to sonship through Jesus Christ, in accordance with his pleasure and will."* A plan was always in place to create, choose, and direct the destinies of those who would become God's children. The plan needed to address sin because God knew in his foreknowledge that the wrong choices would be willfully made by the first two people. From the beginning, God had to create a perfect plan to fix things he knew that man would, unfortunately, choose to do.

No one can have a relationship with God--much less be with him in heaven--unless someone fixes the issue of sin. God is perfect; he cannot be in a relationship with sinful people. Therefore, God chose to have his Son provide the reconciliation and the defeat of sin and death itself. Once that was done fully and completely on the cross, the plan of "adoption," and "sonship" could be offered to us through Jesus Christ, his promised Savior. That has been promised since Adam and Eve's original sin because God knew all along he would have to do this for his sons and daughters then and now.

God extends that promise to us today. Not through our own work, good deeds, or personal accomplishments can we ever earn God's forgiveness, reconciliation, and adoption. They are God's gift to give and God's alone. Though reconciliation and forgiveness are offered to all, and we need only respond to it and accept it, God knows who will ultimately respond to him and who will reject him. He calls those who he knew would respond to him and follow him his "*elect.*" Before God created the universe and all life upon this earth, his foreknowledge already informed him of who among his created "image-bearers" would be the recipients of his love, his reconciliation, and his offer of eternal life with him. It is a sobering thought to realize that he already knew his *elect.*

Charles Spurgeon describes God's omniscience in his sermon below:

> *"From all eternity He (Christ) is rejoicing in His whole world and delighting in mankind. His thoughts rolled onward to the time when His elect should be born into the world; He viewed them in the mirror of His foreknowledge. 'All the days ordained for me were written in your book before one of them*

came to be,' (Ps. 139:16). When the world was set upon its pillars, He was there...The Son of Man (Christ) visited His people. Because His Son delighted in them, He could not rest away from them, for His heart longed after them. They were never absent from His heart, for He had written their names on His hands, and etched them on His side...We may often forget to meditate upon the perfections of our Lord, but He never ceases to remember us. Let's chide ourselves for past forgetfulness, and always pray for grace to keep Him in our fondest memory."[1]

There is nothing that you have or have not done that surprises God. He was there all along and knows your story, because he created you and can see and hear what is happening within your heart. He knows what you have or have not done. He knows what you will do in the future. He has crafted and executed his plan for forgiveness, grace, reconciliation, and eternal life with him. Simply reach out and grasp his promises.

* * *

A Divine Coffee Break

Many years ago, I was spending my lunch hour sitting at my favorite coffee shop that I frequented almost daily. On this particular day, I was heavy-hearted about a few things, and I was reading at a table outdoors while gripping my steaming cup of freshly roasted coffee. Suddenly, my dear friend, Deb, popped her head right in my face and smiled. She had another woman with her whom I didn't know. I suddenly felt such joy as I stood up and instinctively hugged her. My bad mood was brightened to see her unexpectedly dropping into my precious sixty minutes of respite from work. I needed to see a friend that afternoon. God knew it, and he sent me someone when I least expected it.

Now, this wasn't an earth-shattering moment, nor was the conversation. It was merely a chance meeting (a God-intended one, of course), on a day when I needed a friendly face to remind me that God had given me Christian sisters to love me and pop in when I least expected it and most needed it. After exchanging a few updates on various things, graciously introducing myself to the unknown lady who accompanied her and warmly speaking with her for a brief moment, they both made their good-byes and walked to their car. I sat down and simply went about the rest of my lunch hour and felt much, much better.

The next day, Deb called me and told me that she had been trying to share God's plan of salvation and reconciliation with that friend she had been with the day before. Deb had already shared her own story of how God had reached into her life and saved her, and she was just trying to reflect God's love to this other woman the best way she could. She was excited to add that her friend had pulled her aside after we had parted company outside the coffee shop the day before, and she had spouted, "*That friend of yours that we just met (me!). I want what she has. I saw God in her eyes! I want what she has.*" Folks, I went from a little sixty-minute pity party I had been wallowing in at that coffee shop the day before to utter euphoria at how God took me at a weak moment and allowed me to reflect him to a stranger. It was an omniscient appointment that God had planned all along.

2 Corinthians 12:9 records what the Apostle Paul learned from God by living with a physical impairment that adversely affected him: *"My grace is sufficient for you, for my power is perfected in weakness. Most gladly, therefore, I will rather boast about my weaknesses, so that the power of Christ may dwell in me."* Mirroring God to someone at a weak moment encouraged me deeply, perhaps as much as it affected the woman who *"saw God in my eyes,"* and *"wanted what I had."* She didn't want me; she wanted the God that she could see in me at my weakest moment. His presence, power, and love appear strongly within us often when we are at a low point in our life and can do nothing except cling to God and his promises. It is there in those desolate times that others see a caring, understanding, and loving God within us.

God is that caring, wise, and all-knowing shepherd who is always near his sheep, even picking us up and carrying us when we cannot move forward. Let people see the Great Shepherd within you, enveloping you when you are at your weakest. Often, when things are going well, and we are confident and independent in our supposed strength, we don't reflect God at all. Strangely, it is in our weaker moments that others see God much more clearly within us.

A friendly demeanor, rather than a morbid face, a warm smile rather than a tight-lipped scowl, and a caring word for a stranger rather than a terse word--or even silent indifference--is what beckons them to God. They see him in us and they admit, albeit not always, that they deeply want what we have. Who would not wish to follow an all-knowing shepherd who is aware of every detail of his sheep's personalities and tendencies, the subtle dips and turns of every path ahead, and who navigates the treacherous journey of life we walk by leading us and simply asking us to follow him?

* * *

Making it real

We can rest in the fact that God both proclaims and demonstrates his omniscience, and that this has profound implications for us. God is omniscient and omnipresent; we can't hide. He knew us, he knows us, and he is quite aware of what each of us is doing and thinking tomorrow, next year, the next decade, and the day we draw our last breath. But, does he truly know what it's like, I mean really like, to be us? He loves his people, he fixes our sinful selves, and he offers us undeserved forgiveness and reconciliation, even though he knows what we've done and worse, what we will still do in the future. Is it even possible for such an all-knowing God to relate to us in some small way and truly know what it feels like to struggle with sin? There is a one-word answer to this: **Jesus**.

Hebrews 4:15 states, *"For we do not have a high priest who is unable to sympathize with our weaknesses, but one who in every respect has been tempted as we are, yet without sin."* There you have it. Because God came into this world to experience it in the body of a man, Jesus the Son, he can relate. Hebrews 4:16 continues: *"Let us then with confidence draw near to the throne of grace, that we may receive mercy and find grace to help in time of need."*

Don't be reticent, simply draw near to him. He is not a distant and detached taskmaster who requires that we perform an endless array of good deeds or adhere to a back-breaking list of rules. Jesus fulfilled all of God's requirements, and Jesus knew what it felt like to be a man. Being fully God and fully man will take a lifetime and then some to truly understand, however it is a blessed assurance. God knows what we feel like, how we think, and what drives us. He can *"sympathize with our weaknesses."* He requires only a response of gratefulness to his gifts of mercy, grace, reconciliation, and forgiveness. He knows what tempts the human heart and his Son, Jesus Christ, overcame sin for us and broke the chains that bind us to it. He paid the debt of sin for us because he knew all along that we would need a Savior, a debt-payer who would satisfy and pay off the debt of our sin and wipe our spiritual account clean.

If you have responded to God's offer of his complete forgiveness, how can you practically, honestly, and regularly reflect God's omniscience in your life? First, you have to be changed by him; you cannot change yourself. That should come as a relief. He knew you before your parents conceived you. He knows who will ultimately respond to him and his gracious gift of eternal life and forgiveness. When he regenerates your heart, he will place within you a desire to know him and beckon you to respond to him. Once you have responded to God's loving offer of forgiveness and reconciliation, his Spirit will have begun working in you to change you into something entirely new. With a new life comes a new story to tell.

Next, you have to be willing and able to share your personal story; it belongs only to you. People want to know why you are different because if you lean on God's omniscient power and let it change you, they're going to notice it. People in your sphere of life are going to notice that, strangely, you are at peace in the tempests that hit you in life. They'll notice that you are confident in your relationship with God and derive strength and peace from him in tough times. When you act like you're a recipient of undeserved favor by a loving God, people are going to find it obvious, even curious; God will make sure that it's infectious.

Who can refute your story of what God has done in your life? Someone who doesn't see your story lived out, doesn't hear your story from your own mouth, and therefore doesn't even know you have such a powerful and personal God-story to tell. Silence isn't golden; it's deadly. God told his story through chosen men who wrote by the inspiration of the Holy Spirit, from Moses to Solomon and David, to the Prophets, to Jesus' apostles. God has authored his story in your life, as well. God's all-knowing presence in our lives will change us and make us new. He knows us better than we know ourselves.

Through his people, God can be known. If you do not yet know the omniscient, gracious, and loving God of creation, draw near to his throne of grace and mercy with confidence that he will indeed welcome you.

* * *

Study Questions:

1. John 3:20b says, *"God is greater than our heart and knows all things."* What blessings come to us because God is omniscient and knows our past, our present, and our future? God knows what you have done and is willing to forgive you; have you forgiven yourself for things you've done in the past? What are you still having trouble letting go of?

2. Hebrews 1:3 says "*The Son is the radiance of God's glory and the exact representation of His being.*" Christ is that perfect "*radiance of God's glory*" and he is also the only one who is the "*exact representation of His being.*" Where do you struggle with desiring to reflect God's glory and radiate it in your own life? In what ways do you think you are reflecting God's glory in your life so others can know Him?

3. In Psalms 139:23-24 David cries out to God saying, "*Search me, O God, and know my heart; try me and know my anxious thoughts; see if there be any hurtful way in me, and lead me in the everlasting way.*" David recognized God's omniscience and asked Him to search the depths of his heart and thoughts and reveal any "*hurtful way*" in him. Are you willing to ask God to do this in your heart on a daily basis and face what he reveals to you that he sees in you? What things within you has he already revealed that are hurtful?

4. Read Ephesians 1:1-14. How does God's foreknowledge of you and his complete knowledge of you inside and out affect you spiritually and in your everyday life (work, relationships, attitudes, etc.)? What verse(s) in this passage particularly speaks to you and why?

5. 2 Corinthians 12:9 tells us, "*My grace is sufficient for you, for my power is perfected in weakness. Most gladly, therefore, I will rather boast about my weaknesses, so that the power of Christ may dwell in me.*" Do you tend to reflect God more when you are in the midst of struggles or difficult circumstances or do you honestly notice that you reflect him less at these

times? Do you struggle with God really knowing what your circumstances are?

6. Matthew 6:8 says, *"Do not be like them, for your Father knows what you need before you ask him."* If this is the case, then why do we need to pray to God if he already knows everything?

7. Hebrews 4:15 says, *"For we do not have a high priest who is unable to sympathize with our weaknesses, but one who in every respect has been tempted as we are, yet without sin."* God the Son, Jesus Christ, knows what it's like to be us, though he was God in the Flesh. How does his knowledge of our weaknesses and temptations affect our walk with him?

8. Because God is omniscient, why is it such good news that he made plans from the beginning of time to restore mankind's relationship with him? What does this mean for you personally and how does this encourage to trust him?

Additional Bible verses on God's omniscience

Do: *Discuss and ponder over these verses, and pray for God to illuminate each one. (For additional context, read the entire Biblical chapter in which each of these verses appears.)*

Proverbs 15:3 - *"The eyes of the Lord are in every place, keeping watch on the evil and the good."*

Psalm 147:5 - *"Great is our Lord, and abundant in power, his understanding is beyond measure."*

. . .

Jeremiah 23:24 - "'Can a man hide himself in secret places so that I cannot see him?' Declares the Lord. 'Do I not fill heaven and earth?' declares the Lord."

Job 28:24 - *"For he looks to the ends of the earth and sees everything under the heavens."*

1 Corinthians 2:11 - *"For who knows a person's thoughts except the spirit of that person, which is in him? So also no one comprehends the thoughts of God except the Spirit of God."*

Matthew 6:8 - *"Do not be like them, for your Father knows what you need before you ask him."*

Revelation 2:23 - *"And I will strike her children dead. And all the churches will know that I am he who searches mind and heart, and I will give to each of you according to your works."*

Memory verse:

2 Corinthians 12:9 - *"My grace is sufficient for you, for my power is perfected in weakness. Most gladly, therefore, I will rather boast about my weaknesses, so that the power of Christ may dwell in me."*

. . .

Action Plan – These are areas of my life where I want to learn to trust in God's omniscience:

1.

2.

3.

Suggested Readings and Resources:

1. *Knowing God*, J. I. Packer, July 1993

2. *The Reason for God: Belief in an Age of Skepticism*, Timothy Keller, August 4, 2009

3. *The Gospel of Ruth: Loving God Enough to Break the Rules*, Carolyn Custis James, Robert L. Hubbard, Jan. 2011

4. *When Life and Beliefs Collide*, Carolyn Custis James, November 2002

Notes:

Chapter Four

THE GREATEST GIFT OF ALL – GOD'S LOVE

1 John 4:7-8 *"Beloved, let us love one another, for love is from God, and whoever loves has been born of God and knows God. Anyone who does not love does not know God, because God is love."*

Deuteronomy 7:9 *"Know therefore that the LORD your God is God, the faithful God who keeps covenant and steadfast love with those who love him and keep his commandments, to a thousand generations"*

Over the last several millennia, the Bible descriptively sings of God's love, and it is a love like none other. Human love is something quite different than God's love; there is no comparison. God is perfect and we are not, thus his love is perfect and ours isn't. God embodies love and *"God is love."* (1 John 4:8b) That should quell any concerns that God is all about rules and no love. Setting the stage for our discussion of

God's love, 1 John 4:8 explains it simply, *"Anyone who does not love does not know God, because God is love."*

We demonstrate what we consider to be love in an infinite number of ways, depending on how we were raised, what our life experiences have been, and how we individually and subjectively define love deep within our own heart. Without a Biblical definition of love, the only other definition is how man defines love, and that is all over the map. Worse, man's definition of love is tainted by sin, therefore it diverges from God's love, which is perfect. Man's love, sad to say, can be anything from highly to subtly conditional, self-serving, authoritarian, legalistic, even sadistic and evil. We have to look to God to define love, since it is embodied in his very essence.

Let's examine what the Bible tells us about love because God didn't keep himself a mystery; love is who he is. He meant it to be quite clear, irrefutable, and accessible. Understanding love is understanding God. If we don't know how to love, then we don't know God. If we don't know God, then we can't reflect his attributes in our lives and show a glimpse of his type of glorious love to others.

The following verses describe God's type of love and some of its unique characteristics:

1 John 4:19, *"We love Him, because He first loved us."*

Deuteronomy 7:9, *"Know therefore that the LORD your God is God, the faithful God who keeps covenant and steadfast love with those who love him and keep his commandments, to a thousand generations"*

. . .

1 Corinthians 13:4-7, *"Love is patient and kind; love does not envy or boast; it is not arrogant or rude. It does not insist on its own way; it is not irritable or resentful; it does not rejoice at wrongdoing, but rejoices with the truth. Love bears* all things, believes all things, hopes all things, endures all things."

Romans 5:8, *"but God shows his love for us in that while we were still sinners, Christ died for us."*

Psalm 52:8, *"But I am like an olive tree flourishing in the house of God; I trust in God's unfailing love for ever and ever."*

What you'll notice is that the overarching characteristic of God's love is that he loves us despite ourselves, and that he made that overture first. He loves us because it is who he is; he cannot be what he isn't. He can only be what he eternally *is,* which is love itself. His love is undergirded with faithfulness, patience, selflessness, and longsuffering, and all of this is unchanging since the beginning of time. God is unchangeable; his love never wanes, runs out, or lapses for a second.

Agape (ἀγάπη) love, in Greek, means a love that is not based upon the merits of the recipient of that love but upon the giver of it. *Agape* love requires no payment in response to that love. It is a tender and personal choice or commitment by the love giver. It is utterly selfless, and it is not based on circumstances. It is also a love that God wants people to have for one another. God makes the first move to demonstrate his *agape* love to people because we are the only thing that is created in his "image," and he has a special place in his heart for his image-bearers (See Genesis 1:26). It is a love based on the giver, for we are most certainly not worthy of it.

The Biblical record provides a plethora of highly specific and descriptive elements of God's love. Let's look at these verses below:

1 John 4:19, "*We love because he first loved us.*"

John 3:16, "*For God so loved the world, that he gave his only Son, that whoever believes in him should not perish but have eternal life.*"

1 Corinthians 13:4-7, "*Love is patient and kind; love does not envy or boast; it is not arrogant or rude. It does not insist on its own way; it is not irritable or resentful; it does not rejoice at wrongdoing, but rejoices with the truth. Love bears all things, believes all things, hopes all things, endures all things.*"

Romans 5:8, "*but God shows his love for us in that while we were still sinners, Christ died for us.*"

Psalm 52:8, "*But I am like a green olive tree in the house of God. I trust in the steadfast love of God forever and ever.*"

Matthew 5:44, "*But I say to you, love your enemies and pray for those who persecute you*"

God's love is also eternal, intensely nurturing, and shockingly unconditional. Flowing from an omniscient and gracious god, his love is woven into the very fabric of his plans for his people. Knowing God gives us access to his healing, transforming, forgiving, and everlasting love, which is part of God's very essence. Through his love for his people he provides direct and open access to himself.

As David poetically says in Psalm 52:8, *"I am like a green olive tree in the house of God. I trust in the steadfast love of God forever and ever."* David knew what it felt like to be loved by his God and described it as something firmly planted, nurturing, and deep-rooted, much like an olive tree. He also proclaims that God's love is *"steadfast"* and always there, unshakeable, and unconditional. This engendered a love for God in David's heart that would last *"for ever and ever."* David likened himself to an olive tree created and planted by God, because the olive tree is deep-rooted, important to human life and sustenance, and it is long-lasting (the Garden of Gethsemane today still has original olive trees that are several thousand years old and they are still producing olives!).

In the ancient world, olive oil was used for cooking, anointing, beauty, and for burning oil lamps to provide light in the darkness. The olive branches were used in ancient Greece as a sign of peace. Deep-rooted, long-lasting faith and peace in God's unfailing love is indeed eternal and unfailing like an olive tree. In deep trials, David knew this kind of tender and nourishing love from God. Later in David's life, amid his adultery, murder, and lying, David still knew God's undying love (though God's fair consequences for David's sins were commensurate with his infractions). Remember, a loving father disciplines his child until the will is bent toward obedience. God's love admonishes like a loving father, but it also feeds, sustains, and gives life to his children.

Charles Spurgeon's sermon entitled "God's Unfailing Love"[1] profoundly speaks of God's choice to love us and begs us to meditate on one of God's most profound attributes:

"Meditate for a while on God's unfailing love. It is a tender love. With a gentle touch, he heals the brokenhearted and binds up their wounds. He is as gracious in the manner of His unfailing love as in the matter of it. It is great unfailing love. There is nothing little in God; His unfailing love is like Himself--it is infinite. You cannot measure it. His unfailing love is so great that it forgives great sins to great sinners, after great lengths of time, and then gives great favors and great privileges, and raises us to great enjoyments in the great heaven of the great God.

It is undeserved unfailing love, as indeed all true unfailing love must be, for deserved unfailing love is only a misnomer for justice. There is no right on the sinner's part to the kind consideration of the Most High; had the rebel been doomed at once to eternal fire, he would have richly deserved the doom. And if delivered from wrath, sovereign love alone has found a cause, for there was none in the sinner himself. It is a rich unfailing love. Some things are great but have little efficacy in them; this love is a cordial to your drooping spirits; a golden ointment to your bleeding wounds; a heavenly bandage to your broken bones; a royal chariot for your weary feet; a bosom of love for your trembling heart. It is manifold mercy and love!...It will never leave you.

If this love is within you, God's love will be with you in temptation to keep you from yielding, with you in trouble to prevent you from sinking, with you living to be the light and life of your countenance; and with you dying to be the joy of your soul when earthly comfort is ebbing fast!"

This is a different type of love than we naturally possess. *Agape* love is what Jesus Christ, God's own Son, shows us in his life. He models it so that we can see and experience what it is like personally. Christ, the promised Savior, is God himself. Yet, some can't believe that God's love is unfailing and *forever and ever*, when they have lived a certain kind of life, done something seemingly unforgivable, or simply waved a dismissive hand and declared long ago that God doesn't exist. Some even pat themselves on the back and gleefully proclaim that they have lived a God-free life. Many in today's culture have given themselves over to the internal quest to become their very own god. Others will choose their career as their god and expectantly look to it for purpose and affirmation.

We know from God's handbook for life that he breathed into existence over several millennia, the Bible, that his love is unconditional, intentional, and everlasting. He then sealed that love with a covenant--a contract with his people--after he reached out to us first. We didn't reach out to him; he initiated the relationship and completed it from beginning to end. When we read Romans 5:8, *"but God shows his love for us in that while we were still sinners, Christ died for us,"* we can deduce clearly that, in our deadness of sin and depravity, God chose to love mankind. We are truly selfish and lost sheep that only the Creator could love and choose to save from own folly.

The Old Testament prophet Isaiah summed it up nicely in the Book of Isaiah, Chapter 53, verse 6: *"All we like sheep have gone astray; we have turned—every one—to his own way; and the Lord has laid on him the iniquity of us all."* God's love of his people is unconditional, and he will go to the ends of the earth to find his sheep, like a good shepherd would do with any stray sheep in the flock which he cares for. A loving, caring shepherd will go to the point of breaking the leg of a stray sheep, gently laying that sheep around his shoulders and neck, and tenderly walking that broken sheep back to the fold to protect it from its own waywardness. God will do the same for his people.

We will explore in greater depth the elements of God's *agape* love and how it is an expression of his character. In doing this we will increasingly see how he is an intentional and dedicated Shepherd who will actively go after his sheep and gather them close to himself in a relationship that he has initiated.

God's Love is Unconditional, Intentional, and Unfailing

Let's explore some of the specific elements of God's love. First, God's love is unconditional. While we were drowning in sin, God reached out to love us first and provided a Savior for us. At the very beginning of creation, he loved his first two human creations that were so carefully crafted by his own hands. Even after God observed Adam and Eve badly exercise their will, intellect, and judgment which lead them down a regrettable path, he loved them. He gave them consequences like a good Father should. What's more, he gave them a promised Savior who would redeem God's people and forever conquer sin. The first two people started a mess; God loved them and cleaned it up.

If God did not offer that free and unearned gift of eternal life through his promised Savior, Jesus Christ, heaven would be empty except for God himself. And, amazingly enough, God is hospitable and wants people to not only walk through his front gates and into his house, but he also wants to provide a feast for them. No quick TV dinners and leftovers in heaven for God's people! He wants to pull out all the stops and provide a bountiful wedding-like feast for us so that we can celebrate our relationship with him. There are no tickets that you have to purchase to enter through heaven's doors. There is no small handmade gift on our part that will get us in the door, either. Heaven takes no bribes. God paid the price for our entrance into his house and his boundless love. That is *agape* love.

Second, God's love is intentional. God's love is his choice, his premeditated and omniscient desire, and his very essence. It is intended to right all our wrongs by the giving of a Great Redeemer, Jesus Christ. Read and ponder over the Apostle Paul's words below from Romans 5:1-11:

1. *Therefore, since we have been justified by faith, we have peace with God through our Lord Jesus Christ.*
2. *Through him we have also obtained access by faith into this grace in which we stand, we rejoice in hope of the glory of God.*
3. *Not only that, but we rejoice in our sufferings, knowing that suffering produces endurance,*
4. *and endurance produces character, and character produces hope,*
5. *and hope does not put us to shame, because God's love has been poured into our hearts through the Holy Spirit who has been given to us.*

6. *For while we were still weak, at the right time Christ died for the ungodly.*

7. *For one will scarcely die for a righteous person—though perhaps for a good person one would dare even to die—*

8. *but God shows his love for us in that while we were still sinners, Christ died for us.*

9. *Since, therefore, we have now been justified by his blood, much more shall we be saved by him from the wrath of God.*

10. *For if while we were enemies we were reconciled to God by the death of his Son, much more, now that we are reconciled, shall we be saved by his life.*

11. *More than that, we also rejoice in God through our Lord Jesus Christ, through whom we have now received reconciliation.*

In God's perfect love, he chooses to reconcile with us first, when we are the ones who have broken our relationship with him. Even more surprising, God desires to enter into a covenant relationship with those who respond to him. The word *covenant* in Hebrew is בְּרִית (bereeth), and it connotes other subtle meanings such as "allied," or a "treaty/contract." Once that contract was broken, when Adam and Eve sinned and they ate from the forbidden tree, God chose to mete out consequences because he is a just God. Next, he started a new covenant, a second chance. We are the recipients of that second chance to return into a personal relationship with God.

The most important promise in this new covenant is that God provided the Savior to right our wrongs, to declare us forgiven, and to cover us in his wooly white cloak of perfect righteousness. God declares us righteous by looking at the

Savior rather than at us. He extends his perfect peace that we will never have on our own, provides his spiritual gift of faith, extends his endless grace, and gives a sure promise of being with him forever. The author of this real-life story of love, forgiveness, redemption, and reconciliation is God himself. He writes and executes the plan from beginning to end.

John 15:16 records Jesus proclaiming: *"You did not choose me, but I chose you and appointed you that you should go and bear fruit and that your fruit should abide, so that whatever you ask the Father in my name, he may give it to you."* God makes it very clear that he alone chooses who to come into a covenant with. He chooses to make his people cleansed from sin and acceptable to him so that he can be in a relationship with them. He wants his people to experience a loving, grace-filled alliance with him in this short life on Earth and forever after. God's covenants with mankind are always his gracious act of love to a world filled with sinful, broken people unable to ever be worthy to be in a relationship with God. His love for people compels him to reach out first, provide the Savior to overcome sin, and declare us worthy to belong to him in a covenant relationship as adopted sons and daughters. We absolutely can never do this on our own, no matter how many good deeds we do, how many vices we abstain from, or how many days we sit in a place of worship. He is the loving covenant maker who does all the cleanup work for us and in return desires obedience and love.

How is God's love intentional when he allows enormous difficulties and trials to plague someone's life? In his omniscience and foreknowledge, God sees the bigger picture and sometimes allows difficulties, intense challenges, and struggles to forge a strong, steely backbone in his people. Difficulty and challenge are like a fiery forge that purifies metal; God some-times will purify and forge our faith in him this way. God's love has a good and perfect purpose and he desires only good for his people, even in difficult circumstances. As we walk through adversity in life, our trust in his intentions and his unconditional affection for us grows stronger, until we learn to trust in his love to conquer all things in this life and the life thereafter.

Finally, God's love is *"unfailing"* and *"forever and ever,"* as David declares in the Psalms 52:8, when he says, *"But I am like a green olive tree in the house of God. I trust in the steadfast love of God forever and ever."* God's unfailing love for his people flows from his steadfast, faithful, and unchanging character. When you belong to him, his covenantal love isn't conditional, nor does it wane when you digress from good behavior and disappoint him. God is faithful and unfailing and exists unchanged for an eternity, so why should his love for you be any different?

A loving father or mother loves their child even when they are disobedient, misbehaved, and disrespectful. A parent's love doesn't fail, and they will always love their child despite their bad behavior. God allows us our will, our choices, and our human intellect to exist in *"concurrence"* with his perfect will, foreknowledge, and omniscience. Mistakes, however, are ours to make. God doesn't learn anything new, and he isn't caught off guard and surprised that we make bad choices at any given moment. His love is not only unfailing, it is a forever love buoyed by a bottomless spring of grace lasting for an eternity.

Because God is unchanging (which we will explore in a later chapter), his love is unchanging, as are his plans. Though circumstances may appear otherwise, God's love and concern for his people does not wane. He does not fail in anything that he does, says, or promises, ever. Unfailing love undergirds his unfailing promises. Once we belong to him, he will never let us go. God fills our hearts and minds with these unchanging assurances:

> Isaiah 41:10, *"Fear not, for I am with you; be not dismayed, for I am your God; I will strengthen you, I will help you, I will uphold you with my righteous right hand."*
> John 10:28. *"I give them eternal life, and they will never perish, and no one will snatch them out of my hand.*
> Isaiah 49:16, *"Behold, I have engraved you on the palms of my hands; your walls are continually before me."*

God's love, plans, covenants, and promises remain forever because he is unchanging. He never fails his people. Once we have responded to his love and allowed him to enter our lives and have his way with us, he declares us his sons and daughters, and we are in his family forever. Nothing can separate us from the love of God. He won't allow it.

Romans 8:38-39 sums it up:

> *"For I am convinced that neither death nor life, neither angels nor demons, neither the present nor the future, nor any powers, neither height nor depth, nor anything else in all creation, will be able to separate us from the love of God that is in Christ Jesus our Lord."*

Making it real

God's unconditional, intentional, and unfailing love is an overwhelming concept to meditate upon. How can we possibly reflect his love to others, when we can't even drive five miles down the street without wildly gesticulating at a person who cut us off on the road? When our children are monstrously disobedient or blatantly disrespectful, how are we to demonstrate God's *agape* love to them? How can we even desire to love that neighbor who refuses to be friendly and turns away at opportunities to get to know you? To be honest, we cannot do it on our own. *Agape* love does not naturally exist in the human heart; it must be put there by God alone. Without knowing God's love, we cannot practice *agape* love. If we walk with God, he will teach us how to reflect his type of love to others. If you have already accepted his gift of grace and forgiveness, then God will give you his gift of *agape* love and show you how to exercise it.

In John 21:16-17, Jesus gives us a clear insight into what we're supposed to do with God's love:

"Jesus said to Simon Peter, 'Simon son of John, do you love me more than these?' 'Yes, Lord,' he said, 'you know that I love you.' Jesus said, 'Feed my lambs.' Again Jesus said, 'Simon son of John, do you love me?' He answered, 'Yes, Lord, you know that I love you.' Jesus said, 'Take care of my sheep.' The third time he said to him, 'Simon son of John, do you love me.' Peter was hurt because Jesus asked him the third time, 'Do you love me.' He said, 'Lord, you know all things; you know that I love you.' Jesus said, 'Feed my sheep.'"

Jesus, God's own Son, declares that if we are in a relationship with him, we are to feed God's love to others. And, when Jesus repeats things three times, he means to emphasize this as extremely important and fundamental to remember. A shepherd leads, protects, loves, feeds, and tends to his sheep. Jesus encourages us to do this with others as a demonstration of his *agape* love. This is precisely what God does with each of us who belong to him, because that is what a good shepherd should do. God is the Great Shepherd whose undying love will always be for his own sheep. He goes to the ends of the earth to find each of his lost sheep who he already knows belongs to him. He finds them, saves them from themselves, and gently brings them back into his sheepfold to tend to them, nurture them, and provide for them.

1 Corinthians 13:4-7 defines how we can love, feed, and take care of others:

"Love is patient and kind; love does not envy or boast; it is not arrogant or rude. It does not insist on its own way; it is not irritable or resentful; it does not rejoice at wrongdoing, but rejoices with the truth. Love bears all things, believes all things, hopes all things, endures all things."

When the Apostle Paul wrote his letter to the new believers in God and his Son, Jesus Christ, in 1st Century Corinth (located in Greece), he wanted to tell them what God is like. He specifically wanted to encourage them about how loving God is, as well as what his kind of love looks like when people share it with others. Paul was practical, and he laid things out simply for the everyday person then and now. He specifies that love looks like patience and kindness and that it is not tainted with envy, rudeness, or arrogant boasting. *Agape* love is not selfish. Love cannot coexist alongside evil and bad intentions. It is fueled by the truth. God's type of love is forgiving and longsuffering, and it is backed by good intentions. This type of love is unfailing and enduring, just like God himself.

If we know God, are we behaving like this and loving like this? Do we reflect this to type of love to others, or is it merely a pleasant concept to mull over on a Sunday morning? When was the last time we were patient and kind with "sister sandpaper," that gratingly annoying person in our life? It's easy to be patient and kind with pleasant people; it is practicing *agape* love when we exercise it with someone who is extremely unlikeable. The next time the cashier at the store makes a mistake, let's remember to dispense with reactive rudeness and give her grace. Keeping our heart and tongue in check the next time others are engaging in slander, gossip, or lies, and consciously choosing not to join in, is a profoundly impactful way to reflect God's type of love. Being genuinely happy when a friend gets a job promotion, while we have been striving for one for years, is practicing a godly love that doesn't envy but rejoices in good. Putting our spouse's needs—or a friend's needs--before our own and bearing with them when they're grumpy or callous, and choosing to not be irritable or resentful in response, is putting Christ-like love into action. This is visible *agape* love in action.

If you are a parent, begin asking for God's help in bearing with your children in patience and love when they are grouchy, lazy, or disobedient. Exhibit to them God's grace and love rather than reacting in anger, as they probably expect you to. Bearing with them doesn't mean you don't discipline; bad behavior needs consequences so you can lovingly and graciously bend their behavior to be pleasing to a loving God.

On the flip side, if they see anger and harsh discipline and no love or grace, they'll perceive that God is like that: harsh, graceless, and unloving. Bear with them, endure with them, and give them hope in a God that loves them and will walk caringly with them all the days of their life in *agape* love. Water them with grace and love so that they will be *"like an olive tree flourishing in the house of God,"* so they will learn to *"trust in God's unfailing love forever and ever." (Psalm 52:8)*

With your spouse or significant other, make an intentional attempt to bear with them, and encourage them. That is what feeding and taking care of God's sheep looks like. In the covenant of marriage, you are one in Christ and are his *"bride,"* and one day will be presented to God clothed in Christ's righteousness. The covenant of marriage is a direct reflection and a foreshadow of your oneness in Christ, both now and in eternity, and Christ's oneness with God, both now and for all eternity. Therefore, feed your covenantal relation-ship with love, honor, encouragement, and hope. Dispense with the arrogance, rudeness, irritableness, resentment, boast-ing, envy--all the things that God says love isn't. Rejoice in truth together as one, and live it out in front of each other. That reflects God's love and oneness so powerfully that others will be encouraged by it. They'll have hope in God and his love through seeing you model visible *agape* love in your marriage relationship.

James 1:19 provides us with a simple, yet powerful, model of how to show others God's kind of love: *"Know this, my beloved brothers: let every person be quick to hear, slow to speak, slow to anger; for the anger of man does not produce the righteousness of God."*

Additionally, in James 1:22-25, we can be assured that modeling God's love will produce blessing for us and others:

(22) But be doers of the word, and not hearers only, deceiving yourselves.

(23) For if anyone is a hearer of the word and not a doer, he is like a man who looks intently at his natural face in a mirror.

(24) For he looks at himself and goes away and at once forgets what he was like.

(25) But the one who looks into the perfect law, the law of liberty, and perseveres, being no hearer who forgets but a doer who acts, he will be blessed in his doing."

James encourages us to simply make God real by modeling his attributes to others. This is what Christ did, he modeled God to others, obeyed him implicitly, and genuinely loved others even unto death. The beginning of Hebrews 1:3 explains it this way, *"The Son is the radiance of God's glory and the exact representation of His being."* Christ was God in the flesh and the *"exact"* representation of himself. When we know God, we become filled with God's Holy Spirit and we can become *"doers"* of the Word and introduce God to others by living, loving, and doing as Christ did. Mind you, we're not perfect, but God expects us to model Christ in our lives once we belong to him. If we are in covenant with God, others should see his *agape* love in us clearly and irrefutably. People are hungry to see it and receive it, however, they must first know that it is real. If we are genuinely desirous of pleasing God and feeding his sheep, we must recognize that sheep follow a loving, knowledgeable shepherd who they trust, know, and respect. If we mirror that type of love to others, they will want to know the God that we follow.

As we complete this chapter's journey into God's type of love, David, in Psalm 145:8, describes God and his precious love like this: "*The Lord is gracious and merciful, slow to anger and abounding in steadfast love.*" A natural outpouring of our relationship with God is to model his grace, mercy, and steadfast love that never fails us, even in our worst moments. Because he is slow to anger and filled with a love that doesn't wane for his people, let us endeavor to commit daily to make every attempt to lean upon his grace, mercy, and love and feed his sheep with that kind of *agape* love. Make every effort to be an *agape* gift giver and be generous with that gift to those around you.

C. S. Lewis, a profoundly insightful author and a devoted disciple of God, encourages us in the practice love with these observations and words of encouragement in his book, *The Four Loves*:

"*To love at all is to be vulnerable. Love anything and your heart will be wrung and possibly broken. If you want to make sure of keeping it intact you must give it to no one, not even an animal. Wrap it carefully round with hobbies and little luxuries; avoid all entanglements. Lock it up safe in the casket or coffin of your selfishness. But in that casket, safe, dark, motionless, airless, it will change. It will not be broken; it will become unbreakable, impenetrable, irredeemable. To love is to be vulnerable.*"[2]

. . .

Be vulnerable, beginning today. Christ made himself vulnerable, bore our sins on the cross, and died for his beloved friends. He did this because he loves us, and his finished work is done. You now need only to receive him and be willing to be vulnerable and repentant, so that he can heal you and declare you righteous by clothing you in his righteousness. Only then can you even begin to desire to practice *agape* love. That desire comes not from you, but from him.

In 1 Corinthians 13, the Apostle Paul gives us a clear description of God's love:

1. *"If I speak in the tongues of men or of angels, but do not have love, I am only a resounding gong or clanging cymbal.*
2. *If I have the gift of prophecy and can fathom all mysteries and all knowledge, and if I have a faith that can move mountains, but do not have love, I am nothing.*
3. *If I give all I possess to the poor and give over my body to hardship that I may boast, but do not have love, I gain nothing.*
4. *Love is patient, love is kind. It does not envy, it does not boast, it is not proud.*
5. *It does not dishonor others, it is not self-seeking, it is not easily angered, it keeps no record of wrongs.*
6. *Love does not delight in evil but rejoices with the truth.*
7. *It always protects, always trusts, always hopes, always perseveres.*
8. *Love never fails. But where there are prophecies, they will cease; where there are tongues, they will be stilled; where there is knowledge, it will pass away.*
9. *For we know in part and we prophesy in part,*
10. *but when completeness comes, what is in part disappears.*

11. *When I was a child, I talked like a child, I thought like a child, I reasoned like a child. When I became a man, I put the ways of childhood behind me.*
12. *For now, we see only a reflection as in a mirror; then we shall see face to face. Now I know in part; then I shall know fully, even as I am fully known.*
13. *And now these three remain: faith, hope and love. But the greatest of these is love."*

God *is* love. He wants us to love him *"because He first loved us."* (1 John 4:19). In the face of such unconditional and undeserved love, *agape* love that is based upon the very essence of God, the Giver, there is nothing more we should wish for than to become love itself to this broken world. Jesus, God in the flesh, says that if we love him, we should go and *"feed his sheep."* If you know God, then begin to do this today. Feed his sheep with a radical, selfless, and sacrificial love that beckons others to follow our Great Shepherd to his sheepfold, heaven itself, safely within the bounds of God's loving and protective arms forever. Once you are in covenant with him, you belong to him and his sheepfold, and he never lets you slip through his hands. His love and his promises are unconditional, intentional, and unfailing.

If you have not yet experienced God's profound love, it is accessible. His love is steadfast and never-ending, and you are beckoned to reach out and receive it now; it is never too late. He has proactively extended a hand of love, forgiveness, and reconciliation to the world; he would like us to respond, reach back, and receive the gift. If you have not yet done so but have a desire to reach out to God, now is the time to respond to his gift of forgiveness, love, and eternal life with him. When you dive into a bottomless ocean of God's *agape* love which he offered us first, it will wash the blinders off of your eyes so that you can clearly see yourself and your need for your loving Creator. It will engender within you a desire to repent from straying far from him. His love will fully refresh your soul and restore you into a relationship with him, much like the shepherd who seeks, finds, and brings back his wayward sheep to his safe and secure sheepfold.

The Apostle Paul, in Ephesians 1:4-5, reminds us: *"For He chose us in Him before the foundation of the world to be holy and blameless in His presence. In love He predestined us for adoption as His sons through Jesus Christ, according to the good pleasure of His will..."*

You can trust God's intensions, which are only for good; a gift of love like this is worth the taking because of he who offers it freely.

Study Questions:

1. Read 1 Corinthians 13:4-7 and write down some of the elements of what God's *agape* love looks like.
   Examine yourself honestly and see where you are struggling with loving others unconditionally, selflessly, and genuinely. Ask God to show you why you struggle in this area.
2. Do you believe that God's love is unconditional,

intentional, and unfailing? Is there an area of your life where you struggle to believe this?

3. 1 John 4:19 says, *"We love Him, because He first loved us."* How do you respond to God on a daily basis with the knowledge that he loves you? Do you agree or disagree with the Biblical concept that God loved and chose us first, and if so, why?

4. When Christ tells Simon Peter three times to feed and take care of His sheep/lambs, what does that mean to you? Where can you step out and try this week to "feed" or "take care" of someone's needs?

5. Romans 8:28 says, *"And we know that in all things God works for the good of those who love him, who have been called according to his purpose."* Where do you struggle with the fact that God loves you? What difficulties or challenges are you experiencing that induce you to feel that he is not working all things out for your good?

6. If *"God works everything together for good for those who love him,"* what does that imply for those who do not yet love him?

7. We have learned that God is omniscient. How do you see that God's love ties in with his omniscience and the fact that he knows everything about you, including what you have done and what you will do in the future?

8. Let's examine C. S. Lewis's comments on love: *"To love at all is to be vulnerable. Love anything and your heart will be wrung and possibly broken. If you want to make sure of keeping it intact you must give it to no one, not even an animal. Wrap it carefully round with hobbies and little luxuries; avoid all entanglements. Lock it up safe in the*

*casket or coffin of your selfishness. But in that casket, safe,
dark, motionless, airless, it will change. It will not be broken;
it will become unbreakable, impenetrable, irredeemable. To
love is to be vulnerable."*

Question: Do you think that God is "vulnerable" when
he chooses to love people? If you struggle with
learning how to love God back, is it because you feel
vulnerable? If so, why? What is holding you back?

Additional Bible verses on God's love

Do: *Discuss and ponder over these verses, and pray for God to illuminate each one. (For additional context, read the entire Biblical chapter
in which each of these verses appears.)*

Ephesians 2:4-5 - *"But God, being rich in mercy, because of the great
love with which he loved us, even when we were dead in our trespasses, made us alive together with Christ— by grace you have been
saved—"*

Proverbs 8:17 - *"I love those who love me, and those who seek me
diligently find me."*

1 John 3:1 - *"See what great love the Father has lavished on us, that
we should be called children of God! And that is what we are! The
reason the world does not know us is that it did not know him."*

1 John 4:8 - *"Whoever does not love does not know God, because God
is love."*

Jeremiah 31:3 - *"The Lord appeared to us in the past, saying: 'I have loved you with an everlasting love; I have drawn you with unfailing kindness."*

Zephaniah 3:17 - *"The Lord your God is with you, the Mighty Warrior who saves. He will take great delight in you; in his love he will no longer rebuke you, but will rejoice over you with singing."*

Romans 5:8 - *"But God demonstrates his own love for us in this: While we were still sinners, Christ died for us."*

Romans 8:37-39 - *(37) No, in all these things we are more than conquerors through him who loved us.*

(38) For I am convinced that neither death nor life, neither angels nor demons, neither the present nor the future, nor any powers, (39) neither height nor depth, nor anything else in all creation, will be able to separate us from the love of God that is in Christ Jesus our Lord."

Memory verse:

1 John 4:19 - *"We love Him, because He first loved us."*

Action Plan - I want to learn how to more openly and effectively share God's agape love with others, but I need God's help with these impediments in my heart:

1.

2.

3.

Suggested Readings and Resources:

1. *The Love of God: An Intimate Look at the Father-Heart of God*, Oswald Chambers, July 14, 2011

2. *The Four Loves*, C. S. Lewis, HarperCollins, February 4, 2017

3. *God's Love: How the Infinite God Cares for His Children*, R. C. Sproul, Sept. 1, 2012

4. *Give Them Grace: Dazzling Your Kids With the Love of Jesus*, Elyse M. Fitzpatrick, Jessica Thompson, Crossway, 2011, Wheaton, IL.

5. *Thinking. Loving. Doing: A Call to Glorify God with Heart and Mind*, John Piper & David Mathis (Contributions by: R. Albert Mohler Jr., R. C. Sproul, Rick Warren, Francis Chan, John Piper, Thabiti Anyabwile), August 15, 2011.

Notes:

Chapter Five

GREAT IS THY FAITHFULNESS – GOD'S FAITHFULNESS

Psalms 89:8 *"O LORD God of hosts, who is mighty as you are, O LORD, with your faithfulness all around you?"*

Deuteronomy 7:9 *"Know therefore that the LORD your God is God, the faithful God who keeps covenant and steadfast love with those who love him and keep his commandments, to a thousand generations"*

Being faithful is to be reliable, trustworthy, unwavering, committed, and steadfast. It is marked by promises kept and an unshakeable adherence to a commitment to someone or something. Furthermore, it is something that one can count on in times of adversity as well as in times of ease. We rely on others to be faithful to their words, motives, and promises; it forms the foundation of human relationships, civil law, foreign relations, and all aspects of civilization.

The problem is, faithfulness is under fire in this present day and age. The very concept of being faithful to the same person for a lifetime in marriage has been replaced by a less binding commitment that can be easily broken. There is less employee faithfulness in the workplace, and the average employer increasingly finds a workforce that will quit on a whim and will scarcely make the two-year mark at any given company. There is an increasing epidemic of loneliness and friendlessness, as people increasingly find that few are willing to be faithful or committed to a meaningful friendship. There is less and less reliability, constancy, or value of long-term relationships because many are trying to please one person above all: the self.

Those who tend to focus upon self-faithfulness and pleasing themselves above all else, are less likely to seek out friendships, long-term commitments, and lasting relationships. They would rather be their own best friend, employer, and significant other; it is easier that way. Yet, when the winds of adversity starting blowing, folks like this lose self-confidence quickly and yearn to cling to someone else as a life preserver —temporarily, of course. When things settle down, they can toss the life preserver back and begin the all-too-familiar self-focused life again. The term, "fair-weather friend," has been around a long, long time. This problem isn't new, it's just more rampant, more visible, and more culturally accepted.

Strangely, most people yearn to find a faithful friend, partner, employer--even pet--yet we find it hard to practice faithfulness consistently ourselves. It takes effort, lots of it, and consistent effort that we may find exhausting, inconvenient, and somewhat unsatisfying if not properly rewarded. When things get tough, it is human nature to want faithfulness and reliability in others, but we waiver when it's expected of us. We might even admit that we consider faithfulness a burden because it just takes too much effort, time, and selflessness at any given moment. In most minds, it is a conditional bilateral agreement of expectations where, "*If you do this, then I'll do that.*"

Now that we have the bad news out of the way, we can move in more positive directions. Faithfulness is a distinct character trait of God. He sticks by his people and he always has their back. In the best of times, and more importantly, in the worst of times, God is faithful to his people. He is faithful because he chooses to keep his promises, contracts, and relationships, even when his people have broken them. It is who he is and is a result of his gracious and loving character. What shepherd would abandon his sheep when the day is beautiful and all is well, or at dusk when the wolf prowls nearby? God is that shepherd who faithfully tends his flock well at all times and in all circumstances, irrespective of how the sheep are behaving.

The Biblical record has much to say about faithfulness, and it is always attributed to God as an integral part of his being, his motives, and his behavior. Read and ponder over the following verses which appear in both the Old Testament and New Testament books of the Bible:

- 1 Corinthians 1:9, "*God is faithful, who has called you into fellowship with his Son, Jesus Christ our Lord.*"

- 1 Corinthians 10:13, "*No temptation has overtaken you except what is common to mankind. And God is faithful; he will not let you be tempted beyond what you can bear. But when you are tempted, he will also provide a way out so that you can endure it."*

- Deuteronomy 7:9, *"Know therefore that the Lord your God is God; he is the faithful God, keeping his covenant of love to a thousand generations of those who love him and keep his commandments."*

- Deuteronomy 32:4, *"He is the Rock, his works are perfect, and all his ways are just. A faithful God who does no wrong, upright and just is he."*

- Psalm 89:8, *"Who is like you, Lord God Almighty? You, Lord, are mighty, and your faithfulness surrounds you."*

- Hebrews 3:6, *"But Christ is faithful as the Son over God's house. And we are his house, if indeed we hold firmly to our confidence and the hope in which we glory."*

- Ruth 1:15-18, *"Ruth said, 'Do not urge me to leave you or to return from following you. For where you go I will go, and where you lodge I will lodge. Your people shall be my people, and your God my God. Where you die I will die, and there will I be buried. May the Lord do so to me and more also if anything but death parts me from you.'"*

. . .

To understand God's faithfulness, we must begin with the Old Testament historical record, because it is a history of God's outreach and faithfulness to his people, and it is a narrative filled with foreshadows of his promised Savior who is the culmination of the most profound kind of faithfulness. The Book of Deuteronomy, written by Moses, gives us several rich descriptions of God's character. In Deuteronomy 7:9 Moses tells the Israelites who God is and what he is like:

"Know therefore that he the Lord your God is God; he is the faithful God, keeping his covenant of love to a thousand generations of those who love him and keep his commandments."

Particularly, Moses tells his people that God is faithful because he keeps his *"covenant of love"* with his people who respond to him, love him, and who *"keep His commandments."* Because God loves his people, he desires to come into a solid and faithful relationship with them. He always remains faithful to that covenant, though his people will often break their end of the contract and not always love him and obey him. However, let it be said that his faithfulness is also tempered by justness—a love of justice—and God must mete out consequences for his people when they choose not to love him and obey him. A loving father, creator, and shepherd would do nothing less. Deuteronomy 32:4 reveals additional descriptive elements about God's faithfulness, telling us, *"He is the Rock, His works are perfect, and all His ways are just. A faithful God who does no wrong, upright and just is he."*

. . .

God's faithfulness is part of his very essence and is likened to a "*rock*," which would suggest that it is unmovable, unyielding, and solid to stand upon and to build with. "*His works are perfect, and all His ways are just,*" assures us that his type of faithfulness is to be fully and permanently trusted because all his works, words, plans, and motives are always "*perfect.*" His faithfulness is backed up by all his motives being "*just.*" This is the type of faithfulness every person yearns for in this life. Only God can—and will—provide this level of perfect, just, rock-solid faithfulness. He provides it to his people, though they will not always return the favor. As innately sinful human beings, we may be unfaithful to God at times, often look to our own needs first, and generally behave like petulant and demanding children, yet God will remain faithful to his own.

A marriage, a friendship, an employment agreement, a promise to a neighbor or friend, and a commitment to another is difficult without first knowing God's perfect faith-fulness. It is a "*fruit of the Spirit,*" given by God to his people, meaning that we do not possess it until he gives it to us. Without God's gift of faithfulness, we don't naturally feel the inclination to practice such a thing at all. It would be too hard, too stressful, too long of a time to commit to, much too inconvenient, and maybe even downright annoying to practice such a demanding thing with anyone for an extended length of time! The best of us may try, but it is a mere minuscule attempt at something that doesn't come naturally.

* * *

Back in 2014, I walked through modern-day Jerusalem with my husband and our Israeli guide. Before entering the Old City, I stood at a nondescript fence and stared through it to gaze upon the still existent Garden of Gethsemane. Our guide mentioned that the olive trees were several thousand years old. I wondered if one of the trees, in particular, had shaded Jesus as he sat and meditated upon his coming act of self-sacrificing faithfulness to his people before he was taken to the cross. I wanted to seize a special moment to contemplate the amazing story of Jesus sitting in this garden and painfully asking God if perhaps he might not need to suffer as he was appointed to. Jesus, the man, struggled with being faithful to the end, yet Jesus, God's own Son, knew that dying for mankind's crushing sin was a final act of faithfulness that must be accomplished. If olive trees could have ears, what a conversation with God they must have heard as Jesus sat beneath one of them and poured out his heart to God, his Father.

Godly faithfulness is painful and comes at a great cost. God loved people so very, very much, that faithfulness led him to sacrifice his own Son, the *"radiance of God's glory, and the exact representation of his being"* (Hebrews 1:3) upon a tree cut and fashioned into a brutal Roman cross. In the Garden of Eden, Adam and Eve partook of one forbidden tree that they were expressly told by God not to eat from. Fast forward several millennia later, and Jesus sat in a garden and contemplated his coming self-sacrifice upon a tree cut and shaped into a cross. That is what faithfulness looks like: taking the lashes, the thorns, the nails, and the sword for those whom he is faithful to, unto death, to wipe our sin slate clean. God is a faithful creator, father, warrior, healer, shepherd, and redeemer who embodies a faithfulness that we hunger for every day of our lives. He offers this costly gift freely, and we need only receive it, acknowledge it, and live a life of gratitude for it. Why? Because God has paid the high cost of that faithfulness.

Portrait of Faithfulness - Hannah

In approximately 1100 B.C. a young housewife struggled with infertility. In her household, she was one of two wives (this was very common in the ancient world). The other wife had several children; Hannah was barren. Her husband Elkanah was a kind and loving husband and admittedly loved Hannah the most. Let's look into Hannah's life, as recorded in the Old Testament Book of 1 Samuel, Chapter 1:4-20:

(4) "Whenever the day came for Elkanah to sacrifice, he would give portions of the meat to his wife Peninnah and to all her sons and daughters.
(5) But to Hannah he gave a double portion because he loved her, and the Lord had closed her womb.
(6) Because the Lord had closed Hannah's womb, her rival kept provoking her in order to irritate her.
(7) This went on year after year. Whenever Hannah went up to the house of the Lord, her rival provoked her till she wept and would not eat.
(8) Her husband Elkanah would say to her, 'Hannah, why are you weeping? Why don't you eat? Why are you downhearted? Don't I mean more to you than ten sons?'
(9) Once when they had finished eating and drinking in Shiloh, Hannah stood up. Now Eli the priest was sitting on his chair by the doorpost of the Lord's house.

(10) In her deep anguish Hannah prayed to the Lord, weeping bitterly.

(11) And she made a vow, saying, 'Lord Almighty, if you will only look on your servant's misery and remember me, and not forget your servant but give her a son, then I will give him to the Lord for all the days of his life, and no razor will ever be used on his head.'

(12) As she kept on praying to the Lord, Eli observed her mouth.

(13) Hannah was praying in her heart, and her lips were moving but her voice was not heard. Eli thought she was drunk

(14) and said to her, 'How long are you going to stay drunk? Put away your wine.'

(15) 'Not so, my lord,' Hannah replied, 'I am a woman who is deeply troubled. I have not been drinking wine or beer; I was pouring out my soul to the Lord.

(16) Do not take your servant for a wicked woman; I have been praying here out of my great anguish and grief.'

(17) Eli answered, 'Go in peace, and may the God of Israel grant you what you have asked of him.'

(18) She said, 'May your servant find favor in your eyes.' Then she went her way and ate something, and her face was no longer downcast.

(19) Early the next morning they arose and worshiped before the Lord and then went back to their home at Ramah. Elkanah made love to his wife Hannah, and the Lord remembered her.

(20) So in the course of time Hannah became pregnant and gave birth to a son. She named him Samuel, saying, 'Because I asked the Lord for him.'

People are people whether they lived three thousand years ago or they are alive today. For a woman, infertility is as devastating today as it was in the ancient world. Worse, it is, unfortunately, human nature that those who have something others don't will often gloat and taunt, basking in their own blessings and mocking those who struggle. The story of Hannah is both true and it is deeply touching because it is a story of pain, disappointment, and even a bit of bullying. The silver lining in Hannah's clouded life was that she knew God and believed he was a faithful God who loved her. Verses 10 and 11 record Hannah's deeply moving cry to him:

> (10) *"In her deep anguish, Hannah prayed to the Lord, weeping bitterly.*
> (11) *And she made a vow, saying, 'Lord Almighty, if you will only look on your servant's misery and remember me, and not forget your servant but give her a son, then I will give him to the Lord for all the days of his life, and no razor will ever be used on his head.'"*

God keeps his covenant with his people who love him, follow him, and believe in him, and he is a God who hears when his people turn to him for help. As we can see in the last part of verse 19 and in verse 20, God answers Hannah:

> (19) *"...the Lord remembered her.*
> (20) *So in the course of time Hannah became pregnant and*

*gave birth to a son. She named him Samuel, saying, 'Because I
asked the Lord for him.'"*

When we are in a covenant relationship with God, like
Hannah was, and we turn to him, trust him, and boldly ask
him to come to our aide, he will answer. His faithfulness to his
people compels him to respond because God's very nature is
to be a rock to his people that they can stand upon confidently. His perfect will is to be faithful to those who belong to
him. He chooses how he will respond in faithfulness. Sometimes God will choose not to grant what we ask—for our own
good—other times he will specifically give us what we pray for.
Yet in all things, Romans 8:28 encourages us that, *"...all things
God works for the good of those who love him, who have been called
according to his purpose."*

If you have not yet come to fully know the Creator, rest
assured that God and his Son, Jesus Christ, are *"the same yesterday, today and forever."* (Hebrews 13:8) They unchangingly
remain gracious, loving, and faithful to those who respond.
God desires to hear from you and for you to turn to him. He
wants to enter into a faithful relationship with you; once he
does, he will never leave you. He will be nothing other than
the faithful, reliable, strong, and steadfast "rock" he always
has been and always will be.

If you have already come to a point in your life where you are
in a covenant relationship with God, he wants you to exercise
his gift of faithfulness, one of the *fruits of the spirit* that he
gives his people. He wants us to show others what his type of
faithfulness looks like and for us to demonstrate and model

his steadfastness, his commitment, and his unshakable relationship with his people. He wants people, his image-bearers,
to respond to him, love him, trust him, and obey him. He
desires faithfulness from us in return.

Now, we will take a brief look at the life of a profoundly brave
and faithful servant of God who lived during World War II.
Her faith and trust in God, and his faithfulness to her, is a
deeply moving testimony of how God faithfully walks alongside his people in the worst of times.

Portrait of Faithfulness - Cornelia "Corrie" ten Boom

There are many life-changing stories of bravery and selflessness during World War II, as well as many testimonies of
God's intervention and faithfulness to the Allies during the
fierce battles against Nazi Germany and their imperialistic
push across Europe. In 1940 the Germans boldly invaded the
Netherlands. There, a woman by the name of Cornelia ten
Boom (her nickname was "Corrie") encountered a Jewish
woman holding a suitcase at her family's door. The woman's
husband had been arrested by the Germans and her son had
already gone into hiding to escape the German authorities in
Amsterdam.

The woman had heard that Corrie's parents had already
helped their Jewish neighbors and asked for them to once
again risk their lives and help her by hiding her from the
Nazis. The ten Boom family, a strong Christian family who
loved God and knew how he had revealed himself to the
people of ancient Israel, loved the Jews and were concerned
for their safety. Corrie's family selflessly opened up a risky

"hiding place" in their humble home for Jews and Dutch resistance members to hide from the Gestapo.

During the ten Boom's dangerous activities in hiding Jews and resistance fighters, Corrie and her family worked unceasingly in providing for their needs. God was continuously faithful to them over a seemingly endless four-year period of hiding refugees and enabled the ten Boom's to do the impossible. Food was highly rationed in Amsterdam and Corrie approached the ration-card offices boldly asking for one hundred cards, rather than just a handful for her family. God was faithful to her and her efforts and granted Corrie what she asked for. She then gave those one hundred ration cards to every Jew she came across.

On February 28, 1944, the ten Boom's brave efforts in hiding Jews and Dutch resistance members were met with a visit by the Nazis at their door. Their illegal activities were revealed by a whistleblower and Corrie's family was imprisoned. God intervened and made certain that none of the six refugees hiding in their home were discovered. After Corrie and her family's arrest, Corrie was placed in solitary confinement and then put on trial. She and her mother were sent to a political concentration camp and later to a women's labor camp in Germany. God had not abandoned them, however. When Corrie was in prison, the refugees who were hiding in her home on the day her family was arrested by the Nazis sent her a letter to alert her that they had all escaped and were safe. God was faithful.

While in the prison work camp, Corrie used a smuggled Bible and her small amounts of free time to lead worship services for the other prisoners. Within their prison-house, God's faithfulness continued with her in surprising ways. The German soldiers usually came into each prison-house to check on the prisoners, but Corrie's house had a terrible infestation of fleas, and none of the German soldiers wanted to venture inside for prisoner checks. Corrie praised God for the fleas because they kept the soldiers from entering and enabled her to continue their worship services inside. Though miserable conditions surrounded Corrie, she remained faithful to God and he steadfastly remained near to her, albeit in amazingly strange ways.

Eventually, due to a strange and unexplainable "clerical error" on the part of the Nazi's managing her prison camp, she was released from the work camp. A week later, Corrie learned that all the women in her age group were killed in the gas chamber; only Corrie had survived by being released one week earlier. Again, she could see God's visible faithfulness to her in miraculous ways. The full story can be read in Corrie's book, *The Hiding Place*.[1]

Hannah and Corrie lived three thousand years apart, yet God's faithfulness to them is the same because God is the same unchanging rock. He forever walks alongside his people, watching every detail of their everyday lives, intervening in miraculous ways, and strengthening them. Though we may falter, make significant miscalculations, or become disheartened, God is there as a firm foundation of faithfulness upon which we can stand in confidence. History and personal experience testify to this truth every day across the millennia.

Fortunately, there is a divine hand extending outward from heaven to each of us directly offering a steadfast grip of faithfulness and a gift of redemption that we are free to take hold of. Hannah's and Corrie's stories occur several millennia apart, yet they are both a tangible and real model of both God's faithfulness to them and their faithfulness to God. Hannah's and Corrie's life are just a snippet of human history and serve as examples of God's direct and visible intervention in the lives of his people. Since the creation, there is an unbroken thread of God's faithfulness, and that promise is as good today as it was at the very beginning of time.

Christ, God's own Son, was and is a faithful friend to the bitter end, unto death, and he is our Savior and friend for all eternity. As if that were not enough, Christ bore upon his shoulders a crushing weight of the horrific sins of the world, every single sin that you and I committed and will commit over a lifetime. John 15:13 defines faithful friendship like this: *"Greater love hath no man than this, that a man lay down his life for his friends."* This is precisely what Jesus did for us. He laid down his life for me, you, and anyone who will accept his hand of friendship and his crown of lordship.

God spent several millennia teaching his covenant people, the ancient Israelites, by walking side by side with them through endless deserts, up steep mountains, and down deep valleys. He drafted a plan to save them because their sin (and our sin) separates us from God. He executed his intentional plan of salvation, reconciliation, and redemption with a promised Savior who would right all of our wrongs. Though God is our heavenly Father and Creator, we can also clearly see him in Christ as a friend who chooses us, sticks with us, forgives us, cleans us up inside out, and crafts a path for us to follow him. He chose to do this because he wants an eternal relationship with his image-bearers. Who wouldn't want a faithful and selfless friend like this?

Making it Real

We have explored how God is eternally faithful to his people. The troubling question for some will be, *"What about people who don't know God yet?"* In this study exploring God's character, I don't pull any punches; I am direct, honest, and forthright with you. We will therefore lay the issue on the table and address it. God knows who his people are; he is omniscient. Some people respond to him early in life, while others will respond to him later on, sometimes at the very end of their lives. A shepherd always knows which sheep are his and will go the ends of the earth to find them, save them, and bring them home. The sheep will wander until they hear the shepherd's voice.

God's faithfulness is to his people, and he makes that abundantly clear to them. His grace, his love, and his compassion are absolutely eternal and boundless; it is for those who belong to him, and he knows who they are. 2 Timothy 2:19 puts it simply, *"the firm foundation of God stands, having this seal, 'The Lord knows those who are His.'"* As we have established thus far, his faithfulness, love, grace, and compassion are unconditional. He loves his wayward sheep before, during, and after they respond to him, because he has always known them. Once we know him and follow him, he provides spiritual gifts that we don't innately have. He provided the model, Jesus Christ, his Son, so that we can see what faithfulness, love, grace, and compassion look like. Those gifts are meant to be used and shared, not hoarded in a dark closet. They are meant to show what God is like to others, in every sphere of life, including friendships, marriage, relationships, family, etc.

Faithfulness in friendships

The challenge for us daily is *being* a friend like this. I have witnessed faithful friendships between women who stood in solidarity with a friend undergoing cancer treatment and hair loss. Those friends willingly went to the salon and had their hair cut off, too, so they could share in their suffering friend's discomfort. Others have stood by a friend who was being abused by a spouse or significant other and helped them get to a safe place. I have watched a young woman and her husband come to another's home while their spouse was deployed in service to our nation, and they spent half of their Saturday mowing and tending to her yard. True friendship and commitment look like this. It is unexpected, inconvenient, costly, and selfless. If we are walking with God, our relationships should look like this.

Faithfulness in marriage

Second, let's honestly address the issue of faithfulness in marriage. The concept of marriage is a covenant based upon Biblical faithfulness, life-long commitment, vows of oneness, and longsuffering together through thick and thin. It was created as a foreshadowing of our oneness with God's Son and his oneness with God. Sadly, many marriages today are not marked by these characteristics. Now, marriages are increasingly initiated as temporary contracts entered into with nothing but a precarious connection of fleeting emotion, hollow promises, and retained independence that neither party is willing to give up. Faithfulness is often absent from relationships—and marriages—from the beginning.

My husband and I have observed the unfortunate reality of unfaithfulness in the lives of many couples who we had befriended early in our marriage. Increasingly, one marriage after the other suddenly broke up, their children's lives were sent into a tailspin, and their vows of faithfulness came to an abrupt end. The recurring issue was infidelity. Over the years we discussed this issue and concluded that faithfulness was being completely redefined. Infidelity was simply the natural outcome of two people who had never become one in the first place. Replacing faithfulness in marriage was a veneration of the self. It appeared that the self has to be satisfied at all costs, irrespective of the collateral damage. Marriage is becoming stripped of the element of selflessness and mutual long-term commitment. Now, being faithful to one's self is paramount.

How can we practice faithfulness with another whom we are in a marriage covenant with for a lifetime? Marriage, we must understand first, is a reflection of our oneness with Christ, and his oneness with God. One of the most human, yet divine, covenants in the ancient world is marriage. 1 Corinthians 11:3 explains the oneness of marriage and its model of unity this way: "*But I want you to understand that the head of every man is Christ, the head of a wife is her husband, and the head of Christ is God.*" There is a divine hierarchy of "oneness" that God ordained marriage to visibly and symbolically reflect: the unity of man and woman under Christ, and the unity of Christ with God. In 1 Corinthians 11:11-12 this concept is illuminated further: "*Nevertheless, in the Lord, woman is not independent of man nor man of woman; for as woman was made from man, so man is now born of woman. And all things are from God.*"

Today, the unity and oneness of a man and a woman within the covenant of marriage have been wholly redefined with a fine-tipped pair of sharp scissors. Society has surgically cut out the God-authored unity of marriage (not to mention crossing out the author's name altogether) and declared that there is a new definition. Separate and equal roles and authority is the new marriage model. Once the Biblical root has been cut, marriage is like a plant that slowly dies because it is starved of the very nutrients of love, oneness, and authority from God which once nourished it. Therefore, today, men and women feel free to cohabit before marriage, practicing an artificial oneness they have mutually manufactured on a trial basis. Ironically, after marriage, many emphasize personal freedom, independence, and separateness, leaving marital unity in the dust after a few years.

Many today within and outside the church will balk at the notion that marriage reflects our oneness with Christ and Christ's unity with God. Most will disagree that there are distinct roles that God made men and women to uniquely play within the boundaries of marriage. Yet, what army functions with all members being equal with no hierarchy of authority, responsibility, commissioning, and roles? None. No challenge could be overcome, no battles fought, and no victories won if there were no generals, no lieutenants, no captains, and no privates. What employment contract at any company would enable someone to join a particular department and decide who they will be, what job responsibilities they will only commit to doing, and who they will decide to work under as a boss if any? No such company exists.

Yet, today, the average person will often step back from God's concept of marriage and redefine it to fit their comfort zone. Thus, faithfulness in today's world is a newly defined contract of marriage that is conveniently retractable, highly conditional at any given moment, and is devoid of the concept of selfless unity for a lifetime. Without the Biblical model of marriage reflecting our unity of flesh, our oneness with Christ, and his unity with God, the marriage covenant today is a house built upon the sand, easily blown away by the slightest tempest.

Faithfulness in parenting

Emanating from the demise of faithfulness and authority in marriage is a crisis of parenting. If the foundational Biblical covenant of marriage has already been redefined, and there is no God-honoring hierarchy of authority, faithfulness, and unity among parents, coupled with no distinct roles, how can parenting the next generation bear good fruit? It often doesn't. Matthew 7:17 states bluntly, *"So, every healthy tree bears good fruit, but the diseased tree bears bad fruit."* You propagate what you are. If you redefine marriage roles of men and women in the family and live by something other than God's plan for marriage and parenting, then you may very well *"bear bad fruit."* Frankly, what else would you expect?

Without following God's model of faithfulness, unity, and authority, people naturally construct their own methodology for raising and nourishing their children. Today we see something even more disturbing. We see families where parents raise children with no parental authority or unity, and where children are treated as their parents' "buddies," a role that children are ill-equipped to play. We must, as parents, be faithful to our God-given roles as parents, even if we find ourselves in a one-parent household. Faithfulness and commitment to God, our Shepherd, will provide the authority and boundaries that we need to surround our children with.

Throughout Biblical history, we see that those who submit to the authority, boundaries, and omnipotence of God can trust him to remain faithful. Children have enormous difficulty in understanding authority and boundaries when they do not exist in the family. They will not submit to boundaries anywhere in life when none have been constructed in the home. Therefore, as marriage and family have broken into fragments, children have turned to surrogate families, such as gangs, peer groups, online communities, etc. with their man-made hierarchy of rules, authority, and morals--or lack thereof.

We have learned through several Biblical accounts of profound faithfulness to God and God's abiding faithfulness to his people, that without commitment to him, we are truly on our own. Shepherding his people is what God does throughout human history. Without his model, what does parenting our little sheep look like? Watch a flock of sheep scatter in a million directions when a threat presents itself, and there is no shepherd to run to for protection and no sheepfold to hide within. It's easy for a predator--or any threat--to pick off the weakest when there is no shepherd tending the flock.

What we can learn from the lives of everyday people who walk with God is that, if they did not submit to him as their shepherd, human history would have woven a very different tale for us to view through today's Biblical lens. Those whose lives God wished to be included in his divinely inspired sixty-six books of the Bible demonstrate important lessons for us today as much as they were instructive to people throughout the ages. In the lives of people like Ruth, Abraham, Noah, Moses, Hannah, etc., God reveals his character attributes, just a few of which we are studying within this book.

The Apostle Paul encourages us in 1 Corinthians 1:9, that *"God is faithful, by whom you were called into the fellowship of his Son, Jesus Christ our Lord."* And in his letter to the Galatians, Paul tells us, *"the fruit of the Spirit is love, joy, peace, patience, kindness, goodness, faithfulness..."* God is faithfulness personified; it is his very essence. However, we as fallen creatures do not possess the natural propensity for faithfulness; it is a gift of the Spirit to be cultivated. It is a gift from God out of his very heart, an attribute of his divine personality that he wishes to share with his people so that we can then go forth and feed others with it.

I cannot end this chapter without sharing a powerful hymn on God's faithfulness written by Thomas Obadiah Chisolm in the 1920s. Chisolm was born in 1866, and he began life with an array of physical ailments that rendered him bedridden and struggling to make ends meet. He decided to give his life to God at the age of 27 and began to walk with him. Chisolm and his close friend, William Runyan, a musician, collaborated on what was to be one of the most well-known hymns of their time, "Great is Thy Faithfulness," published in 1923. The inspiration came from Chisolm's favorite verse, Lamentations 3:22-23, *"It is of the Lord's mercies that we are not consumed, because His compassions fail not. They are new every morning: great is Thy faithfulness."*

Let's look specifically at the third line of lyrics and the well-known chorus of this moving hymn which reflects Chisolm's personal experience with God's tender and steadfast presence in his life:

> *Great is Thy faithfulness, O God my Father,*
> *There is no shadow of turning with Thee;*
> *Thou changest not, Thy compassions, they fail not.*
> *As Thou hast been Thou forever wilt be.*
>
> *Great is Thy faithfulness! Great is Thy faithfulness!*
> *Morning by morning new mercies I see;*
> *All I have needed Thy hand hath provided--*
> *Great is Thy faithfulness, Lord, unto me!*
>
> *Pardon for sin and a peace that endureth,*
> *Thine own dear presence to cheer and to guide;*
> *Strength for today and bright hope for tomorrow,*
> *Blessings all mine, with ten thousand beside!*

This is one of my favorite hymns because it is filled with glorious descriptions of God's unchanging faithfulness bound up in mercy, forgiveness, caring provision, and perfect peace. It is Chisolm's personal testimony of his relationship with the God who changed his life. This same God, unchanging and faithful, is waiting for us to walk with him today, to seek his mercy, peace, and provision, and to know him. God has shown us throughout history that he is a God to be trusted because his unchanging and unending faithfulness is a solid rock upon which we can stand, live, and thrive. God is a sure, steadfast, unchanging, and reliable footing upon which you can firmly plant your present and your future. Once you stand with him, there is nothing that can erode his love and commitment to you. There are no mistakes you can make which will shake his faithfulness to you.

I leave you to ponder over Psalms 119:90 as a powerful conclusion to our journey through God's attribute of faithfulness:

"Your faithfulness endures to all generations; you have established the earth, and it stands fast."

Study Questions

1. Read 1 Corinthians 10:13: *"No temptation has overtaken you except what is common to mankind. And God is faithful; he will not let you be tempted beyond what you can bear. But when you are tempted, he will also provide a way out so that you can endure it."* In what areas of life do you see God's faithfulness to you? Are there areas where you don't see it and feel that you are *"beyond what you can bear"*?

2. Read Deuteronomy 32:4: *"He is the Rock, his works are perfect, and all his ways are just. A faithful God who does no wrong, upright and just is he."* Knowing that God's faithfulness is perfect and his works and ways are just and upright, where do you see that this is true in your life? Where do you have trouble trusting in God's perfect works and ways and are struggling with standing firmly upon him as a "Rock"?

3. God is faithful to us even when we are not always faithful to him. When do you tend to be lax in your faithfulness to God?

4. What did you learn from the Biblical passages about Hannah that helps you see the outcomes of faithfulness to God and his faithfulness to those who trust him?

5. Do you see more clearly how God's faithfulness to you must be practiced in your own life with others? How so? Where do you struggle with being faithful in your life (relationships? commitments? promises? etc.)

6. Deuteronomy 7:9 says, *"Know therefore that he the Lord your God is God; he is the faithful God, keeping his covenant of love to a thousand generations of those who love him and keep his commandments."* How is God's love inextricably tied to his faithfulness?

7. One of the most profound verses in the song, "Great is Thy Faithfulness" is:

> *Great is Thy faithfulness, O God my Father,*
> *There is no shadow of turning with Thee;*
> *Thou changest not, Thy compassions, they fail not.*
> *As Thou hast been Thou forever wilt be.*

What does it mean that God is faithful and compassionate and *"changest not"* (does not ever change)? What are the implications of this?

8. What do you see today in the world around you that is missing a basic element of faithfulness? Is faithfulness considered a virtue today? Why or why not? Does the culture around you define faithfulness very differently than God's type of faithfulness?

. . .

Additional Bible verses on God's faithfulness

Do: *Discuss and ponder over these verses, and pray for God to illuminate each one. (For additional context, read the entire Biblical chapter in which each of these verses appears.)*

Romans 8:38-39 - *"For I am convinced that neither death nor life, neither angels nor demons, neither the present nor the future, nor any powers, neither height nor depth, nor anything else in all creation, will be able to separate us from the love of God that is in Christ Jesus our Lord."*

Lamentations 3:22-23 - *"The LORD'S lovingkindnesses indeed never cease, For His compassions never fail. They are new every morning; Great is Your faithfulness."*

Psalms 119:90 - *"Your faithfulness endures to all generations; you have established the earth, and it stands fast."*

1 Corinthians 1:9 - *"God is faithful, by whom you were called into the fellowship of his Son, Jesus Christ our Lord."*

1 John 1:9 - *"If we confess our sins, he is faithful and just and will forgive us our sins and purify us from all unrighteousness."*

Hebrews 10:23 - *"Let us hold fast the confession of our hope without wavering, for he who promised is faithful."*

Romans 3:3-4a - *What if some were unfaithful? Does their faithlessness nullify the faith of God? (4) By no means! Let God be true though every one were a liar"*

Memory verses:

<u>Psalm 89:8</u>: *"Who is like you, Lord God Almighty? You, Lord, are mighty, and your faithfulness surrounds you."*

<u>Deuteronomy 7:9</u>: *"Know therefore that the Lord your God is God; he is the faithful God, keeping his covenant of love to a thousand generations of those who love him and keep his commandments."*

<u>Action Plan</u> - I want to be more faithful to others, to my commitments, and to God. This is where I need God's help:

1.

2.

3.

<u>Suggested Readings and Resources:</u>

1. *The Hiding Place, Corrie ten Boom,* Elizabeth and John Sherrill, Chosen Books, Grand Rapids, MI, 2006

2. *The Gospel of Ruth: Loving God Enough to Break the Rules,* Carolyn Custis James & Robert L. Hubbard, Harper Collins Publishing, August 2009

3. *God is Faithful: A Daily Invitation Into the Father Heart of God,* David Wilkerson, Chosen Books, Bloomington, Minnesota, 2012

<u>Notes:</u>

Chapter Six

PATIENCE IS A VIRTUE – GOD'S PATIENCE

2 Peter 3:15a *"And regard the patience of our Lord as salvation"*

Romans 2:4 *"Or do you think lightly of the riches of His kindness and tolerance and patience, not knowing that the kindness of God leads you to repentance?"*

The human battle with learning and exercising patience can be seen in the life of any toddler, teen, or today's young adult. Just watch a three or four-year-old wait patiently for their birthday party to begin and presents to be opened. It's painfully impossible for them to stand the suspense! Stand back and observe a teen who is sweating bullets by the phone waiting for a friend who promised to call them. Or, look at a young adult today and watch them impatiently swerve in and out of traffic just to try to make that yellow light that is several hundred yards ahead of them. Patience is not innate to the human psyche.

It is instructive to look at a simple dictionary definition of patience: Patience is the ability to endure difficult circumstances such as perseverance in the face of delay; tolerating provocation without responding in annoyance or anger; or exhibiting forbearance when under strain, especially when faced with longer-term difficulties. Some elements of this definition are relevant and can be attributed to God's patience with us, however, there is much, much more to be said. God's character infuses his patience with attributes that are uniquely his. His patience is completely different from ours because he is very different than you and me.

Let's begin by looking at God's definition of patience as it is proclaimed and illustrated in the Bible. God's definition of patience is synonymous with the word *longsuffering*, and is marked by willful endurance and intentional withholding of his righteous anger over a long period of time. Moses records in Exodus 34:6 as an eye witness account: *"The Lord passed by in front of him (Moses) and proclaimed, 'The Lord, the Lord God, compassionate and gracious, slow to anger, and abounding in lovingkindness and truth.'"* Because God tells Moses—and us-- that he is compassionate and gracious, he decides to be *"slow to anger."* What God intentionally demonstrates is that he offers patience with his people when he is rightfully angry with us. His patience is justifiable judgment and wrath that is kept in check for a very long time. His patience has extended to all of us across the millennia since the creation.

The word *patience* is rarely found in the Old Testament books of the Bible, although the Prophet Isaiah records God's conversation with him in Isaiah 48:9, *"For the sake of My name I delay My wrath, And for My praise I restrain it for you, In order not to cut you off."* God is patient by choosing to delay and restrain his wrath (which ancient Israel deserved for turning to false gods and engaging in a shockingly diverse array of forbidden activities). God's patience is a loving and merciful offshoot of his willful restraint. Much of what we learn of God's patient character, as recorded by Moses and the Old Testament Prophets, is that by God being *"merciful and slow to anger"* (See Exodus 34:6, Numbers 14:18, Nehemiah 9:17, Psalm 86:15), he is demonstrating his willful patience. He wants that patience to be recognized, experienced, and to change those who follow him. His patience involves extending mercy, withholding justifiable anger, and showing undeserved grace and compassion. This is a significantly different type of patience than our mere dictionary definition, to be sure.

In the New Testament, the word *patience* appears much more frequently, however, it is most often discussed in the context of people learning to exercise patience (as they wait for God), holding steadfastly to him in hope, loving others through patience with them, bearing with one another, and charity. We learn to wait on God in quiet and trusting expectation, to be willing to face a delay, and to bear calmly and with self-control.[1] The Book of Matthew, Chapter 18, leads us into a discussion of God's patience, as modeled and taught by Jesus Christ. Who better than Jesus Christ, God's own promised Savior and Son, to model for us God's longsuffering and patience? Let's delve into Matthew 18, verse 21 onward, and read through the parable of the unforgiving (and impatient) servant:

(21) "Then Peter came up and said to him, 'Lord, how often will my brother sin against me, and I forgive him? As many as seven times?'

(22) Jesus said to him, 'I do not say to you seven times, but seventy-seven times.

(23) Therefore the kingdom of heaven may be compared to a king who wished to settle accounts with his servants.

(24) When he began to settle, one was brought to him who owed him ten thousand talents.

(25) And since he could not pay, his master ordered him to be sold, with his wife and children and all that he had, and payment to be made.

(26) So the servant fell on his knees, imploring him, 'Have patience with me, and I will pay you everything.'

(27) And out of pity for him, the master of that servant released him and forgave him the debt.

(28) But when that same servant went out, he found one of his fellow servants who owed him a hundred denarii, and seizing him, he began to choke him, saying, 'Pay what you owe.'

(29) So his fellow servant fell down and pleaded with him, 'Have patience with me, and I will pay you.'

(30) He refused and went and put him in prison until he should pay the debt.

(31) When his fellow servants saw what had taken place, they were greatly distressed, and they went and reported to their master all that had taken place.

(32) Then his master summoned him and said to him, 'You wicked servant! I forgave you all that debt because you pleaded with me.

(33) And should not you have had mercy on your fellow servant, as I had mercy on you?'

(34) And in anger his master delivered him to the jailers, until

he should pay all his debt.
(35) So also my heavenly Father will do to every one of you, if
you do not forgive your brother from your heart."'

Let's be clear that patience is a *"fruit of the Spirit,"* given by God to those who come into a relationship with him. Without God's imparting of it to us, we don't have it, except in a weak and sinful human form. This parable outlines what natural human impatience looks like. We can all relate to it, as all of us have made weak attempts throughout our lives to practice patience with another, only to lose it and lapse into something far uglier. It also highlights what God's type of patience looks like, as well. In this passage, Jesus is using a simple story to illustrate a point: God exercises patience and dispenses mercy, though we mess up time and time again. But, tempering that fact is an admonition to us to offer patience and mercy to others, as God has done to us. Paying it forward is what God expects of us, for he has put up with us with a level of patience and mercy that we frankly do not deserve.

Alistair Begg, pastor, author, and profoundly gifted Christian speaker, explains God's patience in one of his sermons when he says, *"When God reveals himself in the Old Testament books of the Bible, he consistently does so in terms that establish the fact of his patience."* As an example of this, Exodus 34:6-7 shows a conversation God has directly with Moses where he defines his divine patience:

(6) "The Lord passed before him (Moses) and
proclaimed, 'The Lord, the Lord, a God merciful and gra-

*cious, slow to anger, and abounding in steadfast love and
faithfulness,
(7) keeping steadfast love for thousands, forgiving iniquity
and transgression and sin but who will by no means clear the
guilty...*[xi]

In this brief passage in Exodus 34, God defines himself to
Moses and explains his divine patience and how it translates
into mercy, grace, slowness of anger, steadfast love, forgiveness, and faithfulness to his people. God sometimes proclaims
to people who he is and therefore what he is like. Patience
doesn't mean the absence of consequences for willful sin,
however. God is a patient heavenly father, but he isn't a
pushover. God's patience, he reminds us, takes the long view
and the purposeful view of things. He teaches his people to
likewise develop patience, trust, and hope, and to cultivate a
long-term view of things, as well. He not only declares that he
is patient, loving, and forgiving, he demonstrates it so that
there is no mistaking it. This is how he reveals himself to
people.

Next, we will look at the life of Abraham, a man who lived
around 1852-1872 BC. This is a historical Biblical narrative,
recorded by Moses, of a man who learned to trust God and
cultivate patience over many, many years. It is also an interesting example of God's remarkably gracious patience with
Abraham and his wife, as you'll see shortly.

Portrait of Patience - Abraham

We will embark upon a journey through the lives of Abram and Sarai in the Biblical narrative (they would later be renamed by God "Abraham" and "Sarah"). Their lives are carefully recorded, including some of their good--and not so good--choices, as well as some of their specific conversations and particular life experiences, so that we can learn what cultivating God-like patience looks like. Moses, (Abraham's great-great-grandson, and writer of the Book of Genesis, Exodus, Leviticus, Numbers, and Deuteronomy), tells us in Genesis of his great-great-grandparents, Abram and Sarai. He records a very human portrait of their impatience and a long-term painfully built foundation of learned patience and trust in God. In the future, Abraham and Sarah's patience and trust in God would beget future descendants for Abraham that God promised would be, *"as numerous as the stars in the sky and as the sand on the seashore."* (Genesis 22:17b)

Sarai, like most of us, struggled with patience and trust. She made a series of long and arduous inter-country moves from Ur (in Mesopotamia) to Haran (which lays within modern-day Syria), a whopping 600+ mile journey. She left her home and dutifully accompanied her husband Abram, who was specifically asked by God to get up and move to their new home in Haran (Genesis 11:27-32). Genesis 12:3 records a profound promise by God that would reward Abram and Sarai's patience and trust in Him: "*I will bless those who bless you, and whoever curses you I will curse; and all peoples on earth will be blessed through you.*"

Sarai barely had the pictures up on the walls and the curtains hung in her new home in Haran when her patience was again tested. She and Abram were instructed by God to move again, this time to Canaan, where they arrived in Shechem, another

400-mile journey. Next, God told them to go further to Bethel, another 20 miles, then later to pick up and go to Egypt, another 225 miles! By now, we find them in Genesis 13 being called by God to subsequently leave Egypt and go 225 miles back to Bethel, and then another 35 miles to Mamre (Hebron). Next, Genesis 14 records more moves, as Sarai and Abram are asked by God to go from Hebron to Hobah (near Damascus in modern-day Syria) about 160 miles away. This was no pleasure cruise; this was a God-initiated journey in obedience, trust, and patience building. This usually tends to involve inconvenience, intense challenge, and a bit of misery and pain. All of this, however, is for an express purpose, make no mistake about it.

Compounding the difficulties of moving multiple times across great distances, Sarai was thus far unable to have children, a devastating issue in the ancient world, much less today. Moses, in Genesis 11:30 records: *"Now Sarai was childless because she was not able to conceive."* This was a crucial problem that would have huge repercussions later on for Sarai, Abram, and their household. Thus far, there were no children to boast of, to lighten the load of life, and to leave their inheritance to.

> Genesis 15:2-6 records for us an important one-on-one conversation between Abram and God, a dialogue foretelling that Sarai will conceive a child within the next year:
> *(2) But Abram said, "O Lord God, what will you give me, for I continue childless, and the heir of my house is Eliezer of Damascus?"*
> *(3) And Abram said, "Behold, you have given me no offspring, and a member of my household will be my heir."*

(4) And behold, the word of the Lord came to him: "This man shall not be your heir; your very own son shall be your heir."
(5) And he brought him outside and said, "Look toward heaven, and number the stars, if you are able to number them." Then he said to him, "So shall your offspring be."
(6) And he believed the Lord, and he counted it to him as righteousness.

As Moses mentions in the historical narrative, Sarai had proven to be unable to conceive a child. Is she patient with God, as well as hopeful and trusting in him to provide children that he promises to her? Genesis 16 gives a glimpse into Sarai's impatient, bitter, untrusting heart. Let's just say that she is a work in progress; she has a long way to go in getting to know God. All of her family's long journeys and constant moving from place to place with God leading the way, all those intimate conversations between her husband and God, even a covenant with God himself, and Sarai was anything but patient. Instead, she was jaded. Sarai was also mistrusting and unbelieving in the God who had walked with her through many, many miles of deserts. She had become a prickly little cactus and it wasn't pretty. Her impatience hatched a plan.

Genesis 16:1-6 tells us:
(1) Now Sarai, Abram's wife, had borne him no children. She had a female Egyptian servant whose name was Hagar.
(2) And Sarai said to Abram, "Behold now, the Lord has prevented me from bearing children. Go into my servant; it may be that I shall obtain children by her." And Abram listened to the voice of Sarai.

(3) So, after Abram had lived ten years in the land of Canaan, Sarai, Abram's wife, took Hagar the Egyptian, her servant, and gave her to Abram her husband as a wife.
(4) And he went into Hagar, and she conceived. And when she saw that she had conceived, she looked with contempt on her mistress.
(5) And Sarai said to Abram, "May the wrong done to me be on you! I gave my servant to your embrace, and when she saw that she had conceived, she looked on me with contempt. May the Lord judge between you and me!"
(6) But Abram said to Sarai, "Behold, your servant is in your power; do to her as you please." Then Sarai dealt harshly with her, and she fled from her.

What does God do when Hagar flees from Sarai's impatience, wrath, and jealousy? He sees what has occurred and he tenderly fixes it. He patiently, graciously, and faithfully endures Sarai's misbehavior and her mean-spirited mistreatment of Hagar. Additionally, God allows Hagar the blessing of conceiving a child, Ishmael. Next, God gently advises Hagar to go back to Sarai's house and resubmit to her mistress's authority. Hagar humbly complies with God's requests, and he tenderly promises her: *"I will increase your descendants so much that they will be too numerous to count."* God honors Hagar's patience and faith in him. She even calls God, *"The One who sees me."* *(Genesis 16:13),* to acknowledge that God had taken notice of her trust and obedience. Hagar knew that God has seen her plight as well as her faithfulness and that he had decided to bless her.

Genesis 17:1-22 follows next, with a covenant that God initiates between himself, Abram, and Sarai. This is the moment where God reveals his special long-term plans for them. Their arduous journey in learning to be patient with God will have its reward:

(1) When Abram was ninety-nine years old the Lord appeared to Abram and said to him, "I am God Almighty; walk before me, and be blameless,

(2) that I may make my covenant between me and you, and may multiply you greatly."

(3) Then Abram fell on his face. And God said to him,

(4) "Behold, my covenant is with you, and you shall be the father of a multitude of nations.

(5) No longer shall your name be called Abram, but your name shall be Abraham, for I have made you the father of a multitude of nations.

(6) I will make you exceedingly fruitful, and I will make you into nations, and kings shall come from you.

(7) And I will establish my covenant between me and you and your offspring after you throughout their generations for an everlasting covenant, to be God to you and to your offspring after you.

(8) And I will give to you and to your offspring after you the land of your sojournings, all the land of Canaan, for an everlasting possession, and I will be their God."

(9) And God said to Abraham, "As for you, you shall keep my covenant, you and your offspring after you throughout their generations.

(10) This is my covenant, which you shall keep, between me and you and your offspring after you: Every male among you shall be circumcised.

(11) You shall be circumcised in the flesh of your foreskins, and it shall be a sign of the covenant between me and you.

(12) He who is eight days old among you shall be circumcised. Every male throughout your generations, whether born in your house or bought with your money from any foreigner who is not of your offspring,

(13) both he who is born in your house and he who is bought with your money shall surely be circumcised. So shall my covenant be in your flesh an everlasting covenant.

(14) Any uncircumcised male who is not circumcised in the flesh of his foreskin shall be cut off from his people; he has broken my covenant."

(15) And God said to Abraham, "As for Sarai your wife, you shall not call her name Sarai, but Sarah shall be her name.

(16) I will bless her, and moreover, I will give you a son by her. I will bless her, and she shall become nations; kings of peoples shall come from her."

(17) Then Abraham fell on his face and laughed and said to himself, "Shall a child be born to a man who is a hundred years old? Shall Sarah, who is ninety years old, bear a child?"

(18) And Abraham said to God, "Oh that Ishmael might live before you!"

(19) God said, "No, but Sarah your wife shall bear you a son, and you shall call his name Isaac. I will establish my covenant with him as an everlasting covenant for his offspring after him.

(20) As for Ishmael, I have heard you; behold, I have blessed him and will make him fruitful and multiply him greatly. He shall father twelve princes, and I will make him into a great nation.

(21) But I will establish my covenant with Isaac, whom Sarah shall bear to you at this time next year."

(22) When he had finished talking with him, God went up from Abraham.

God rewards Abraham's trust, belief, and patience in him, re-emphasizes his caring and sovereign lordship over Abram and Sarai by renaming them Abraham and Sarah (a sign of headship over them), sets up an everlasting covenant with them, and promises children to them who will become "*kings*" and "*nation builders.*" (The descendants of Abraham and Sarah are the Jewish people.) God doesn't forget Hagar, and Ishmael is promised the blessing of many children and they will be "*princes.*" (The descendants of Hagar and Abraham are the Arab people.) In his foreknowledge, God knows that in the future Abraham's descendants, the Israelites, would not adhere to God's covenant with him. God's omniscience informs him that they will have to endure much spiritual correction over the millennia.

This historical record highlights God's profound patience and faithfulness juxtaposed with Sarah's impatience and weak faith. God chooses to be patient and longsuffering with this couple and gives them grace and blessing. He chooses to promise Sarah that she will indeed have children, despite her longtime barrenness. Has Sarah earned any of this? Heavens, no! At this point, Sarah should be overjoyed, patiently awaiting God's promises, and resting in God's covenant of love and faithfulness.

By now, in Genesis 18, Sarah is ninety years old and should have learned some semblance of patience and trust in God at this point. Not quite. Genesis 18 records Abraham meeting up with three "*visitors*," one of whom promises Abraham that he will indeed by a father the following year. Now, at that point, Abraham is one hundred years old and Sarah is ninety; they're no spring chickens who are ripe for childbearing. They are physically past the point of being able to sire children, especially Sarah, who has thus far still proven unable to conceive. Her patience with God's covenant and his previous promise of children and her being "*The mother of many nations*," has run dry, it would seem.

Let's look at Genesis 18:9-15 to see where Sarah's patience and trust are at this point:

> *(9) They said to him, "Where is Sarah your wife?" And he said, "She is in the tent."*
>
> *(10) The Lord said, "I will surely return to you about this time next year, and Sarah your wife shall have a son." And Sarah was listening at the tent door behind him.*
>
> *(11) Now Abraham and Sarah were old, advanced in years. The way of women had ceased to be with Sarah.*
>
> *(12) So Sarah laughed to herself, saying, "After I am worn out, and my lord is old, shall I have pleasure?"*
>
> *(13) The Lord said to Abraham, "Why did Sarah laugh and say, 'Shall I indeed bear a child, now that I am old?'*
>
> *(14) Is anything too hard for the Lord? At the appointed time I will return to you, about this time next year, and Sarah shall have a son."*
>
> *(15) But Sarah denied it, saying, "I did not laugh," for she was afraid. He said, "No, but you did laugh."*

After years and years of opportunities to learn patience, trust, and peace in God's plans and provision, Sarah eavesdrops on her husband's conversation with their visitors (one of who appears to be an angel of the Lord, or some divine manifestation, for he knows the future, and that Sarah will conceive a son specifically by *"this time next year."*). Then, Sarah sarcastically laughs beneath her breath and mumbles to herself about her old age and how it was quite a stretch to believe that God could provide her a promised child at this late date. Compounding this, Sarah lies when the divine visitor asks Abraham (did you notice he didn't ask Sarah?) why she laughed at this prophetic news.

Despite Sarah's sarcasm and mistrust of God's promises to her and her husband, God patiently and graciously blesses them with the child he has promised. As recorded in Genesis 21:1-7, we see God's promise kept:

(1) The Lord visited Sarah as he had said, and the Lord did to Sarah as he had promised.

(2) And Sarah conceived and bore Abraham a son in his old age at the time of which God had spoken to him.

(3) Abraham called the name of his son who was born to him, whom Sarah bore him, Isaac.

(4) And Abraham circumcised his son Isaac when he was eight days old, as God had commanded him.

(5) Abraham was a hundred years old when his son Isaac was born to him.

(6) And Sarah said, "God has made laughter for me; everyone who hears will laugh over me."

(7) And she said, "Who would have said to Abraham that

Sarah would nurse children? Yet I have borne him a son in his
old age."

We have journeyed together through this long and quite
eventful life story of a husband and wife who were far from
perfect, yet they walked with God and learned a type of
patience and grace from him that was not based on personal
merit. Despite Sarah's jadedness, disbelief, and mistrust of
God, he used Sarah's life to demonstrate a longsuffering type
of patience with her that is filled with grace, compassion, and
mercy. And, as a result of their experiences, both Abraham
and Sarah grew in greater patience in God and a deeper trust
in him as they walked with him over a long period to time.

Making it Real

Much like Sarah And Abraham, God chooses to endure us
and desires to be patient in a fatherly way that belies his love
and his commitment to us when we belong to him. He is longsuffering in watching us fumble the ball over and over again,
and yet he is still patient with us. God's mercy, grace, love,
and long-term patience is a portrait of God's character is
declared and demonstrated consistently from Genesis
through Revelation, in all sixty-six books of the Bible. It is
God's patient and gracious character threading its way
through the frayed fabric of human existence from the
creation onward.

God's very first two people, Adam and Eve, were no better
and no worse than Abraham and Sarah. The entrance of sin

into a once-perfect world God created was man's intentional choice right from the very beginning. And from there, God has had to patiently work out a plan to fix what we have ruined. He has loved us patiently and provided a Savior to right our wrongs and bear all of our sins, none of which he committed. He is still patiently waiting for people to accept his gift of eternal life. He is waiting patiently for us to respond to him, confess our sin to him, and to live an abundant life with and through him.

In light of this, how do we reflect godly patience to others and give people a glimpse of what God's perfect patience looks like? Our patience will not be perfect, mind you, because we, too, are works in progress just like Abraham and Sarah and others in the Biblical historical narrative. However, that being said, we have to endeavor to cultivate godly patience that exhibits an undertone of love, selflessness, and grace, traits that we do not naturally possess. To exhibit godly patience, therefore, we have to be infused with God's own son, Jesus Christ, so that we are wearing his imputed coat of righteousness and we are given his spiritual gift of patience.

Charles Spurgeon's sermon, "Wait for the Lord - Psalm 27:14" encourages us to consider how our patience will be necessarily tested by God over a long period to ensure that he forges a godly desire within us to wait for him patiently in all circumstances:

> *"It may seem an easy thing to wait, but it is one of the postures which a Christian doesn't learn without years of teaching. Marching and quick-marching are much easier for God's soldiers than standing still. There are hours of perplexity when the most willing spirit, anxiously desirous to serve the*

Lord, doesn't know what part to take. Then what shall it do?
Vex itself by despair? Fly back to cowardice, turn to the right
hand in fear, or rush forward in presumption? No, but simply
wait. Wait in prayer, however. Call upon God, and spread the
situation before Him; tell Him your difficulty and plead His
promise of aid. In dilemmas between one duty and another, it
is sweet to be humble as a child and wait with simplicity of
soul upon the Lord. It is sure to be well with us when we feel
and know our folly, and are heartily willing to be guided by
the will of God. But wait in faith. Express your unstaggering
confidence in him; for unfaithful, untrusting waiting is an
insult to the Lord. Believe that if he keeps you busy even until
midnight, yet he will come at the right time; the vision shall
come and shall not linger. Wait in quiet patience, not rebelling
because you are under the affliction, but blessing your God for
it. Never murmur against the second cause, as the children of
Israel did against Moses; never wish you could go back to the
world again, but accept the situation as it is, and put it as it
stands, simply and with your whole heart, without any self-
will, into the hand of your covenant God, saying, "Now, Lord,
not my will, but Yours be done. I don't know what to do; I am
brought to extremities, but I will wait until You shall halt the
floods, or drive back my foes. I will wait, if You keep me many
a day, for my heart is fixed upon You alone, O God, and my
spirit waits for You in the full conviction that You will yet be
my joy and my salvation, my refuge and my strong tower."[2]

God's imputed gift of longsuffering leading to patience, trust,
and hope in him is a painful, yet necessary, journey each of us
must make from the depths of sin to the summit of salvation
in Christ. Romans 3:23 is an ever-present reminder that we are
no better and no worse than anyone else: "*For all have sinned*

and fall short of the glory of God." This verse is an admonition that we must recognize our own depravity before we can look to our patient Creator and Redeemer and receive his gift of grace and salvation from our sins. Only by receiving him, honoring him, walking with him, waiting on him, and enduring for him, can we begin to cultivate and practice godly patience with others.

For those who endure long and protracted trials, such as illnesses, difficult marriages, wayward children, broken families, etc., patience seems impossible. Benign everyday issues of misbehavior on the part of a child or a coworker, a driver on the road, or a bad customer service experience, all temporarily test our patience. We call it our "hot buttons," but that glosses over the real issue, which is patience. Yet, in all of these circumstances, the test is in waiting upon God, trusting that he is good, and believe that his timing and his ways are perfect. That, in turn, fuels our patience in ways that our own will or personal strength cannot.

With that said, how do we even begin to exercise godly patience? The only way is by trusting in the One who walks by our side at all times and is master over our circumstances. One of my favorite missionary autobiographies is written by Hudson Taylor, the 19th-century medical student who was called to share God's message of reconciliation, forgiveness, and salvation in China. Hudson Taylor endured a long list of back-breaking hardships, harsh struggles, and grievous losses in his mission to teach others about who God is and to share the good news of salvation through Jesus Christ with the Chinese people. Taylor called God the *"Great Master Circumstance"* and proclaimed that if he remained always within God's will and followed his lead, he was always within God's will and circumstances and knew all would work out well.[3]

Hudson Taylor's words from over 150 years ago are a reminder that, if we trust God's goodness and grace in our lives in all circumstances, everything will work out for good for us, for that is God's promise to his people. That creates within us a deep and abiding godly patience that is not of our own making, it is something wholly attributable to God alone. We need only to turn to Romans 8:28 to be reminded of these truths: *"And we know that for those who love God all things work together for good, for those who are called according to his purpose."*

If we have committed ourselves to a relationship with God, we must look for opportunities to utilize God-like patience with others. Looking at one of my favorite practical Christian living books, *Respectable Sins: Confronting the Sins We Tolerate*, by Jerry Bridges, we can glean insight into where the everyday challenges to patience-building are hiding. It is at home, with family, in the familiar areas of our lives, Bridges says. In these comfort zones, we often expect others to conform to our expectations because we feel that people who are familiar with us should know what we want, how we want it, and when we want it.[4] "Familiarity breeds contempt" is the underlying lesson. Thus, to overcome the challenge of exercising godly patience with others, we have to make an extra effort to practice it (remember, 1 Corinthians 13 says, "Love is patient..."). God-like patience is exercised out of love. And, love is strengthened by patience. The two are inextricably woven together.

Furthermore, Jerry Bridges points out that impatience is often the response with those who know us well; those who are strangers are not expected to know how to be as pleasing to us, so we will be more forgiving, sometimes. Continued regular practice of impatience then leads to irritability, which further stresses and strains our relationships with those who are closer to us. Case in point, as a grandmother, it is far easier for me to endure my grandson's disobedience and be patient with him than it is for his mother (my daughter) who is with him from dawn to dusk. She has taught my grandson what behavior she expects. If he misbehaves, he knows he is not pleasing her. I, on the other hand, don't expect as much spotless behavior from my grandson, because he doesn't know what I expect of him as keenly as his mother does. But, that being said, I am less patient with my own husband's ways than someone else in our family, for I expect my husband to know what I do—and don't—like for him to do; I expect that he should know what my pet peeves are by now, and I expect him to refrain from testing them.

With a stranger, such as an inconsiderate driver on the road, a slow cashier at the market, or a neglectful waitress at a restaurant, we have to wait and take a deep breath before responding, for we are unsure of how they may respond. Yet, if we remember at the moment God's grace to us, we just might exercise a little more forgiveness, understanding, and patience with someone who doesn't behave in a manner pleasing to us. It is a practiced trait, another *fruit of the Spirit*, which we must partake of from God's hand so that this gift of patience can be used to reflect him in our responses to others. The other alternative is responding with our sinful nature, which is tainted with sin and unreliable at best.

From the Garden of Eden, where sin and impatience with God's commandments first emerged, to our world today where we desire everything instantaneously, we all struggle with patience with God, patience with others, even patience with ourselves. Let us wait upon God, and in doing so, learn to bear with each other in grace, love, and patience, which he freely extends to us, though none of us deserve it.

I leave you with the Apostle Paul's words from Ephesians 4:1⁻7:

> *(1) As a prisoner for the Lord, then, I urge you to live a life worthy of the calling you have received.*
> *(2) Be completely humble and gentle; be patient, bearing with one another in love.*
> *(3) Make every effort to keep the unity of the Spirit through the bond of peace.*
> *(4) There is one body and one Spirit, just as you were called to one hope when you were called;*
> *(5) one Lord, one faith, one baptism;*
> *(6) one God and Father of all, who is over all and through all and in all.*
> *(7) But to each one of us grace has been given as Christ apportioned it.*

May we truly desire the divine gift of patience from God, who so freely exercises it with us. If we claim to truly walk with God, let us pray for, cultivate, and practice godly patience with others, as well as with God, the giver of it. Those within our sphere of life will then catch a glimpse of how long-suffering and patient the Creator is with us. Reflecting God's patience to others is a truly life-saving gift that beckons others to respond to a holy God who is a loving Father exercising profound patience with a world of wayward children.

If you have not yet responded to God and committed to walking with him, know that he chooses at this very moment to be *"patient with you, not wishing that any should perish, but that all should reach repentance."* (2 Peter 3:9b) Today, God is still waiting patiently for his gift of reconciliation, forgiveness, and eternal life with him to be accepted. If you have not yet reached back to grasp his gift, he asks you to simply pray for the humility to do so.

He will do the rest.

* * *

Study Questions:

1. Who else in the Bible has portrayed a life that exhibits godly patience? Who do you know in your own life who exhibits this type of patience?
2. Do you believe that Romans 8:28 is true for you? Do you struggle with this verse and if so, why?
3. In your life, what struggles, mistreatment, and hardships are hard for you to accept? Do you struggle with God allowing difficult things to happen in your own life that you feel you don't deserve?
4. In what areas of your life do you have trouble waiting on God? Why do you think this is the case?
5. 2 Peter 3:9b says that God is *"patient with you, not wishing that any should perish, but that all should reach repentance."* For those who do not yet know God and

follow him, what does this mean? Why is God so patient with people who wish to live apart from him?

6. Reread the Biblical passages which provide the story of Abraham and Sarah. Where can you relate to their life experiences and their responses to God? How does God's patience with them encourage you?

7. Reread the Charles Spurgeon's sermon, "*Wait for the Lord* - Psalm 27:14" earlier in this chapter. What can you learn from this?

8. Patience can directly affect our grace, compassion, and love for others. How so?

Additional Bible verses on God's patience

Do: *Discuss and ponder over these verses, and pray for God to illuminate each one. (For additional context, read the entire Biblical chapter in which each of these verses appears.)*

Romans 9:22-24 - *"What if God, although willing to demonstrate His wrath and to make His power known, endured with much patience vessels of wrath prepared for destruction? And He did so to make known the riches of His glory upon vessels of mercy, which He prepared beforehand for glory, even us, whom He also called, not from among Jews only, but also from among Gentiles."*

Psalm 78:38 - *"But He, being compassionate, forgave their iniquity and did not destroy them; And often He restrained His anger and did not arouse all His wrath."*

2 Peter 3:9 - *"The Lord is not slow about His promise, as some count slowness, but is patient toward you, not wishing for any to perish but for all to come to repentance."*

Isaiah 48:9 - *"For the sake of My name I delay My wrath, And for My praise I restrain it for you, In order not to cut you off."*

1 Corinthians 13:4 - *"Love is patient and kind"*

Memory verse:

Ephesians 4:1-2 - *"I therefore, a prisoner for the Lord, urge you to walk in a manner worthy of the calling to which you have been called, with all humility and gentleness, with patience, bearing with one another in love"*

Action Plan - I need God's help in developing godly patience in my life in these areas:

1.

2.

3.

Suggested Readings and Resources:

1. *When the Darkness Will Not Lift: Doing What We Can While We Wait for God and Joy*, John Piper, December 2006

2. *Waiting on God: Strength for Today and Hope for Tomorrow*, Charles Stanley, January 2015

Notes:

Chapter Seven

FORGIVE AND FORGET – GOD'S FORGIVENESS

Ephesians 1:7 *"In him, we have redemption through his blood, the forgiveness of sins, in accordance with the riches of God's grace."*

Acts 3:19 *"Repent, then, and turn to God, so that your sins may be wiped out, that times of refreshing may come from the Lord."*

I want to introduce you to John L. His story is inspiring because it is living proof of a forgiving God. We met John in 2019 at church while visiting an adult Sunday school group. Being a lover of languages, I immediately noticed John had a strange accent that I couldn't identify. Someone gently whispered in my ear that John's accent was a "prison accent." John was kind, gracious, welcoming, and very enthusiastic about

God; he was a man who had been visibly and permanently changed, and it radiated from within him.

John's story began early in his childhood and the story was painful. His home life was fraught with abuse. At the age of fourteen, he dropped out of school and ran away from a home devoid of love. It was an act of desperation and self-preservation; his earthly father failed him, injured him, and nearly destroyed him. John ran as far from home as he could go and ended up at a truck stop. There, he spent fifteen months washing dishes for $.90 an hour and lived there with room and board offered to him. Sadly, the truck stop owner attempted to sexually abuse him. John resisted, and he was fired. John decided to escape to California continuing to run from despair and disillusionment. He would tell you that all he had ever wanted was to be loved and accepted; up to that point in his life, he had experienced neither.

Later, John found a new "family" who adopted him as one of their own. They were the Sons of Satan motorcycle gang. They introduced John to new miseries: drugs, alcohol, and crime. Being part of that gang had life-changing consequences for John. Though they accepted him and provided a pseudo family to belong to, he was forced to prove his loyalty by running drugs, engaging in bank robberies, etc. At the tender age of seventeen, he was a full member of the gang. John came to realize that all he had ever learned from them was to be "indiscriminate, impressionable, and insensitive," (these are John's own words). What he earned from this gang's activities was two prison terms adding up to forty years. His first incarceration was for eleven years in the most violent prison in the United States. He swore to himself he would never go back to prison again.

John returned to drug addiction after his first prison term ended, and he soon became plugged into the world of drugs and various criminal activities. Two years later, he ended up in prison again, this time with a life sentence. That was sobering for John; he knew he had done terrible things and had been willingly sucked into a godless world, blaming others for his choices. While in solitary confinement, John read Harold Morris' story, *Twice Pardoned.*[1] Harold's story, similar to John's, touched his heart and brought him to tears. He hadn't cried since he had been a child. Morris's story was John's story, and it made John realize who God and Jesus Christ are, that they are real, and that they change lives visibly and irrevocably. If God could change Harold Morris' heart, he could change John's heart, mind, and life.

On November 17, 1990, John will tell you that, "*I surrendered my heart, my life, and my will to Jesus Christ. I was tired of living like an animal. I wanted God to change me into something new.*"[2] God made John realize that he needed a relationship with him where John would be willing to learn to be humble, teachable, and hungry for God and his revealed Word, the Bible. God used the Bible to pierce deeply into John's heart, and he saw changes in his life that were so dramatic he could scarcely believe what was happening. God's message of hope, reconciliation, and forgiveness was changing John from the inside out, shaping his character into something new and better, and transforming him into a follower of Jesus Christ. He wasn't doing this, God was.

John will tell you that he learned to be a "*real man,*" and that involved being bold and confident in walking in God's power and forgiveness. He learned to look expectantly every day for

God's hand working in his life; he saw it daily, and he was continuously changed by it. These were changes that John declares that he never could have made for himself. God's forgiveness had ushered in a life-changing rejuvenation of John into an entirely new person. He felt compelled, even in times of adversity in prison, that he needed to set himself aside to help others. He refused to be self-absorbed any longer. He willingly gave up self-pity and bitterness and became so busy helping and encouraging others, he did not have time to attend his *"own pity party."* He became sensitive to the needs of others through suffering so much himself. He became encouraging to others and shared what God was doing in his own life.

God intervened in John's life so visibly and personally it completely altered his heart, his mind, his tendencies, and his worldview. John moved away from self-pity and bitterness to God's outstretched hand that provided him transformation of the heart, mind, and soul in real and tangible ways. God taught John integrity, empathy, encouragement, strength in God alone, and self-sacrifice for others. God's forgiveness, reconciliation, and personal relationship made John a new man. While in prison, John earned a Master's Degree and then a Doctorate in Theology and Religious Philosophy. He also became a licensed and ordained minister. John had initially entered prison an angry, bitter, and destructive man without a relationship with God. He emerged forty years later walking hand in hand with the real living God who radically changes lives, intentionally desires relationships with people, and chooses to change them into something new.

* * *

God's forgiveness is an underlying attribute of his character that is woven throughout the fabric of human history. He created a perfect world, created two individuals in his *"own image,"* (Genesis 1:26), and then watched those two image-bearers choose to rebel against him. In the Garden of Eden, God observed man's sinful will and intellect carefully weigh the rules versus the potential consequences and subsequently choose the self over God. From that point onward, a side-by-side concurrence of God's perfect will with man's broken and depraved will walked forward into history together, with God establishing a plan to fix this mess himself.

God needed to address mankind's selfish and rebellious will. He chose to exercise his sovereign power to make all things right in his appointed time. If he had not done so, God, in his perfection, would not have been able to have a relationship with people ever again. His forgiveness and carefully crafted consequences ushered in the Creator's tender and intentional plan to mend the brokenness of people's hearts and souls. God formed a plan at the foundation of the world to eventually come and dwell amongst people face to face in the person of a promised Savior who would destroy permanently the sin that entered God's once perfect creation.

On a trip to Israel in 2014, my husband and I and our private Israeli tour guide walked and talked together as we moved up the steps of the *Via Dolorosa* in Jerusalem. I was hot and tired after touring many other places that day, so I asked everyone to stop at a humble little pomegranate juice shop. Our guide,

Ron, reached into a bowl of massive pomegranates, and I assumed he was selecting one or two for the shop worker to use in his complicated pomegranate juicing machine. But, no, Ron was a talker, and once again that day he had something very interesting to say to his two Christian customers. He picked up a particularly large bulbous pomegranate in his huge hand, lifted it in the air slightly, and looked at me and my husband offering a rather snide comment. He told us, "*See this pomegranate, do you know what we Jews say about these things?*" I shook my head and was secretly hoping he'd just hand the piece of fruit to the worker and have him pop that softball-sized thing into the juicer and have at it. I was thirsty and not much in the mood for a teachable moment. Ron was in no hurry to hand over the pomegranate, however. He continued, "*We Jews say that a pomegranate and all its seeds represent the 613 Jewish Laws handed down to us by God in ancient times.*" He looked very, very sober, if not angry when he said this. Ron then disdainfully tossed the pomegranate to the shop worker who subsequently juiced all of those estimated 613 seeds into a rich, red, tart juice for me.

Ron, you see, had told us in so many words that he hated all those laws of his people's faith and history, and that he resented them.. It irked him to no end, and he made sure that we knew that. He resented the weight of those laws and chose to steer far away from them and simply live in his secular corner where no one told him what to do, God included. He saw a walk with God as a religious ball and chain around his neck and wanted to be free of that weight on his shoulders. His perception of God was rules, rules, and more rules, so Ron lived by no rules, and he liked it that way. Long ago he had chosen to live a life intentionally and willfully separate from God. Ron preferred to be his own god, boss, leader, and savior. He looked for opportunities to tell us this.

The first five books of the Bible record God's creation of the universe, his personal, purposeful, and his intentional outreach and covenants with specifically chosen people such as Adam, Noah, Abraham, and Moses. It also recorded God's provision of specific laws to his people, the Israelites. God's desire for a relationship with a fallen world resulted in commandments, beginning with an easy ten at first, then more religious, social, ceremonial, and civil laws, all of which he expected his people to follow. Those laws kept his people in line and close to him, much like a bit and bridle keeps a horse close to its master. God's people were to be a *"light to the nations"* (Isaiah 51:4) so they could visibly reflect to the polytheistic world who the one and only God is. Those laws were backed by constant sacrifices of animals as an act of atonement for man's sin. God had openly proclaimed and promised that a final sacrificial lamb, a Savior, would be the once-and-for-all sacrifice on behalf of all who would accept him. That Savior would fulfill the laws and be the final reconciler between God and man.

Fast forward to today, the very thought of constantly keeping all of those laws had personally exhausted our Israeli guide and many others a long time ago. However, God is a very forgiving Creator, and he provided his promised final sacrifice for sin, his Savior and Son, Jesus Christ, so that all those ancient laws are fulfilled. We tried to spend our time with Ron discussing this and sharing the good news that those laws don't reconcile us with God anymore. God knew that no one could ever perfectly keep all of those laws. The final sacrifice, Jesus Christ, promised for several thousand years, had done the job and satisfied all 613 of those laws for Ron, for me and my husband, and all mankind. Ron didn't quite comprehend all of this, but he looked intrigued.

We continued chatting with Ron and told him that God reached out of his own accord to chosen people throughout history and loved them despite their wayward selves. Endlessly withholding his wrath, protecting and providing for people who whined, complained, and ungratefully wished for an enslaved life that they used to have back in Egypt, all points to a God who tenderly forgives over and over and over. We explained that the promised Savior, who would eventually enter human history, was foretold specifically and repetitively throughout the Old Testament books of the Bible. When that Savior entered human history, he came specifically as promised, and he turned the world upside down by conquering sin itself.

We emphasized to Ron that the promised Savior said he did not come to abolish the old laws. Instead, he came to fulfill them, as promised. We explained that Christ's work is done, finished, perfect, and no one can add a single bit of extra elbow grease or puny acts of righteousness to that completed work. After dying willingly on a cruel Roman cross thereby conquering sin, evil, and death, the promised, foretold, and repeatedly prophesied Savior rose from the dead. Afterward, he visibly appeared to his disciples and over five hundred people, and then ascended to heaven to sit at his Father's right hand. The ultimate plan of forgiveness was accomplished.

God's forgiveness is a direct offshoot of his grace, love, patience, faithfulness, and omniscience. First, God's patience and forgiveness enable him to withhold his wrath. Second, his forgiveness is permanent; he doesn't withdraw forgiveness after he has given it. Additionally, he forgets our sins *"as far as the east is from the west, so far has he removed our transgressions from us,"* (Psalm 103:12), as part of his perfect plan. No one can earn God's forgiveness. It is the Giver's choice to bestow it on whom he wills. That makes it all the more humbling when we know we are undeserving recipients of this amazing gift.

Ron then shared an interesting anecdote with us as we walked up the steps of the Temple Mount in Jerusalem, and we stood upon the steps to turn and look at the thoroughfare of bustling Jerusalem below us. He mused out loud that one of his previous customers, Neil Armstrong (the first man on the moon), had walked up these steps with him several years earlier, and he stood pretty much where we were by the wide steps where the moneychangers placed their tables to conduct business in the first century. This spot was where Jesus would have duked it out with the infamous moneychangers whose tables he angrily turned over. Neil Armstrong knelt to the stone steps and humbly wept, Ron soberly related to us. Apparently, the astronaut was so completely overcome with God's love, grace, and forgiveness in Christ, that no moon landing or space flight even scratched the surface of his abject awe for what God had done for him. That perplexed Ron, quite frankly, but he respected that depth of faith in a man. God's offer of an outstretched hand, permanent forgiveness, and salvation to us should bring us to our knees, too.

In Psalm 103, David enshrined his awe of God's love and forgiveness in the most descriptive of terms:

(1) "Bless the Lord, O my soul, and all that is within me, bless his holy name!

(2) Bless the Lord, O my soul, and forget not all his benefits,

(3) who forgives all your iniquity, who heals all your diseases,

(4) who redeems your life from the pit, who crowns you with steadfast love and mercy,

(5) who satisfies you with good so that your youth is renewed like the eagle's.

(6) The Lord works righteousness and justice for all who are oppressed.

(7) He made known his ways to Moses, his acts to the people of Israel.

(8) The Lord is merciful and gracious, slow to anger and abounding in steadfast love.

(9) He will not always chide, nor will he keep his anger forever.

(10) He does not deal with us according to our sins, nor repay us according to our iniquities.

(11) For as high as the heavens are above the earth, so great is his steadfast love toward those who fear him;

(12) as far as the east is from the west, so far does he remove our transgressions from us.

(13) As a father shows compassion to his children, so the Lord shows compassion to those who fear him.

(14) For he knows our frame; he remembers that we are dust.

(15) As for man, his days are like grass; he flourishes like a flower of the field;

(16) for the wind passes over it, and it is gone, and its place knows it no more.

(17) But the steadfast love of the Lord is from everlasting to everlasting on those who fear him, and his righteousness to children's children,

(18) to those who keep his covenant and remember to do his commandments.
(19) The Lord has established his throne in the heavens, and his kingdom rules over all.
(20) Bless the Lord, O you his angels, you mighty ones who do his word, obeying the voice of his word!
(21) Bless the Lord, all his hosts, his ministers, who do his will!
(22) Bless the Lord, all his works, in all places of his dominion. Bless the Lord, O my soul!

Let's unpack this powerful Psalm, for David's praises to God within Psalm 103 are rich with a multitude of descriptive elements of God's character, all of which work in perfect unison with his awe-inspiring forgiveness to mankind. David begins by praising God for who he is, for the holiness of his name, and for all the wonderful benefits to mankind which come only from God. Verse 3 then begins a praising overview of God's attributes, beginning with his forgiveness. David first focuses upon God's forgiveness of all of his people's sins. He does this because it is who God is; he is a God who chooses to forgive. This will mean much more to David later on as his own life progresses and his sinful propensities are exposed time and time again.

David proclaims that, because of God's holiness and forgiveness of all the sins of his people, he heals them from physical disease according to his will, he redeems them from affliction, and he righteously works out injustices endured at the hands of others. David likens God's personality to a king who bestows upon his people his *"crown of his steadfast love and mercy."* David lauds God's righteousness manifested in mercy, grace, slowness to anger (patience), steadfast love, healing, and reconciliation. In verse 9-12 David describes to us that these attributes lead God to *"not always chide, nor will he keep his anger forever. He does not deal with us according to our sins, nor repay us according to our iniquities. For as high as the heavens are above the earth, so great is his steadfast love toward those who fear him; as far as the east is from the west, so far does he remove transgressions from us."* God's forgiveness to his people is depicted as total, complete, and limitless. This made David awash with gratitude.

Forgiveness, David continues further in verses 13 and 14, is evident in God's role as a father who shows *"compassion to his children, so the Lord shows compassion to those who fear him. For he knows our frame; he remembers that we are dust."* And, as God's forgiveness is limitless and everlasting, so is his love. David says in verses 17-18: *"But the steadfast love of the Lord is from everlasting to everlasting on those who fear him, and his righteousness to children's children, to those who keep his covenant and remember to do his commandments."* God's character is unchanging and his gifts are everlasting. Man cannot do any amount of work to add to who God is and what he has done for us. That leads us to the promised Savior who completed the final work of redeeming us and providing victory over sin, ushering in God's forgiveness to this broken world.

Jesus, the foretold and promised Messiah, who would conquer sin and open the veil between us and God's mercy seat, was God's ultimate gift of redemption and forgiveness. In the Old Testament, written before the entrance of God's promised

Savior at the appointed time in history (the 1st century A.D.), the continuously required sacrifices of unblemished lambs were used to atone for the Israelites' sin and satisfy God's righteous wrath and judgement. When God ushered into the world his own Son, an unblemished perfect lamb, he required him to die upon a tree (the cross); this points to that original tree in the Garden of Eden where sin first began. Through Christ, God provided us the final and once-and-for-all perfect sacrifice for our sins. By doing this, Jesus Christ redeemed us from being enslaved to our sin, which separates us from God. The Hebrew and the Greek word for *"redeem"* in the Biblical record means "a purchase" or a "ransom." In ancient times a slave was "redeemed" when someone paid a price for them to be given their freedom. This is precisely what God did for his people through his own Son, Jesus Christ.

The Biblical narrative is filled with specific declarations and demonstrations of God providing mankind atonement for sin and offering forgiveness and reconciliation. It is the foundation of God's plan from the very beginning of creation. In the New Testament, the Book of Hebrews, chapter 9, verse 22 declares, *"Without the shedding of blood, there is no forgiveness."* By shedding his blood on the cross, Christ paid the price for our sins and redeemed us (bought us back from sin), purchased God's forgiveness for us, and permanently conquered sin and death for those who are in a relationship with him. In the New Testament, Ephesians 1:7 assures us, *"In him we have redemption through his blood, the forgiveness of sins, in accordance with the riches of God's grace."* Also, 1 Peter 3:18 sums it up clearly: *"For Christ died for sins once for all, the righteous for the unrighteous, to bring you to God."*

The Old Testament prophet Micah (6th century B.C.) describes it this way, *"Who is a God like you, pardoning iniquity and passing over transgression for the remnant of his inheritance? He does not retain his anger forever, because he delights in steadfast love."* *(Micah 7:18-19)* God chooses to pardon and forgive repentant people, and he elects to withhold his holy anger and judgment against us for our sinful ways, for he *"delights in steadfast love."* That is true forgiveness and an intentional commitment and willingness to stick by us even when we are disappointing to God.

Upon paying a steep price unto death to buy us back from sin and death, God extends to us forgiveness underpinned by self-sacrifice, grace, and love. This kind of forgiveness comes from the heart of a God who desires to share his heavenly courts not with lofty, perfect people, but with sinful beggars whose lives have been saved and bought at a great price. Folks, we are those "beggars," and eternally grateful beggars we should be. And, not only are our filthy rags of personal piety, hidden sin, and dingy motives washed clean, our shoulders are then cloaked with a lovely robe of Christ's righteousness, and our table is set with a bottomless bowl of spiritual fruits of *"love, joy, peace, patience, kindness, goodness, faithfulness, and self-control."* (Galatians 5:22-23a)

This logically brings us to the Book of John, Chapter 3. It is here that Jesus' conversation with the Pharisee (High Priest), Nicodemus, illustrates the necessity of being a truly repentant person before God, and that God's Holy Spirit must regenerate each person in the newness of life. Nicodemus was a Pharisee, one who diligently practiced Old Testament Law. He looked to the keeping of that law to make him righteous before God. Jesus turned Nicodemus' understanding of God

upside down. Jesus told him that every person, both Jew and
non-Jew (Gentile), must be reborn in the Spirit (not the Law).
Let's eavesdrop on their conversation:

> (1) "Now there was a man of the Pharisees named Nicode-
> mus, a ruler of the Jews.
> (2) This man came to Jesus by night and said to him, 'Rab-
> bi, we know that you are a teacher come from God, for no one
> can do these signs that you do unless God is with him.'
> (3) Jesus answered him, 'Truly, truly, I say to you, unless one
> is born again he cannot see the kingdom of God.'
> (4) Nicodemus said to him, 'How can a man be born when he
> is old? Can he enter a second time into his mother's womb and
> be born?'
> (5) Jesus answered, 'Truly, truly, I say to you, unless one is
> born of water and the Spirit, he cannot enter the kingdom
> of God.
> (6) That which is born of the flesh is flesh, and that which is
> born of the Spirit is spirit.
> (7) Do not marvel that I said to you, 'You must be born again.'
> (8) The wind blows where it wishes, and you hear its sound,
> but you do not know where it comes from or where it goes. So
> it is with everyone who is born of the Spirit.'
> (9) Nicodemus said to him, 'How can these things be?'
> (10) Jesus answered him, 'Are you the teacher of Israel and yet
> you do not understand these things? (11) Truly, truly, I say to
> you, we speak of what we know, and bear witness to what we
> have seen, but you do not receive our testimony.
> (12) If I have told you earthly things and you do not believe,
> how can you believe if I tell you heavenly things?
> (13) No one has ascended into heaven except he who descended
> from heaven, the Son of Man.

(14) And as Moses lifted up the serpent in the wilderness, so must the Son of Man be lifted up,

(15) that whoever believes in him may have eternal life.

(16) For God so loved the world, that he gave his only Son, that whoever believes in him should not perish but have eternal life.

(17) For God did not send his Son into the world to condemn the world, but in order that the world might be saved through him.

(18) Whoever believes in him is not condemned, but whoever does not believe is condemned already, because he has not believed in the name of the only Son of God.

(19) And this is the judgment: the light has come into the world, and people loved the darkness rather than the light because their works were evil.

(20) For everyone who does wicked things hates the light and does not come to the light, lest his works should be exposed.

(21) But whoever does what is true comes to the light, so that it may be clearly seen that his works have been carried out in God."'

In this passage, Jesus speaks to Nicodemus and to us today, pointing to rebirth through repentance by the power of the Holy Spirit, not by keeping of old laws. No earthly birth is implied here; Jesus declares that he was sent to save and bring rebirth to those who trust in his conquering of sin. The Law was going to be fulfilled in Christ's one-time sacrifice upon the cross, and true repentance would bring about a new kind of rebirth under the power of something other than the Old Testament Israelite Law: The Holy Spirit.

This was earth-shattering to Nicodemus. He could no longer count on his work in keeping the Law, for that was not underpinned by repentance, nor was it fueled by the power of the Holy Spirit. Repentance and acceptance of the promised Savior was the door to the kingdom of heaven now. Jesus, the promised Savior, was going to fulfill the Law, the endless sacrifices, and the temporary atonement that ancient Israelite religious practices offered under Israelite Law. This conversation knocked both Nicodemus and every person on the earth then and now off of their self-made pedestals of self-righteousness.

Our meager attempts at holiness and self-righteousness are, like the Old Testament Prophet Isaiah warned, *"like filthy rags; we all shrivel up like a leaf, and like the wind, our sins sweep us away."* (Is. 64:6). The endless laws could never be perfectly kept and were all fulfilled by the promised Savior. Now, there is nothing that anyone must do but repent and accept God's gift of salvation from sin and eternal life through Jesus, the promised Messiah. Now, because God loved mankind so much, *"he gave his only Son, that whoever believes in him should not perish but have eternal life. For God did not send his Son into the world to condemn the world, but so that the world might be saved through him. Whoever believes in him is not condemned, but whoever does not believe is condemned already, because he has not believed in the name of the only Son of God. (John 3:16-18)*

The Apostle Paul, in Romans 3:21-26, clearly explains Christ's finished work and God's imputed forgiveness and righteousness to believers:

(21) *"But now the righteousness of God has been manifested apart from the law, although The Law and the Prophets bear witness to it—*

(22) the righteousness of God through faith in Jesus Christ for all who believe. For there is no distinction:
(23) for all have sinned and fall short of the glory of God,
(24) and are justified by his grace as a gift, through the redemption that is in Christ Jesus,
(25) whom God put forward as a propitiation by his blood, to be received by faith. This was to show God's righteousness, because in his divine forbearance he had passed over former sins.
(26) It was to show his righteousness at the present time, so that he might be just and the justifier of the one who has faith in Jesus."

Who better to model God's infinite forgiveness in his life than God's own Son and promised Savior, Jesus Christ? Let's delve into various segments of Jesus' life and see how forgiveness is integral to his interactions with people, his message, and his mission.

Portrait of Forgiveness – Jesus Christ

Jesus demonstrated to the people of the 1st century, as well as to us today, sacrificial forgiveness. At the hands of others, Jesus willingly endured mistreatment, misunderstanding, misrepresentation, malice, betrayal, sin, and death. He did this for the people because he loved them, forgave them, healed them, and promised them eternal life. His sacrificial death made believers in Jesus wholly forgiven by God.

As we have explored previously, original sin, authored my man, started with a tree (Adam and Eve chose to disobey God —sin--by eating from the forbidden tree in the Garden of Eden). Thousands of years later, sin was conquered by Jesus' death upon a tree formed into a Roman cross. 2 Corinthians 5:21 adds further to this: *"For our sake He (God) made Him (Christ) to be sin who knew no sin, so that in Him we might become the righteousness of God."* Jesus was the "second Adam," this time bringing through his perfect life and sacrificial death a complete and total victory over sin that began with the first Adam. He laid down his life for *"his friends,"* and neither his word or his work comes back void or wasted. It delivers forgiveness, redemption from sin and death, and reconciliation with the Creator who wishes to offer forgiveness.

Throughout the thirty-three years of Jesus' life upon this earth, he modeled for us a depth of forgiveness that should light a fire under us to offer the same forgiveness to others. Forgiving and then bearing the brunt of another's bad choices, their evil and destructive behavior, and their ill intentions, is something that none of us would choose to do. It simply isn't in us. Few, if any, would desire to forgive--much less die--for another's bad choices. Yet, with the entrance of Christ into the world, things changed drastically and eternally. He operated by vastly different rules. Jesus warned about ceasing the law of *"an eye for an eye, and a tooth for a tooth,"* and instead ushered in a host of new ways of living.

See Matthew 5:3-12 and you will get a taste for what people of Jesus' time saw as a radically different set of laws to live by. These were laws of the heart; these were no longer obligatory mandates. A heart circumcised by the Holy Spirit, not by the Law, provided fulfillment of the old ways and ushered in a new era of blessing. In Matthew 5:3-12, Jesus tells his disciples (and all who follow him):

> *(3) "Blessed are the poor in spirit, for theirs is the kingdom of heaven.*
>
> *(4) Blessed are those who mourn, for they shall be comforted.*
>
> *(5) Blessed are the meek, for they shall inherit the earth.*
>
> *(6) Blessed are those who hunger and thirst for righteousness, for they shall be satisfied.*
>
> *(7) Blessed are the merciful, for they shall receive mercy.*
>
> *(8) Blessed are the pure in heart, for they shall see God.*
>
> *(9) Blessed are the peacemakers, for they shall be called sons of God.*
>
> *(10) Blessed are those who are persecuted for righteousness' sake, for theirs is the kingdom of heaven.*
>
> *(11) Blessed are you when others revile you and persecute you and utter all kinds of evil against you falsely on my account.*
>
> *(12) Rejoice and be glad, for your reward is great in heaven, for so they persecuted the prophets who were before you."*

Matthew specifically records Jesus assuring his disciples that they—and we--are *"blessed"* if we have a humble spirit, meekness, mercy, and purity of heart, all of which bring us a *"reward"* that is *"great in heaven."* No adherence to endless Old Testament laws had ever altered the human heart. Now, *"an eye for an eye"* is replaced by Jesus's new directive, in Matthew 5:38-48:

(38) "You have heard that it was said, 'An eye for an eye and a tooth for a tooth.'

(39) But I say to you, do not resist the one who is evil. But if anyone slaps you on the right cheek, turn to him the other also.

(40) And if anyone would sue you and take your tunic, let him have your cloak as well.

(41) And if anyone forces you to go one mile, go with him two miles.

(42) Give to the one who begs from you, and do not refuse the one who would borrow from you.

(43) You have heard that it was said, 'You shall love your neighbor and hate your enemy.'

(44) But I say to you, love your enemies and pray for those who persecute you,

(45) so that you may be sons of your Father who is in heaven. For he makes his sun rise on the evil and on the good, and sends rain on the just and on the unjust.

(46) For if you love those who love you, what reward do you have? Do not even the tax collectors do the same?

(47) And if you greet only your brothers, what more are you doing than others? Do not even the Gentiles do the same?

(48) You therefore must be perfect, as your heavenly Father is perfect."

Christ not only tells us, but he also shows us what forgiveness and mercy look like, now that the Kingdom of God is at hand and he has arrived to fulfill the Law as the promised and foretold Savior. He asks us to endure and to stand firm with him in the face of adversity or persecution and to confidently face it head-on. He tells us to have a heart that gives more than we are even asked for. This means going the extra mile for someone, even if they don't ask you to; Jesus did that for us. He lovingly admonishes us to love our enemies, and not only that, to pray for them; Jesus did that for us. Jesus tells us to be perfect, just like he and his father are. Only through Christ's imputed righteousness can we do any of these things. Only by God looking at Christ—not us—can we be seen as acceptable by God.

Christ is the perfect sacrifice, the only who willingly laid down his life for his friends. By leaning upon and believing in his finished work and sacrifice on our behalf, we are deemed acceptable and forgiven by God. In the power of Christ, we, too, can begin to practice forgiveness in a way that we never desired before.

A life that is illustrative of Christ-like forgiveness is that of Elisabeth Elliott.

Portrait of forgiveness – Elisabeth Elliott

In the mid-20th century, Elisabeth Elliott and her husband, Jim, initially worked in Quito, Ecuador, to bring the good news of God's forgiveness through Jesus Christ to the Quichua Indians. Jim had hoped to find a heretofore "unreachable" tribe and teach them about the God of the Bible and his forgiving and gracious plan of salvation from sin. Later, an unreached tribe, the Auca/Huaorani was found to be in a particular locale in Ecuador, and Jim and his four other missionary colleagues decided to come into contact with them to share the good news of Jesus Christ. This tribe was known to have killed anyone who had attempted to interact with them. Jim and his four friends entered the Auca/Huaorani village to initiate a relationship with them and to tell the tribe about Jesus Christ. Shortly thereafter, Jim and all of his colleagues were mercilessly speared to death before they could do more than meet up with three members of the tribe. At the time, Elisabeth and Jim had a 10-month-old daughter and Elisabeth was left a widow. It appears to be a heartbreaking tale, but God had a plan; all was not lost.

Elisabeth did not choose to go home to the U.S. and seethe in vengeance, inconsolable mourning, or unforgiveness. Instead, she and her infant daughter stayed in Ecuador. She continued working with the Quichua Indians herself. Elisabeth met two Auca/Huaorani women from the tribe who had killed her husband and fellow missionaries. Forgivingly and selflessly Elisabeth allowed them to live with her for one year and they taught her the language of the Huaorani people. These Huaorani women became the lynchpin for Elisabeth eventually approaching the tribe. This tribe trusted Elisabeth after she allowed two of their women to live with her, and they allowed her to live with them for two years. During that time, no harm came to her, even though they knew she was the wife of Jim Elliott, the man who they had killed. God became real to them through Elisabeth's forgiveness and loving service to them.[3]

This is forgiveness of the most powerful kind. Elisabeth loved, prayed for, and ministered to her enemies, just as Christ asks us to do. Elisabeth lovingly brought the Gospel of forgiveness and redemption to the Auca/Huaorani, because she trusted God and visibly demonstrated incredible forgiveness, selfless service, and genuine love. This is selfless, sacrificial, almost impossible to understand, and it is real. This is what Christ lived out authentically to others so that he could be a face-to-face example for us. Selfless forgiveness is a gift that we must have from God so we can subsequently practice it with others. Elisabeth Elliot made a loving and forgiving God real, visible, and knowable to the Auca/Huaorani people, and they came to believe in God as a result.

If you have not yet come to know God and experience his profound forgiveness that, as you have learned in this chapter, is completely undeserved, yet offered to you, now is a good time. He waits patiently, graciously, lovingly, and compassionately for you to respond to him. He has all-encompassing forgiveness to offer you, despite anything you may have done or not done in life. He desires to offer forgiveness and to forget what you and I have done. Psalm 103:12 assures you and I that, *"as far as the east is from the west, so far does he remove our transgressions from us."*

Making it real

Forgiving ourselves, forgiving others, and even forgiving God are three areas in which many people struggle at one time or another. The ability to truly forgive is from the power of the Holy Spirit; we can't do this ourselves. Jesus demonstrated this and gave us examples to live by. Elisabeth Elliot demonstrated God's kind of forgiveness because she had the power of the Spirit within her enabling her to stand firm in the face of those who killed her husband and colleagues and forgive them, love them, and serve them.

Forgiving ourselves is that internal release from the guilt that handcuffs us and robs us of freedom to live in peace. There are inevitably some areas in life where we have significantly dropped the ball, gravely disappointed someone, or done something that we consider unforgivable. Unforgiveness of the self is a festering, deep wound that gives rise to self-loathing, self-destructive behavior, and an inability to forgive others. If God can forgive us and forget things permanently, we must accept God's promises, power, and limitless forgiveness to truly heal us. Only then can we take the next step, forgiving others.

We often become comfortable and familiar with this enemy, unforgiveness, and we exercise it as a tool to correct, discipline, or punish those around us. Left unchecked, it evolves into other things such as malice, slander, gossip, and physical and/or psychological mistreatment of others. Matthew 6:14-15 puts it bluntly, *"For if you forgive others their trespasses, your heavenly Father will also forgive you, but if you do not forgive others their trespasses, neither will your Father forgive you."* If we are refraining from forgiving others, we are in a state of unforgiveness before God. Additionally, God asks us not to approach him in worship if we have unforgiveness and unreconciled differences with another. God asks that we go to that person and directly and decisively deal with the unresolved issue, and only then come back and worship him. Essentially, remaining in a willful state of unforgiveness toward another, we are choosing to remain separated from God.

Finally, we must touch upon the subject of forgiveness toward God. This one also hits close to home, for many suffer from deep-seated anger and refusal to forgive God for something that they perceive he has done, that he has not done, or that he has--or has not allowed--to occur. Those who do not know God will inadvertently harbor anger and unforgiveness toward some entity who they consider to be "in control." This is the innate desire to blame someone else for something that went wrong or unexpectedly. It is hedging one's bet that, if there truly is a god, then he isn't very powerful and certainly isn't in control. It all boils down to a false perception of God, which stems from not knowing him.

When we truly know that God is gracious, loving, compassionate, forgiving, and merciful, we can take refuge in him when life gets tough and the losses are huge. But when we do not know God, or we fashion a god of our own making, it becomes frightening and disappointing when circumstances look overwhelming. When we know God, we can rest in who he truly is. We can trust that he keeps his promises and that he is powerful enough to fulfill them. History has proven that God always keeps his promises. He does not promise that life will be perfect, however. Quite the contrary, Jesus warns that we will be *"reviled and persecuted for His name's sake."* (Mat. 5:11)

God's forgiveness is a life-changing gift. It is an integral part of who he is. A world bent on vengeance, self-righteous vigilante-ism, and frivolous litigation will find an act of forgiveness shocking, other-worldly, and possibly absurd. Responding to God, and accepting his forgiveness, reconciliation, and the free gift of eternal life will begin to create visible changes in our worldview, our personality, our behavior, and our motives. Belonging to God will impute his Son's righteousness to us;

that should—and does—change us so that those changes are visible to others. Though we may be mocked, disbelieved, misunderstood, and perhaps persecuted privately and publicly, God desires us to respond to his forgiveness and to derive strength and peace from it.

Are you willing to be a risk-taker, a forgiver, and a forgetter, and be forever refreshed in God and his Son, Jesus Christ? Are you willing to be like Elisabeth Elliott or John L., wholly resting in a God who transforms the heart and sets you upon a path of forgiveness, service, and love toward others? If so, God is waiting patiently for you to grasp his outstretched hand of forgiveness and reconciliation so you can be forever changed, refreshed, and strengthened by it. Once you grasp it, he will never let you go.

Acts 3:19 leaves us on an encouraging note: *"Repent, then, and turn to God, so that your sins may be wiped out, that times of refreshing may come from the Lord."*

* * *

Study Questions:

1. Which part of Psalm 103 particularly speaks to you concerning the subject of forgiveness? Why?
2. What does Hebrews 9:22 mean when it says, *"Without the shedding of blood, there is no forgiveness"*?
3. Who do you know that seems to model godly forgiveness? How do they demonstrate it?
4. Knowing that God desires to forgive people who respond to him in repentance and faith, how does

this change the way you want to live your life? What would you do differently?

5. Read Matthew 5:38-48 again (which we discussed earlier in this chapter). In light of this passage and what it says about forgiveness, where do you still struggle with this issue?

6. Acts 3:19 says, *"Repent, then, and turn to God, so that your sins may be wiped out, that times of refreshing may come from the Lord."* How is repentance (from sin) tied to God's forgiveness?

7. How do you reconcile God's forgiveness with justice and consequences? Give examples.

8. Ephesians 4:32 says - *"Be kind and compassionate to one another, forgiving each other, just as in Christ God forgave you."* How do you think kindness and compassion are directly related to forgiving others?

Additional Bible verses on God's forgiveness

Do: *Discuss and ponder over these verses, and pray for God to illuminate each one. (For additional context, read the entire Biblical chapter in which each of these verses appears.)*

Psalm 86:5 - *"You, Lord, are forgiving and good, abounding in love to all who call to you."*

Micah 7:18 - *"Who is a God like you, who pardons sin and forgives the transgression of the remnant of his inheritance? You do not stay angry forever but delight to show mercy."*

. . .

Matthew 6:14 – *"For if you forgive other people when they sin against you, your heavenly Father will also forgive you."*

Colossians 3:13 – *"Bear with each other and forgive one another if any of you has a grievance against someone. Forgive as the Lord forgave you."*

Ephesians 4:32 – *"Be kind and compassionate to one another, forgiving each other, just as in Christ God forgave you."*

Memory verse

Psalm 103:2-4 – *"Bless the Lord, O my soul, and forget not all his benefits, who forgives all your iniquity, who heals all your diseases, who redeems your life from the pit, who crowns you with steadfast love and mercy"*

Recommended reading:

Through Gates of Splendor, Elisabeth Elliot, Tyndale Momentum, Revised, Updated edition, June 1981.

Let It Go: Forgive So You Can Be Forgiven, T. D. Jakes, Atria Books, Simon & Schuster, Inc., New York, 2012.

. . .

<u>Action Plan</u>: I want to practice forgiveness toward myself, toward others, and toward God. These are some areas where I know I need God's help:

1)

2)

3)

<u>Notes:</u>

Chapter Eight

THE SAME YESTERDAY, TODAY AND FOREVER – GOD'S IMMUTABILITY (UNCHANGING NATURE)

Hebrews 13:8 *"Jesus Christ is the same yesterday and today and forever."*

Malachi 3:6 *"For I, the LORD, do not change; therefore you, O sons of Jacob, are not consumed."*

The Book of Hebrews states in Chapter 13, verse 8: *"Jesus Christ is the same yesterday, today and forever."* There you have it. God (and his Son, Jesus Christ) are unchanging and, therefore, are the same yesterday, now, and forever. God's immutability, i.e. his unchanging nature, never was, never is, and never will be altered. His unchanging nature also applies to sin. He hates it, will not tolerate it, and always will respond this way. He does not hate sin in the past yet tolerate it today. God must deal with it because it is unequivocally unacceptable to him and always will be.

The Old Testament Book of the Prophet Malachi, Chapter 3, verse 6, sheds clear light on the subject of God's unchanging nature: *"I the LORD do not change; therefore you, O children of Jacob, are not consumed."* God describes himself as being *"The Lord* "who possesses a character that does *"not change."* As a result of that personal declaration, God subsequently explains that, in light of his unchanging nature, he offers mercy to his people and comforts them with his self-control in choosing to *not* consume them (i.e. pour out his wrath upon them) for their offensive sin. This implies that, because God is an unchanging God of mercy, longsuffering, self-control, and compassion, he exercises enormous restraint with his people.

Despite man's propensity to be selfish, wayward, and disobedient, God's unchanging nature of love, graciousness, holiness, patience, compassion, and forgiveness fuels his choice to spare people the wrath they deserve. Though we are constantly changing our minds, motives, decisions, and propensities on a moment-by-moment basis, God remains his unchanging self. This is much like a firm and loving parent who raises a strong-willed child and stands unwavering in loving their child, offering grace and forgiveness to them, yet without allowing the child's bad behavior to be tolerated. A good parent stays the course through their child's ups and downs. God the Father, is an immovably strong and loving Creator and a divine parent who stands firm as an unwavering and unchanging pillar of strength to his children.

Immutability is a foundational element of God's character upon which all other attributes exist in perpetuity. When God introduces himself in history to people, he remains true to himself and his covenants with them. Despite his people's backsliding, unbelief, disobedience, idolatry, disrespect, discontentment, etc., God will not be changed by it, nor will he change his plans and promises. He will not break his promises, though we may break ours. That is reassuring. A God who always keeps his promises is a God worth knowing.

Additionally, a foundation of total immutability allows for God's other attributes to continuously flow from himself to his people forever. There is no ebb in God's character flowing through history; he remains himself at all times. A God whose very nature is wholly unchanging allows his grace and unmerited favor to continue being given to naughty children (yes, this is us), who don't deserve it. Furthermore, his immovable and immutable nature allows all of the elements of God's character to remain unchanged despite how much we test it. Now, this in no way implies that God, a loving Father, will not mete out justice and discipline. No good parent would refrain from molding their child into something far better than they naturally are by withholding much-needed discipline.

2 Timothy 2:13 adds to our understanding of God's unchanging character: "*If we are faithless, he remains faithful, for he cannot disown himself.*" God keeps his promises, his contracts, and covenants with his people, and he never deviates from his plans for each of us as well as for all of human history. He will not act out of a fleeting moment of newly felt spite or wrath, nor will he elect to rewrite his preconceived plans mapped out for each of us, because he suddenly learns something new that necessitates a change in course for some of us. His faithfulness to his people is solid and immovable. On the other hand, his promised judgment for those who refuse to come into a relationship with him is also unchanging and unwavering.

What does this mean for us as we seek to understand the very personality and nature of God in the context of his immutability? An unchanging God implies many wonderful things. Let's examine three distinct implications of God's unchanging character. First, God does not change his mind regarding the plans and choices that he makes. Thus, God does not break promises, contracts, or covenants because something or someone induces him to break rank and go another direction. Why is that? Because he is perfectly loving, perfectly righteous, perfectly gracious, perfectly just, perfectly patient, perfectly compassionate, and perfectly forgiving, therefore, he need not—and will not—change. Anything changing from a state of perfection is taking a step down to a diminished state of being that is less than perfect.

The Apostle Paul says in Romans 8:28-30: *"And we know that in all things God works for the good of those who love him, who have been called according to his purpose. For those God foreknew he also predestined to be conformed to the image of his Son, that he might be the firstborn among many brothers and sisters. And those he predestined, he also called; those he called, he also justified; those he justified, he also glorified."* This means that God has purposes and plans already laid out because he foreknows all things and therefore pre-plans all things, including plans for his people, so that the outcome complies with his sovereign will. In light of that, God never changes those plans, for they were set long ago, and despite what we do, we cannot foil them.

The key here is that God promises to weave together for good everything his people do, say, or think—or not do, not say, or not think—and he keeps to his plans that he has already made for each of us. Furthermore, God will challenge us to trust his plans and purposes when we belong to him. We need do nothing but follow him based upon who he is. His roadmap for his people is sure to lead to a perfect destination, though there will most assuredly be hurdles, bumps, and bruises along the way. These challenges are placed there to shape our character. Though we are given a will and intellect to make choices, his perfect and unchanging plans for us move forward, despite what we do to throw ourselves off the best possible course.

Hebrews 6:13-19 delves deeper into God's unchanging nature and its direct effect upon his keeping of promises to do good for his people according to his unchanging plans:

> *(13) "When God made his promise to Abraham, since there was no one greater for him to swear by, he swore by himself,*
> *(14) saying, 'I will surely bless you and give you many descendants.'*
> *(15) And so, after waiting patiently, Abraham received what was promised.*
> *(16) People swear by someone greater than themselves, and the oath confirms what is said and puts an end to all argument.*
> *(17) Because God wanted to make the unchanging nature of his purpose very clear to the heirs of what was promised, he confirmed it with an oath.*
> *(18) God did this so that, by two unchangeable things in which it is impossible for God to lie, we who have fled to take hold of the hope set before us may be greatly encouraged.*
> *(19) We have this hope as an anchor for the soul, firm and secure."*

Verse 17 hits the nail on the head: *"Because God wanted to make the unchanging nature of his purpose very clear to the heirs of what was promised, he confirmed it with an oath."* God's immutable personality produces unchanging plans, and he makes an unbreakable promise to stick to those plans, despite our protestations or meddling. That is an assurance that we know we can lean on yesterday, today, and forever. When we know God and are in a relationship with him, he deems us to be "*the heirs of what was promised.*" Verses 18 and 19 assure us that God never lies, and that we can hope in who he is. Rather than being a boat adrift in the sea of life, we can lean upon God's unchanging nature as a solid and unmoving *"anchor for the soul, firm and secure."*

Let's not refrain from also addressing what this means for any individual who does not yet believe in God and does not yet trust in his promised and provided Savior, Jesus Christ. Until such a time as one responds to and puts their faith in God and his Savior, one does not belong to God and is therefore not his heir. If we are not God's children, then we are not his heirs, therefore there is no promise or guarantee that anything will be "good" if we choose to go it on our own and follow our self-made blueprint for our lives. Living, choosing, and planning one's life apart from God is a lonely road promising very little at the end but an assured eternal separation from God. Those who are not with him are subject to God's unchanging declaration that, *"Whoever is not with me is against me, and whoever does not gather with me scatters."* (Matthew 12:30)

Second, God's immutable character coupled with his foreknowledge of the future, his knowledge of every person's thoughts and motives, and his perfect plans for his people, can never learn something new that changes his decisions. Though God observes and hears all that occurs deep in the hearts of people as well as all that has, is, and will occur, he does not learn anything new and is not surprised by anything. He allows all people their concurrent will alongside his sovereign will, however, there is no change or addition to God's knowledge of things. We may make the wrong choices, harbor flawed and selfish motives, misbehave blatantly or in secret, yet God knew it all along. He is unchanging, therefore his character, his knowledge, and his plans will not change, despite our choices. Like his finger writing the Ten Commandments, God's character, his knowledge, and his plans are set in stone, for they are the only perfect, solid, and unchanging rock upon which to inscribe a blueprint for each of his people's lives.

Finally, God's unchanging character tempers his righteous wrath and holy justice which he rightfully should mete out in disciplining a disobedient world of wayward people, yet doesn't. Instead, God meted out the punishment for sin on his promised sacrificial Lamb, his Son Jesus Christ. Jesus took the hit for our follies. Despite ourselves, God keeps his covenants with his people and therefore willfully withholds his righteous and holy wrath upon us lawbreakers. God intentionally withholds his wrath from literally destroying us and keeps his promises to his own, though they may fall away, deliberately disobey, or worse, worship other things. He provides the promised Savior for his people to bear the discipline, punishment, and death for our bad choices, so that we are not judged for them ourselves. If we were judged for our own sins, all of us would be condemned, and heaven would be empty except for God. We have explored this previously. This does not mean God will not discipline and correct bad behavior and disobedience, however. I cannot emphasize that enough. He allows the necessary consequences to teach and to mold us.

Malachi 3:6-7, which we have touched upon briefly earlier in this chapter, bears repeating:

> *(6) I the Lord do not change. So, you, the descendants of Jacob,*
> *are not destroyed.*
> *(7) Ever since the time of your ancestors you have turned*
> *away from my decrees and have not kept them. Return to me,*
> *and I will return to you, says the Lord Almighty.*

When we belong to God and are his heirs, he does not disinherit us; he keeps intact his promises, covenants, and our inheritance of his kingdom, despite our bumbling mistakes and willful disobedience.

* * *

Next, let's look at the Apostle Paul. He was many things, and I will list some of them: Paul (also called Saul), was a Jew of the tribe of Benjamin, born around the year 5 A.D. He was a Pharisee (a religious sect adhering strictly to Israelite Law), and he was a highly educated man. Paul was a vocal and well-known Christian persecutor; he hunted down people who followed Jesus and had them jailed, executed, and even cruelly compelled them to blaspheme against God. Despite this dubious resume, God had plans for Paul all along.

On a dusty Damascus road (in what is modern-day Syria), the unchanging eternal God's Son, Jesus Christ, began a conversation with Paul that would chart a course of profound change in this man's life forever. God had plans all along to use this particular man to turn the world upside down. God would change this man's heart, mind, body, and soul forever amidst a plume of dust and blinding light. They began the conversation like this, as recorded in the Book of Acts, Chapter 9:

(1) "Meanwhile, Saul (Paul) was still breathing out murderous threats against the Lord's disciples. He went to the high priest

(2) and asked him for letters to the synagogues in Damascus, so that if he found any there who belonged to the Way, whether men or women, he might take them as prisoners to Jerusalem.

(3) As he neared Damascus on his journey, suddenly a light from heaven flashed around him.

(4) He fell to the ground and heard a voice say to him, 'Saul, Saul, why do you persecute me?'

(5) 'Who are you, Lord?' Saul asked. 'I am Jesus, whom you are persecuting,' he replied.

(6) 'Now get up and go into the city, and you will be told what you must do.'

(7) The men traveling with Saul stood there speechless; they heard the sound but did not see anyone.

(8) Saul got up from the ground, but when he opened his eyes, he could see nothing. So, they led him by the hand into Damascus.

(9) For three days he was blind, and did not eat or drink anything.

(10) In Damascus there was a disciple named Ananias. The

Lord called to him in a vision, 'Ananias!' 'Yes, Lord,' he answered.

(11) The Lord told him, 'Go to the house of Judas on Straight Street and ask for a man from Tarsus named Saul, for he is praying.

(12) In a vision he has seen a man named Ananias come and place his hands on him to restore his sight.'

(13) 'Lord,' Ananias answered, 'I have heard many reports about this man and all the harm he has done to your holy people in Jerusalem.

(14) And he has come here with authority from the chief priests to arrest all who call on your name.'

(15) But the Lord said to Ananias, 'Go! This man is my chosen instrument to proclaim my name to the Gentiles and their kings and to the people of Israel.

(16) I will show him how much he must suffer for my name.'

(17) Then Ananias went to the house and entered it. Placing his hands on Saul, he said, 'Brother Saul, the Lord—Jesus, who appeared to you on the road as you were coming here— has sent me so that you may see again and be filled with the Holy Spirit.'

(18) Immediately, something like scales fell from Saul's eyes, and he could see again. He got up and was baptized,

(19) and after taking some food, he regained his strength."

Let's begin to unpack this narrative. We'll begin first by clarifying that Jesus and God are one, as Jesus declared throughout his life and God verified to the world. John 10:30 records Jesus stating plainly, *"I and my Father are one."* John 14:9 tells us that Jesus said, *"...whoever has seen me has seen the father..."* Jesus' encounter on the Damascus road focused on Paul's persecution of Jesus (and his followers), for Paul was then severely persecuting those who followed Jesus Christ and recognized that he was the promised Messiah/Savior. At that point in Paul's life he was no friend to Jesus Christ or his followers. Interestingly enough, a Pharisee like Paul would know specific prophecies about who the Messiah would be. He had studied the Old Testament writings all of his life and the prophecies of Gods' coming Savior, yet he remained willfully blind to the foretold Messiah, Jesus, when he appeared. At the time, Jews were severely persecuted by Rome, and they were hungry for a political messiah who would save them from Roman persecution. Not everyone was interested in a spiritual Savior at that time.

In this passage, Jesus knocks Paul/Saul to the ground on that Damascus road, as he washes him in blindingly bright light. God temporarily takes away Paul's sight and speech, and he is rendered incapacitated, blind, and mute. Jesus' voice is the only one audible, and he calls out Saul's name twice and poses a simple question: *"Saul, Saul, why do you persecute me?"* Jesus, God the Son, directly accuses Saul of persecuting him (and his followers). Jesus lets him answer the question, yet Saul, like a good Pharisee, answers the question with a question. Verse 5 records: *"Who are you, Lord, Saul asked."* (Saul knows exactly who is speaking, and he rightly calls him *"Lord."*)

Jesus's response (vs. 5 and 6) is: *"I am Jesus, whom you are persecuting,"* he replied. *"Now get up and go into the city, and you will be told what you must do."* This is the very last day Paul would be living according to his own plans. God always had a plan for him, but now was the appointed time to reveal it; the plan was a game-changer. God specifically instructs a man,

Ananias, to go to a specific individual's house and meet up with Paul, whose infamy against Christians Ananias knew very well. Paul's bad reputation preceded him.

Verses 15 and 16 drops the bombshell: "*But the Lord said to Ananias, 'Go! This man is my chosen instrument to proclaim my name to the Gentiles (non-Jews) and their kings and to the people of Israel. I will show him how much he must suffer for my name.'*" God has always planned on using Paul and calls him "*my chosen instrument to proclaim my name to the Gentiles and their kings and to the people of Israel.*" God even goes a step further and mentions that Paul will be given knowledge of what God's plans for him will entail, for there will be much suffering on the horizon.

From there, Ananias obeys Jesus' directive, and he goes directly over to the home where Saul is:

> (vs 17) "*Placing his hands on Saul, he said, 'Brother Saul, the Lord—Jesus, who appeared to you on the road as you were coming here—has sent me so that you may see again and be filled with the Holy Spirit.'*
> *(18) Immediately, something like scales fell from Saul's eyes, and he could see again. He got up and was baptized,*
> *(19) and after taking some food, he regained his strength.*"

The lesson here is that no matter how awful and depraved one can be, God has a plan for you, if he knows you from the foundation of the world as one of his children. He will seek you out, find you, and turn your plans upside down until they are in synch with his. All he requires is that you respond. For Paul, the appointed time to learn God's very particular plans for him had come. God had, in his perfect foreknowledge, waited for just the right time to knock Paul off his socks and make him a new man. Verses 20 onward to the end of Acts Chapter 9 depicts Paul as a new man who spoke reverently of God, his kingdom, and his plans for his people. After a lifetime of studying and following tradition and attacking followers of Jesus, Paul began sharing with the 1st-century world that Jesus was the foretold Messiah people had been expecting for several thousand years. Paul was intimately and inextricably woven into God's plan and never saw it coming.

The purpose of taking a brief journey through the Apostle Paul's life and his encounter with God and Jesus Christ, his Son, is to illustrate an important point about God's character. Though you may make exceedingly bad decisions, commit unspeakable crimes, think the most murderous thoughts, and generally spend your life in sinful offense to God and others, God never changes, nor do his plans for you. If he has chosen you to belong to him, he will work everything together for good, even in the life of a Christian-hating Pharisee, and bring hope, healing, forgiveness, and eternal life to you. Those who God already knows will eventually respond to him and embrace his promises. In this case, God took the most grievous offender and made him a *"chosen instrument to proclaim my name to the Gentiles and their kings and to the people of Israel."* Why? Because God had always planned that Paul would belong to him and be his emissary of the good news of Jesus Christ and God's plan of salvation and reconciliation.

Making it Real

We can see that part of the foundation of God's personality is that he is unchanging, as are his plans and his knowledge of all things past, present, and future. He does not change his mind about who his children are, and he does not withdraw their inheritance because they have erred in some area of life. Jesus, God's Son, has covered all those offenses that God knows about in the past, the present, and offenses we will commit in the future. The key is that, if we respond to God in faith, love, and submission to his perfect will, we belong to him; he has done all the rest of the leg work. He already knew who would belong to him and respond to him in faith. He chooses his people and always has. When we belong to him, our inheritance in him is never going to be taken away from us. Why? Because he doesn't change his plans, his covenants, or his promises, ever. Likewise, he does not change any of his other personality attributes such as his love, patience, compassion, forgiveness, faithfulness, nor his grace. They all remain in unchanging perfect perpetuity forever.

Yet, if we desire to follow and obey God and his Son, how are we to embrace and model God's immutability in our own lives, so that people around us can see what he is like? Is there any way to model, as Christ did, the concept of God's unchanging nature when we struggle with keeping commitments, following through on promises, and remaining steady in the midst of life's storms? Yes, there are simple ways to do this. My husband and I used to put it to our children bluntly, "Make your "*yes's*" yes, and your "*no's*" no." We did this because Matthew 5:37 says it plainly. It's easy to start there. We told our kids that when they say "*yes*" to a commitment, they needed to make every attempt to follow through. This flowed into areas such as committing to playing a musical instrument

and not quitting, to remaining involved with important organizations they agreed to join, etc. The same applied if they
said "*no*" to something. If they said it then they had to mean
it. We reminded our kids of this—and ourselves—over and
over throughout the years. We did this because we are
surrounded by a culture of "*Maybe*," and "*We'll see*" and W*well,
if I have time*," and "*Oh, I know I said that but...*".

Let's discuss how God's unchanging nature can be modeled in
marriage and family life. Today, no longer looking at marriage
as a permanent covenant commitment, adults often look
upon marriage as a "*let's see how long this works*" joy-ride
together, at least until the joy runs out. Plans based on perma-
nence and unchanging commitment to another is considered
unbearable, archaic, and personally inconvenient! We are a
culture of convenience, rather than of unwavering commitment to promises made, vows taken, and contracts signed. In
our family, we wanted our children to rest in God's eternal
commitment to them and emulate that in their own lives, and
in their future marriage relationships. Today, both of our children are married to strong believers in God and Jesus Christ,
and we see a deep level of long-term commitment that hear-
kens back to their upbringing.

In the workplace, a strong commitment to hard work and
fulfilling the job description one said "*yes*" to is often replaced
by the concept of one's work commitment being a highly
temporary arrangement that may or may not be satisfying
enough to stick to long term. If you find yourself in the position of an employer, you'll often find that people today base
their decisions on a whim and day-to-day happiness, both of
which are fleeting. Likewise, if they do not find a job, a relationship, a promise, a purchase, or anything else happy-

producing, they'll drop it like a lead balloon (or, just ship it back to Amazon). If a job exacts too much toll on them on any given day, they will storm off in a huff and look for another job that might dole out a bigger spoonful of sensitivity to affirm their fragile sense of self.

Planning and adhering to a blueprint is vital in construction and architecture, otherwise, a building, a bridge, or any structure may topple over or collapse. Cultivating a commitment to following a plan and executing it to completion is a strong foundation for success. Building in flexibility for unforeseen situations is a must. But, being willing to commit to and follow through on what we say, what we plan, or what we know we should do, is modeling God's immutability. Adhering to a contract we have signed and endeavoring to fulfill our end of a bargain is showing strength, commitment, and integrity, all of which others hunger for but seldom wish to cultivate in themselves. That is how we can model God's unchanging and unwavering promises, covenants, and plans. It can happen in everyday life and yet mirror a heavenly attribute of God's character in the smallest of everyday circumstances.

In friendships and other relationships, the concept of being unchanging leads to a reliable, strong friendship that overcomes time, distance, and disagreements. The friendships that impressed us the most were ones that lasted, even when we moved—or they moved—and when hard times fell upon one of us and the other stood by and spent time investing in us, or us in them. A precious example to us are friends who, after decades of all of us moving away from each other geographically, never abandoned our friendship. When we moved across the country back to our home state of California after several years of living in the Dallas-Ft. Worth area in Texas, we kindled a close and caring friendship with a wonderful couple. Twenty-five years later, when we moved back to Texas, we reconnected with our dear friends, and our relationship struck up right where we had left off. We all looked older, more wizened, had several more children than when we last saw each other, and we had all experienced many unexpected things over the decades. Yet, when we reconnected, nothing had changed. That is a friendship that is immutable, solid, permanent, and God-like. That type of friendship is hard to forge today. We value it highly.

On the flip side, a propensity to change one's mind at any given moment, constantly vacillating on decisions, or even canceling a relationship that ceases to provide us benefit, is the opposite of immutability. Worse, it leads to discontentment with things, circumstances, and people, and it fosters underlying unfaithfulness in decisions made. Are we modeling God's rock-solid unchanging character when we say *"yes"* to too many things and plan to withdraw from half of them? When we become unfaithful to a long-time friend or a spouse because things have changed, and it feels easier to cut off the relationship, does this reflect God's immutability to others? No. If there is a seemingly endless undertone of discontentment in our heart that leads us to callously hop from one job to the next, one church to the next, or one relationship to the next, are we attracting others to God, or simply modeling a wishy-washy character that endlessly serves our momentary convenience? These are questions to ponder over.

Following is something that I do, which I'd like to share. It is simple, genuine, and powerful. Daily, I begin the morning with this prayer from Psalms 139:23-24:

"Search me, O God, and know my heart! Try me and know my thoughts! And see if there be any grievous way in me, and lead me in the way everlasting!"

Just as David prayed to God in the midst of the severest of trials, I also choose to reach out daily to God by praying his own Scriptures back to him in this way. By saying *"Search me, O God,"* we declare that we are willing to open up the door to our innermost thoughts and motives and ask God to take a look inside, knowing it will be ugly. Opening ourselves up to God's probing eyes that see into our heart, we then ask him to *"see if there be any grievous way in me."* By saying this, we admit that unpleasant things are likely there, but we willingly submit to God's bright light that will illuminate what is deep down in the hidden basement of our hearts. Finally, letting God pull out the broom and dustpan and sweep out what he exposes, you can then finish, as David did, by saying, *"and lead me in the way everlasting!"* What is *"everlasting"* is God's way, which is unchanging and perfect, the narrow path that God wants to lead us upon, with him walking right beside us. That *"everlasting way"* is heaven itself. And, as God is unchanging, so are his plans for us to walk with him on the *"everlasting way,"* sealed with a covenant he will never change or break.

God's unchanging nature is a solid foundation of his character which enables us to consistently experience all other facets of his personality. We can rest in his unchanging plans, his perfect foreknowledge, and eternal adherence to his promises and covenants. There is no foundation on this earth as solid as God's unchanging nature and all the eternal traits that emanate from that: love, grace, patience, forgiveness, compassion, holiness, justice, and many, many more attributes beyond what I have chosen to focus upon in this book.

Matthew 7:24-27 adds to this further when it records Jesus saying:

> (24) *"Therefore everyone who hears these words of mine and puts them into practice is like a wise man who built his house on the rock.*
>
> (25) *The rain came down, the streams rose, and the winds blew and beat against that house, yet it did not fall, because it had its foundation on the rock.*
>
> (26) *But everyone who hears these words of mine and does not put them into practice is like a foolish man who built his house on sand.*
>
> (27) *The rain came down, the streams rose, and the winds blew and beat against that house, and it fell with a great crash."*

We can surely stand firmly upon the unchanging rock of God's immutable character and his unchanging promises, plans, and provision when we belong to him. Going through life completely our own, without a relationship with God, we are that person who builds their *"house on sand."* As soon as the winds of difficulty and trials arise, our lives, plans, and possessions will fall *"with a great crash."* The rock-solid unchanging character of God is a sure foundation to stand upon. It is far more reliable than our own shifting sands that we tend to sprinkle beneath our own feet and later wonder why our life feels shaky and unsure.

James 1:17 sums up God's unchanging character, *"Every good and perfect gift is from above, coming down from the Father of the heavenly lights, who does not change like shifting shadows."* God's very self and his plans remain firm and solid, with no shifting shadows or grey areas he hasn't quite worked out yet. He is perfect and holds all knowledge of past, present and future. His perfect plans need no rethinking, no alteration in course, and not even the most minuscule changes. God's perfect and holy character does not wax or wane or move like a shadow. He need not and will not change, nor will his promises.

That is a God one can depend on.

* * *

Study Questions:

1. What does Malachi 3:6 tell us about God's unchanging nature? What implications does that have for how God deals with sin?
2. Romans 8:28-30 tells us how God works, based upon his unchanging self. What does this mean if you are a believer in God and his Son, Jesus Christ?
3. How do God's unchanging nature and his foreknowledge of all things affect a Christian's life?
4. Why do you think that God never changes, yet he expects us to change?
5. Read Matthew 7:24-27. How is God's unchanging character a rock upon which you can stand in good times as well as in times of acute struggle?
6. Numbers 23:19 says, *"God is not man, that he should lie, or a son of man, that he should change his mind. Has he said, and will he not do it? Or has he spoken, and will he not*

fulfill it?" What does it mean that God does not change his mind and adheres to his plans no matter what the circumstances? In what ways is it encouraging to you that God does not change his mind? Is this discouraging to you? If so, why?

7. In Acts 9, what aspects of Paul's encounter with Jesus (and God) on the Damascus road tell you about how God works in changing his people's lives? Is there an area of your life which you need to give to God, so that he can make those changes in your heart and in your life?

8. In what areas of your own life do you see a pattern of frequently changing your mind? What are the consequences of this (negative or positive)?

Additional Bible verses on God's immutability/unchanging nature

Do: *Discuss and ponder over these verses, and pray for God to illuminate each one. (For additional context, read the entire Biblical chapter in which each of these verses appears.)*

Psalm 102:25-27 - *"Of old you laid the foundation of the earth, and the heavens are the work of your hands. They will perish, but you will remain. They will all wear out like a garment. You will change them like a robe, and they will pass away, but you are the same, and your years have no end."*

James 1:17 - *"Every good thing given and every perfect gift is from above, coming down from the Father of lights, with whom there is no variation or shifting shadow."*

Psalm 55:19 - *"God will hear and answer them-- Even the one who sits enthroned from of old—Selah...With whom there is no change, and who do not fear God."*

Psalm 33:11 - *"The counsel of the Lord stands forever, the plans of his heart to all generations."*

Deuteronomy 33:27 - *"The eternal God is your dwelling place, and underneath are the everlasting arms."*

Memory verse

Hebrews 13:8 - *"Jesus Christ is the same yesterday, today and forever."*

Malachi 3:6a - *"I the LORD do not change"*

Action Plan: I want to begin to model godly, unwavering commitment in my life. These are the areas of my life where I know I need God's help:

1)

2)

3)

. . .

Recommended reading:

1. *Knowing God*, J. I. Packer, InterVarsity Press; 20th Anniversary ed. edition (June 24, 1993)
2. *The Unchanging God of Love: Thomas Aquinas and Contemporary Theology on Divine Immutability, Second Edition*, Michael J. Dodds, The Catholic University of America Press, 2008

Notes:

Chapter Nine

BE HOLY, FOR I AM HOLY – GOD'S HOLINESS

Leviticus 11:45 *"For I am the Lord who brought you up out of the land of Egypt to be your God. You shall therefore be holy, for I am holy."*

2 Thessalonians 4:7 *"God has not called us for impurity, but in holiness."*

Explaining and describing God's holiness is more challenging than any other aspect of his character. We might attribute this to the fact that holiness is something quite hard to put one's finger on in this world. Though we can say that we know someone or have read of someone who is really quite nice, selfless, serving, and fueled with good motives, that is subjective and a set of assumptions and observations. The concept of holiness varies from culture to culture, religion to religion, country to country. A cow is holy in India; in Texas, we raise them to barbeque. A particular rock is considered holy in one culture, while a tree is considered holy in another.

Let's dig down to the very root of holiness by examining the word in the original Hebrew. The word is (*kaddash*) קָדוֹשׁ. *Kaddash* means holiness, purity, otherness, something wholly set apart, and sacredness. This word is used multiple times in the Bible in the books of Leviticus and Numbers as well as several places in Exodus, where God says that he is *kaddash*, (and in some places *kadasheem* – a plural form of *kaddash*). That word is also used when God tells his people to be *kaddash* like he is (Leviticus 11:44 and 1 Peter 1:16). When God says, *"For I am the Lord who brought you up out of the land of Egypt to be your God. You shall therefore be holy, for I am holy,"* (Leviticus 11:45), he says that he is holy and he wants his people to be pure, other than everyone else in the pagan world, set apart, and sacred. God says he is holy and he wants those who associate with him to be the same.

God's holiness (the word *kaddash* used in Exodus Chapter 3) radiated to the very bush and the ground where Moses encountered God on Mount Horeb. Moses quickly unstrapped his sandals and stood barefoot and reverent near a profoundly *kaddash* God. God's holiness elicited indescribable reverence and fear in Moses. Holiness just does that to people. In the presence of such holiness, *Moses "hid his face, for he was afraid to look at God."* (Exodus 3:6) We can understand God's holiness from the context of personal experience of it. Moses was one individual who experienced a major dose of holiness confronting him face to face on a lonely mountain. Moses records in Exodus 3 that God spoke to him:

(1) Now Moses was keeping the flock of his father-in-law, Jethro, the priest of Midian, and he led his flock to the west side of the wilderness and came to Horeb, the mountain of God.

(2) And the angel of the Lord appeared to him in a flame of fire out of the midst of a bush. He looked, and behold, the bush was burning, yet it was not consumed.

(3) And Moses said, "I will turn aside to see this great sight, why the bush is not burned."

(4) When the Lord saw that he turned aside to see, God called to him out of the bush, "Moses, Moses!" And he said, "Here I am."

(5) Then he said, "Do not come near; take your sandals off your feet, for the place on which you are standing is holy ground."

(6) And he said, "I am the God of your father, the God of Abraham, the God of Isaac, and the God of Jacob." And Moses hid his face, for he was afraid to look at God."

God's innate and all-encompassing holiness radiated to a mere bush (yet didn't burn it up), and it rendered the ground near the bush holy, as well. God's holiness emanated outward to such a powerful extent, that Moses was asked to take off his sandals in reverence and acknowledgment that the very ground beneath his feet was infused with God's holiness by its very proximity to God. This is a defining moment when God introduces himself up close and personally to Moses and communicates that, "This is what holiness is: Me." God also implies that Moses is not innately holy, and that he must recognize that from the get-go and unstrap those sandals before approaching. That "otherness" and "set apartness" is what *kaddash* is; it is something *other* than us. Moses felt it, saw it, and experienced its frightening implications. Off came the sandals.

Proverbs 9:10 also uses the word *kaddash* for "*Holy One*" and pluralizes it: "*The fear of the Lord is the beginning of wisdom, and the knowledge of the Holy One is insight.*" In Proverbs, King Solomon (King David's son,) writes of God in the plural and calls him what God called himself in Exodus: holy, set apart, other, sacred, *kaddash*. God, the *Holy One*, wants his people to be set apart, pure, sacred, and fundamentally *other* than everyone else. God wants all people who love and respond to him to be prepared to be set apart, holy, *kaddash*. He wants them to be different than the unholy world around them. He wants them to stand out and be obviously different as believers in and followers of the one true God.

In the New Testament books of the Biblical record, written in Greek, the word for God's holiness is ἁγίου (*hagios*) and means: *full of awe, otherness, different, sacred*. It is similar to *kaddash*. In the New Testament, the word *hagios* is also used for the other member of the Holy Trinity, God's three-part being: The Holy Spirit.[1] God is set apart and innately different than us. Amazingly, he wants to impart that *kaddash and hagios* type of sacredness to his people. We must pause and take that in for a moment. When God calls people to himself, he makes them holy, because he is. He wants every person who responds to him to be trusting, willing, and ready to be made holy, set apart, and visibly different than others around them. He wants his people to be game changers and to stand out.

It is important to point out that he doesn't expect us to change ourselves and become holy by our thoughts, words, deeds, or personal merit. Holiness can never be accomplished that way. Any religion, self-improvement book, course, or program that teaches us that we can make ourselves holy or reach a state of holiness on our own is selling you lies. The purity, sacredness, righteousness, set-apartness, and otherness of God's holiness is simply not attainable on one's own. Instead, God imputes it--bestows it--upon his people. How does he do this? He accomplished this through someone holy: Jesus Christ, God's Son, his promised Redeemer. His perfect Son bridges the vast chasm between holiness and unholiness, the chasm between God and us.

The Apostle Paul put it succinctly to the Christians of ancient Corinth in the 1ˢᵗ century when he declared to them in 1 Corinthians 3:17: *"If anyone destroys God's temple, God will destroy him. For God's temple is holy, and you are that temple."* Again, in 1 Corinthians 6:19, Paul continues explaining what we become when we belong to God: *"Or do you not know that your body is the temple of the Holy Spirit within you, whom you have from God? You are not your own."* The word Paul uses for God's Holy Spirit in that verse is *hagios*. Through Jesus, God imparts his holiness to his people, though we are innately unholy on our own.

It is God's holiness that required a Savior to fix this broken world that simply isn't holy. Every one of us is like a child whose room is given to us newly built, perfectly cleaned and decorated, and filled with every toy we could imagine, and all that we do in response is render ourselves and our surroundings an absolute disaster. That is what mankind has done to this world from the very beginning. It is why a holy God cannot stomach such unholiness. He is set apart from such things, and he cannot allow this world to be forever filled with disobedient, messy, and generally unlikeable little brats. We messy and disobedient children cannot clean things up, and most don't even want to.

God looks at his creation, and he loves the only thing that he made in his image: people. His love, being that he is holy and "*is love*" itself (1 John 4:16), extends an arm over the mess we make of ourselves and our world, and he reaches out and cleans things up. He wants to change our filthy clothes, tussle our head in fatherly love, and smile upon us when we are without merit and deserve nothing but a royal spanking. As if that weren't enough, he crafts a personal plan for repairing our brokenness. When he draws us to himself through his irresistible grace and gives us the ability to respond to him through his Son, Jesus Christ, God wraps a cloak of his holiness and righteousness around our shoulders and adopts us as sons and daughters for an eternal walk beside him. He must do it all, though. God, the Giver, must impart his holiness, for the receiver has none, and nothing he/she can do can ever merit the Giver's favor.

He willingly, mercifully, and intentionally imparts his "*mysterium tremendum*" (Latin for God's mysterious and powerful holiness that is frighteningly and indescribably awe-inspiring) to unholy things by his sheer presence and his perfect will.[2] The tremendous and mysterious *otherness* of God that sets him apart from all other things, people included, is his very perfection that underpins his holiness. To know him, we must face his perfection and his holiness and be prepared to be bowled over by such majesty. We must cherish it because it doesn't exist in anyone or anything in this world or outside of it. What we cherish we come to love, and vice versa.

Most earthly things that we consider of great value are assumed to be perfectly made, without flaw, and better than other similar things. Our response is to set such things upon an untouchable pedestal, and we tend to gaze upon these things with awe. Ironically, those things are usually manmade. God was not fashioned by anyone. He is self-existing, infinite, unmakeable, unshakeable, and unchanging. Perfection doesn't need to change or improve upon itself. Yet, why do we often worship created things because we consider them perfect, and yet we resist knowing our perfect and holy God?

Perfection scares us, it intimidates us, yet it beckons us to come near to gaze upon it with strange curiosity. Who doesn't go to a museum and have an unquenchable desire to reach out and touch a seemingly perfect sculpture or painting? Try doing this and see the irritation and horror upon the faces of the docents who are breathing down your neck waiting to catch you in the act. Manmade inanimate objects that we consider "perfect" compel us to draw near. Yet, why do many run from a perfect and holy God? We should wish to reach out and touch him if that was possible, but we don't. His perfection and otherness can be frightening to most of us, because we sense something we are not, and we don't like a perfect God telling us that we're anything but perfect. Many detest or resent perfection that they sense in others.

We're fine with a perfectly painted Mona Lisa from Leonardo Da Vinci and impeccably molded Pieta sculptures from Michelangelo. Yet, we don't feel comfortable with a perfect and holy God, because his perfection makes us feel uncomfortably aware of our imperfection and sinfulness. That is the point, isn't it? A perfect Monet painting at the Musee' D'Orsay in Paris stirs our hearts to draw near to it, yet a perfect and holy God sends some of us running for the hills while others cautiously tip-toe toward him in bizarre curiosity. It is just a few who run toward him with open arms.

When I visited the Louvre in Paris many years ago, I admired many fine pieces of art from the ancient world, the Renaissance, and other eras. However, my "bucket list" experience was to gaze upon that which I considered perfection: the Mona Lisa. As we entered a crowded room, drawing closer to the wall that held my long-awaited painting, the lady's face suddenly came into view. I stood breathless and blinked a few times to be sure I could see clearly over everyone's heads. I stared into the mysterious eyes of da Vinci's Mona Lisa. She smirked at me across the crowded room through a cube of plexiglass. My heart and eyes were truly stirred for a moment by the perfection of this strangely small work of art many call a masterpiece of Da Vinci's work. But, then the feeling of awe was gone; it lasted all of 30 seconds. I realized that the painting was far darker than I had expected. The size was considerably smaller than I had assumed. Her taunting smirk was strangely disturbing and didn't leave me with a good feeling (she reminded me of a docent hovering nearby scowling at those who tried to cross the rope and come up too close to Ms. Mona Lisa.) It didn't look *perfect*; others had deemed it so, but by what criteria, I thought? Strangely, I was a bit disappointed and deflated.

It hit me like a ton of bricks that this wasn't at all what I expected. I realized that nothing on this earth that is manmade is really perfect. Everything man makes can always be just a bit better. If I could have filled out a survey about my perception of the Mona Lisa, I would have suggested that Da Vinci use lighter colors, so her face would stand out more from the background. I would have asked that Da Vinci redo her mouth and either make her obviously smile or most definitely frown; the smirk wasn't pleasant at all. Finally, I would have suggested that we not be visually and physically separated from that painting by a thick cube of plexiglass which all but ruined the experience.

A few decades later, while I stood in St. Peter's Basilica in Vatican City, I wondered out loud where *"my favorite sculpture in the world was."* My Italian tour guide of the Vatican moved my shoulders to the right so I could pivot and look through the main hall into a side room where I could see it, the *Pieta*, Michelangelo's breathtaking sculpture of Mary holding Christ laying limp within her motherly arms. The same feeling struck me as it had decades before in Paris. It wasn't as perfect as I had imagined once I walked closer to it. And, much to my surprise, the tour guide told me this was one of many *Pieta* sculptures that Michelangelo had made. This one wasn't unique or the only one in the world. That was rather deflating. I felt compelled to go out into St. Peter's Square and buy a postcard of my favorite sculpture; the real thing was strangely disappointing, though beautiful in its own right.

The *Pieta* wasn't unshakeable and eternal, either, as I had imagined it. In 1972 a geologist by the name of Laszlo Toth approached the *Pieta* sculpture in St. Peter's Basilica (in Vatican City) with a geologist's hammer in hand. Without warning, he jumped over the protective fencing and attacked that masterpiece severely, knocking off Mary's arm, parts of her nose and eyelids, and dislodged portions of the sculpture into hundreds of pieces with fifteen fatal blows of a hammer. Nothing manmade is eternal or immune to damage. A once world-renowned sculpture was massively damaged in a minute. It took years and many experts' hands to fix the damage.

Why do we ascribe perfection to manmade things when they are so easily fallible? We do this because others with more knowledge than us will declare that this or that item is a "perfect" example of so and so's work. Perfection is in the eye of the beholder. Yet, in contrast to an innately perfect and holy God, earthly things do not embody perfection, eternalness, or infallibility. They are only deemed to be set apart as special based on others' declaration that such a thing has value. It is a manmade value ascribed to a manmade object.

The point is that God's unchanging and infallible holiness, woven with unchangeable threads of his perfection, needs no person's stamp of approval to ascribe perfection to him. He *is* perfect, set apart, other than the rest of us. He is holy because he is all of those things whether or not we believe it, declare it is or isn't so, or compare him to something else and decide he is just one of many other gods. That is why we are astonished and simultaneously joyous and humbled when we find out that God, since the beginning of time, chooses his people, overlooks their imperfections, and still desires to come into a relationship with them and provide an eternal solution for their unholiness.

What powerful and regal king of this earth would fraternize with a dirty, disrespectful, and ugly pauper? None. Yet, a holy and perfect God sees us for what we are, willingly and lovingly extends a hand to us, and he offers something better than we can do for ourselves. That is the *"mysterium tremendum,"* the tremendous mystery of God's perfection and holiness that would come down to earth and walk among the common and give to those who respond to him a set-apartness, a *"kaddash/ hagios,"* holiness that isn't ours naturally. His holiness lovingly renders the common and the ordinary *uncommon*.

What are we to do in response to such a holy and perfect God? We simply need to respond, repent of the mess that we are, not to mention the messes we've created around ourselves, and allow God's unique holiness to envelope us, clean us up, and fix our broken and innately unholy selves. Once he does all of that for us, he then clothes us in his choicest of attire, a robe woven with gilded threads of his holiness fashioned into a garment of pure white righteousness we couldn't create or purchase for ourselves, even if we tried to.

How does he do such a massive spring cleaning within his people, set us apart for himself, and clothe us anew in Christ's righteousness? He sent a promised Savior embodying and radiating God's very holiness and perfection to this mess of a world. His promised Savior, God The Son--Jesus Christ-- carried no money in his pockets; he purchased the broken in this world with his own life. He redeemed us, and he bought us back from our self-made pit of sin, disobedience, and death. He brings us home, cleans us up, and he clothes us in *kaddash/hagios* holiness. It is a gift to an undeserving, imperfect, and disobedient person. It is an eternal gift for life and for eternity. All we must do is reach back and respond to his holy outstretched arm.

. . .

Making it Real

How do we experience God's holiness? We get to know him. You simply cannot know what holiness is, if you do not know the Holy One. Amazingly enough, he makes a concerted effort to get to know us first. Though he is set apart, sacred, and very different than us, he wants to know me and you. False god figures compel you to do things for them in reverence for their self-made holiness; they never desire to know you or to love you. Inanimate objects—even nature itself—are worshipped as "gods," but they are merely the created; they are not the Creator.

The unfortunate reality is that most people on this earth and throughout human history spend a sizeable portion of their lives looking for things to cram into their lives, their hearts, and their minds, until they could not see or hear God if he stood in a burning bush in front of them and audibly told them to take off their shoes. Fortunately, the Holy One is a patient God, and he will wait. He will wait until perhaps we reach rock bottom and recognize we have reached some unprecedented low point we cannot extricate ourselves from. Only at that point do many yearn for someone other than what this world and other false "gods" have to offer.

When times are empty, tough, or hopeless, no Mona Lisa or perfect Michelangelo sculpture is going to calm a weary soul. We all innately know that. Something merely manmade can never satisfy. No high dollar retirement plan or stock portfolio, and no grand home with priceless décor and vast manicured gardens will truly satisfy. God won't allow it. He wants us to only be satisfied with him and him alone. However, those who choose to reject him, well, he allows that choice to stand. He isn't surprised when it happens. He knows who will respond to him and who will not. When hearts turn away from him and reject him, he is not taken off guard and surprised. He is the Shepherd who knows his sheep already, and yet it talks awhile for each one of his sheep to respond to his voice.

God's holiness requires that people who respond to him be perfect and holy, too. He knows that we need to understand his holiness, see examples of it, and better grasp what it means and what it looks like. That is why his Savior, Jesus Christ, promised from the beginning of human history, was *God's kaddash* holiness face to face, so that people could see it with their own eyes and hear what holiness is with their ears. Holiness demonstrated becomes holiness understood, for those who respond to his holiness with repentance, faith, and life-altering gratitude.

The best way to understand something is to see it, hear it, experience it, and meditate upon it. Our five senses enable us to do this. God gave these to us for a reason. Seeing and understanding God's holiness is first done through reading the book which reveals God's character and his presence throughout history: The Bible. Sixty-six synergetic and detailed "books" in the Bible record God's self-introduction through his creation and throughout human history to people whom he chose to come into covenant with and to walk with.

Understanding God is also furthered via experiences with others who exude God's Holy Spirit in their lives. God wants to be visible to us, but he often prefers to show his plans, his power, and his character through others' lives, as if he desired to fill human history with a hand-picked collection of mirrors.

We can often say we've met a handful of people who exude a sort of other-worldly holiness we can't explain, but we know it when we see it. I have. Let me tell you about it.

* * *

In my younger adult years, I had been in awe of a particular person who had suffered a terrible accident that had rendered her a quadriplegic. This person, whose life story I had read of, had lost all sense of movement and feeling from the neck down, yet she hungered for and drew near to God despite a body rendered numb and seemingly lifeless. God's very holiness seemed to fill the void in her life, and it took on new directions that would impact the world. She selflessly served others and painstakingly pulled together manpower, funds, and a compassionate vision for helping the disabled. She rolled her wheelchair onto airplanes year after year ceaselessly organizing the shipment and delivery of thousands of wheelchairs to the disabled in other parts of the world, where they were forgotten "throw-away" people who dragged themselves through the streets unnoticed and dismissed. This person was Joni Eareckson Tada.

One day, back in the mid-1990s, when I returned to my home church in Calabasas, California after four years living out of state, I noticed Joni Eareckson Tada was present at the church. When I first saw her there, the entire sanctuary seemed to be filled with sizzling electricity and the presence of God, as if the burning bush was nearby. There is no other way to describe it. I hadn't realized Joni had joined our humble church. Whenever I was near her, I felt in humble awe of her. She exuded the very holiness of God in her words, her smile, her strength and persistence, her patience, and her hunger to minister to others like her, who had lost their mobility. And, she was likely unaware that she was affecting me this way, for she was quite jovial, humble, and approachable. But Joni was like a burning bush to me, with God's presence palpably near. Make no mistake, I was not feeling as if she were God himself; Joni was simply exuding his presence, and it was visible and real.

After her accident had rendered her seemingly helpless and powerless, she had responded to and loved a holy God, who drew her to himself and dressed her in a robe of his holiness that was only his to give. And she wore it and lived with it draped around her shoulders rendering her holy, too. She had lost everything, died to herself, lost all feeling in her limbs and torso, yet her heart was beating and yearning to know God; her heart was far from crippled. God had rendered her set apart, other-worldly, holy, and he transformed her into a living mirror of his holiness. This radiated to others around her and profoundly affected me as well as thousands of lives throughout the world. She engendered within me a new sense of compassion for the disabled, and her work encouraged me years later to welcome a disabled young Armenian girl into our home as an exchange student. Joni's life and her radiance of God's very holiness had changed me, as it changed others around her.

* * *

My Encounter with God's Holiness

In 1984, almost a decade before, I encountered my personal defining moment in my walk with God. Over the previous three years, I had been spending hours on the beaches of La Jolla, California, fervently studying political science and French at the University of California, San Diego. It was a time when I was fairly self-absorbed, focused on amassing worldly knowledge, and minimally paying attention to God. I loved him, knew him, and followed him, but I had chosen to let our relationship grow cold rather than allow it to infuse my college years.

Things were about change unexpectedly. One day during the last quarter of my senior year in college, I began to notice that the sand beneath me didn't feel quite right when I lay on my stomach studying for hours on end. Something was odd, and it increasingly began to concern me. I decided to mention it to my mother, who immediately dispatched me to the doctor to have a look at what could be amiss. It appeared that something was very wrong. It had apparently been deemed a tumor, though no one could be quite sure until surgery was done. I began withdrawing from all my courses, put off my last quarter of college, and found myself in UCSD's Medical Center, a cutting-edge teaching hospital.

There, on one distinct night in April 1984, I faced a disturbing reality. I may have cancer, though no one could be sure yet. I felt deep trepidation and a sense of some turning point that was close on the horizon. Let's just call it fear; that was what it was. I'm a control freak, and this situation had left me powerless and helpless. No amount of worldly head knowledge and self-development in college could have instructed me on how to take control and get out of this situation. I was helpless and teetering on the edge of the unknown, perhaps even death.

A distinct presence entered my room the night before my surgery, as I sat up on the bright white sheets in the minimalist hospital room and felt someone in there with me as tangible and real as any object in the room. The hair on my arms stood on end, and a blanket of profound peace and well-being filled me within and without, like a heavy, warm robe on a cold night. I was standing on holy ground; God's very presence was in my room. When it happens, you know it. I knew who was in there with me. Suddenly, fear was no longer present. Peace filled me to the brim and overflowed so profoundly, that I slept peacefully. God himself had come to stand beside his wandering sheep—me. His holiness filled the room and was so thick you could have cut it with a knife.

The next morning, I was not the same person. I joked with the orderlies who rolled me into a cold operating room prep area filled with the smells of alcohol and glimmering with stainless steel. A pleasant anesthesiologist asked me something, and I quipped back to him with a funny word or two and laughed. The peace never left me as I quickly drifted into la-la-land, thanks to the prompt flow of anesthetics through my veins. When I awoke groggy and disoriented, I still felt that profound peace of God's nearness. I had an instantaneous concern that I voiced immediately: *"Am I okay, and am I going to be able to have children?"* The answer I was given was two-fold: *"Yes, you're okay...but we had to take out quite a few things. It's not anything terminal."* No one answered my last question: *"Am I going to be able to have children?"* Through the thick fog of still-lingering anesthesia, I noticed it.

Several months later, after a nice recovery and much self-introspection, I found myself seated at an infertility specialist's office. The doctor was a very close and dear friend of our family. He smiled warmly at me across his desk like a father would at his very own daughter. I liked him because he was kind and talkative, and I knew he was choosing his words carefully, because they were likely going to be difficult. He told me that I would have a very, very hard time having children, if any. He wasn't smiling now. The room was glaringly silent after he made this statement. I was speechless. Who wouldn't be? Then he flashed his huge warm smile again and like a reassuring father he urged me to marry at some point in the near future, if it worked out that way, and to try to start having children immediately. He stressed the word, "*immediately.*" He said soberly that it would be very difficult to conceive, but I must try. There was essentially nothing he could do at that point, he added. Later, he might intervene if things didn't go well, he finished with an honest, sober look on his face.

I felt powerless and helpless; the doctor nearly said the same for himself, though he was nice about it. At that moment I knew I needed to leave behind the self-centered college lifestyle, go back in the Fall and finish up and finish well, and that I needed to hunger for and desire God more than I ever had before. I had walked with God all my life, yet the turning point had come. In my darkest hour, he had lovingly approached me, shared his holiness and peace with me, and stood beside me. I needed to know God better, trust him more, and form a bond with him where I could truly entrust to him my deepest longings. I wanted children more than anything else in the world. I knew that my God could make that happen if he wished. I cherished the verse from 2 Corinthians 12:9, "*My grace is sufficient for you. For my power is perfected in weakness. Therefore I will boast all the more gladly of my weaknesses, so that the power of Christ may rest upon me."* That became one of my favorite verses, and it still is today; I say it to myself daily as a reminder of this profound truth.

Like Joni Eareckson Tada, I had reached a turning point of complete and utter helplessness and powerlessness at that point in my life. My childhood journey with God had reached a new level of sobering adulthood. I realized that I needed to know him better and in a deeper way and that I needed to desire his holiness. To know him better was to love him better and therefore trust him better. A childhood journey thus far had now become a steep uphill journey, but his peace never left me, not then, not now, not ever. In early childhood, God had drawn me to himself and I knew I belonged to him. He had regenerated my heart from its naturally sinful state, given me the gift of faith which I did not have naturally, and now he was challenging me to exercise that faith and trust in him in a profound and frightening new way.

I spent the next year finishing college, graduating, finding my first job, and moving away from home from San Diego up to Los Angeles. I filled my life with prayer with a fervency and vehemence that I had never had before. I asked God daily to grant me a miracle and his continued grace when the time came that I met someone of his choosing and began a life as a married woman. I read the Bible more carefully, meditated on it more deeply, and drew closer to God. I was coming to truly know him in a real way because I knew what it felt like to have him walk with me through the fire, rather than pluck me out of it. His refining of my heart, mind, and soul became glaringly evident to me, yet I had done none of it.

Within six months of moving away and starting life as an adult, fully off the family dole and into the world with a paycheck and a roof over my head, I met my husband-to-be. Moving the clock forward into my third year of marriage, God's grace and compassion had moved swiftly and surely. We had decided to begin trying to have our first child, and it occurred within the first couple of months of effort, smashing all the doctors' sober warnings that I probably wouldn't have children. God brought us our precious daughter, a miracle, a child of God's grace, healing, and mercy. The steep up-hill walk with the Holy One beside me had brought me to a destination I wasn't sure I'd reach, a summit I could never reach without him carrying me up himself.

An encounter with God's holiness will not leave you unchanged. My pursuit of it could only be fueled by God's omniscience, grace, mercy, and love. Without him, I would never have desired to pursue holiness and get to know him better, much less pursue it daily in my own life. With that up close and personal experience with the holy presence of God, I was forever changed. He lifted my weak shoulders, drew near to me, and wrapped his robes of holiness and righteousness around me. He blanketed me inside and out with a *"peace that transcends all understanding."* A life verse I repeat to myself every day is Philippians 4:6-7, *"do not be anxious about anything, but in everything by prayer and supplication with thanksgiving let your requests be made known to God. And the peace of God, which surpasses all understanding, will guard your hearts and your minds in Christ Jesus."*

Each day, I am still in awe of God, and what he has done for me personally, tangibly, and tenderly. I gaze into the eyes of my daughter and my son (who came 2.5 years later), and I see clearly that God decided to grant me not one, but two miracles. God imparted to me a *set-apartness* that yanked me out of the ranks of dour statistics which portended that I'd likely not have any children. He tenderly transformed me into a state of *otherness*, where he could create something miraculous out of a broken and helpless person.

Making it Real

In light of my own experience, and the encounters that anyone can have with the Holy One, how do we then live if we have drawn near to and embraced a holy God? We remain set apart, other, and visibly different than the unholy world around us. That takes effort, vigilance, and constant prayer. Without God's imputed holiness to his people, it simply cannot be done. We need to be like a child's *I Spy* book, where out-of-place items are strewn throughout a picture book scene (let's say a beach scene), and amongst the expected things like sand, buckets and shovels, fish, whales, and shells, you see a glaringly misplaced object that stands out, like a cowboy or a diamond ring. We need to be that cowboy or that diamond ring, shockingly different, set apart, other--kaddash--amid a world strewn with ugliness, selfishness, materialism, and unholiness.

If you have not yet drawn near to the Holy One, you can look at the life of Jesus Christ, eyes wide open, ears tuned to listening, and see holiness bright and clear. Better yet, his well-documented life recorded in the Bible, replete with eyewitness experiences, clearly shows that sparkling diamond in the middle of a dingy scene where it looks as if he doesn't belong. God knew we would have a tough time understanding him, so he decided from the beginning to bring someone into the world that people could see, touch, and lean on to be holiness personified. And, he promised that person right from the beginning of time. He promised his Son, Jesus Christ, the Savior, and he kept that promise down to the very last detail. God keeps his promises—all of them.

Now, that is a God who wants folks to understand him, love him, desire him, and subsequently reflect him to others so that they can know him too. A holy God, who is so set apart from us, sent a part of himself, Jesus the Son, to visit with us and draw near to us. The Book of Hebrews Chapter 1, verse 3, describes Jesus this way: *"The Son is the radiance of God's glory and the exact representation of His nature, upholding all things by His powerful word. After He had provided purification for sins, He sat down at the right hand of the majesty in heaven."*

God drew near to us in this broken world through Jesus Christ being born into it. John 1:14 tells us, *"The Word became flesh and dwelt among us, and we have seen his glory, glory of the only Son from the Father, full of grace and truth."* Drawing near to Jesus was drawing near to God in the flesh. Listening to what Jesus stated clearly, *"Repent, for the king of heaven is at hand,"* (Matthew 3:2) was and is God's direct hand extended to people. He simply said, *"repent"* of sin. He asks us to relinquish our own sinful will and our flawed plans and recognize that they're rotten from the inside out.

Next, Jesus asks for focused and selfless obedience: *"If anyone would follow me, let him deny himself and take up his cross daily and follow me."* (Luke 9:22-23). That is the simple response God wants from us. He gives us his Holy Spirit to do this; he knows we can't—and won't—do it ourselves. Once we respond to his gracious call to come to him, he drapes us with his robe of holiness and perfection we could never manufacture on our own, and he walks the life journey with us until we meet up face to face at the end. And when we do, God will look at Jesus—not us—and declare us acceptable, because of Jesus' perfection alone.

If we have responded to God, then what about that journey through the rest of our lives? It must be a life lived in pursuit of holiness one might say. This is where people get an opportunity to see God's holiness in you. Galatians 2:20 (written by the Apostle Paul) says, *"I have been crucified with Christ and I no longer live, Christ lives in me. The life I live in this body I live by faith in the Son of God, who loved me and gave Himself for me."* The challenge to us is to live life moment by moment through faith in the Son of God, which is pursuing a life that reflects God's holiness.

Practically speaking, we can do this in several ways, always drawing on the power of Christ in us, once we belong to him. On our own, without him, we can do nothing. Take Galatians 2:20 and break it down into steps:

1. Because God's perfect Son, Jesus Christ, lived a perfect life and conquered sin in your life and the lives of everyone in this world, you need to step aside and leave behind all that displeases him.
2. Let Christ live in you. When he does, God's Holy Spirit lives within you, as well. Let him fuel all that you do, say, and think, rather than maintaining control your continued control, which is imperfect and tainted by sin. God is perfect, Christ is perfect, The Holy Spirit is perfect. Allow them to lovingly

control your heart, mind, body, and spirit. Always
remain willing to give up the unholy things in your
life.

3. Live your life moment by moment only by faith in the
   Son of God. Why? Because he loved you and gave up
   himself for you. He fully purchased your freedom
   from sin and separation from God with his own life.
   He has set you apart for himself and paid a steep
   price—unto death—for you.

Next, we must pursue holiness by carefully selecting what
goes into our eyes, ears, and minds. This world is replete with
too much noise, news, media, entertainment, the quest for
eternal youth, and an insatiable addiction to social media.
But, while we're at war with these insidious adversaries, the
Apostle Paul, in his letter to the Philippians, explains to us
what we need to do, as he also told the Christians of ancient
Philippi. In Philippians 4:8 he says: *"Finally, brothers, whatever
is true, whatever is honorable, whatever is just, whatever is pure,
whatever is lovely, whatever is commendable, if there is any excellence, if there is anything worthy of praise, think about these things."*

Translating this into today's language and challenges, we can
glean from Paul that we must think about, watch, listen to,
and fill our lives with experiences that emphasize truth,
honor, justice, goodness, purity, beauty, and excellence. What
does this look like? Here are some practical steps to employ
below. We must begin to look at what we do every day and
honestly assess whether our routines, rituals, and experiences
are pouring goodness into our eyes, ears, and minds, or not.

1. Take a news "fast" regularly and look away from

incessant and repetitive news that makes the heart and mind weary.

2. Take an intentional social media break. Be intentional about it and choose to do this for a specific amount of time (a day, a week, a month, etc.). Don't check it, don't post anything, and don't even talk about it. If necessary, eliminate it. If it's like a cancer in your life, cut it out.

3. Choose to only watch movies or television productions that are free from filthy language, graphic sexual scenes, depraved characters, and unhealthy plots.

4. Read a book, perhaps a biography, about someone whose life emanated holiness and faith in God. Take a "fiction fast" and instead choose to read about someone whose life was and is a reflection of God's holiness. Delving into other Christians' lives can change yours.

5. If we honestly listen to some of our favorite music, and we hear self-destructive lyrics, filthy language, strong sexual connotations, and ugly themes, we need to delete or throw it away and cease listening to it. Our minds and ears can become easily jaded and desensitized to profanity and unholy themes if we hear it over and over again.

6. Honestly assess your innate tendencies to whine, complain, ridicule, or envy others, such as a coworker, a boss, a neighbor, or a family member, and pray for God to temper that a bit—or a lot. Looking for ungodly patterns and propensities in your behaviors can lead to prayer and repentance.

7. Look for opportunities to build up others (family

members, coworkers, neighbors, etc.) and attempt to
take notice of situations where you find yourself
easily critical, verbally damaging, angry, or frustrated.
None of this mirrors God's holiness, goodness, or
kindness.

Underlaying all of our painful self-examination should be
prayer. We cannot change ourselves; God has to do it. Thus,
we have to identify what is not pure, not honorable, unjust,
unlovely, not commendable, and not praise-worthy in
ourselves, and we need to confess it to God and get it out on
the table. Guaranteed, it's going to be ugly. Sin is ugly, and it
hides so nicely behind good intentions, addictions, excuses,
and in groups of others who do the very same things. Without
the power of God's Holy Spirit to change these tendencies in
us, there is no way we'll get rid of these unholy habits,
fetishes, propensities, patterns, and addictions.

That is precisely why one has to listen to what God says and
then go and do it. He asks us to acknowledge him, repent of
our ugly ways, and give our lives to him. He makes it quite
simple and clear. Then, the Holy One, the *Kaddash One*, will
pick up our broken lives like shards of sharp, ugly glass strewn
about the ground and set us apart for himself. By his power
alone, he will remake each of us into a new, shiny, highly
reflective mirror ready to reflect his *kaddash/hagios* holiness.
Yes, we will innately be sinful and fog up the mirror daily. But,
with God's power within us, and a repentant heart, we can ask
God to wipe off the fog and make us clean mirrors of him
again and again and again. Only then, when we are set apart
for God, will people even begin to see holiness in this world.
Only then will others begin to know him and love him too.

Keep this verse in mind daily: *"But as he who called you is holy, you also be holy in all your conduct, since it is written, 'You shall be holy, for I am holy.'"* <u>1 Peter 1:15-16</u>

* * *

<u>Study Questions:</u>

1. What seems impossible about the verses where God tells His people, *"Be holy for I am holy"*? (Lev. 11:44-45, 1 Pet. 1:15-16) What is God telling you about being "holy" in your own life?

2. The Hebrew word, *"kaddash"* is mentioned often in this chapter. One meaning of this word is "set apart." In what areas of your life do you know that you need to be different and set apart? Why does God want to set you apart from the rest of the world?

3. Who have you met in your life that reflects God's holiness? How does this person affect you spiritually? What can you learn from them and emulate?

4. Where do you struggle most with denying yourself certain habits in your life that you sense are not pleasing to God? Are you willing today to begin giving those up to God?

5. Jesus, God's Son, was literally *"The radiance of God's glory and the exact representation of His being,"* (Heb. 1:3) What aspects of Jesus' behavior emulate God's glory?

6. Read Psalm 139:23-24. What does it mean when you are willing to ask God to search your heart and see what is ugly and unacceptable to him? If he sees a

"hurtful way" in you, what action can you and should you take?

7. Read Exodus 3:1-6. In this passage describing Moses and God encountering each other at the burning bush, what do you learn about God's type of holiness? How does a holy life affect others around you?

8. Read Galatians 2:20. What steps can you take to live a life that is reflective of being *"crucified with Christ, and I no longer live, Christ lives in me"*?

What do you think it means to *"live by faith in the Son of God"*? Are you willing to take an honest assessment of yourself through prayer and hear what God shows you that he would like to change in you? What things do you suspect he might see in your life that are not reflective of Christ living within you?

Additional Bible verses on God's holiness

Do: *Discuss and ponder over these verses, and pray for God to illuminate each one. (For additional context, read the entire Biblical chapter in which each of these verses appears.)*

1 Samuel 2:2 - *"There is none holy like the Lord; there is none besides you; there is no rock like our God.*

2 Timothy 1:9 - *"Who saved us and called us to a holy calling, not because of our works but because of his own purpose and grace, which he gave us in Christ Jesus before the ages began"*

Deuteronomy 7:6 - *"For you are a people holy to the Lord your God. The Lord your God has chosen you to be a people for his treasured possession, out of all the peoples who are on the face of the earth."*

1 John 2:29 - *"If you know that he is righteous, you may be sure that everyone who practices righteousness has been born of him."*

1 Peter 1:15-16 (ESV): *"But as he who called you is holy, you also be holy in all your conduct, since it is written, 'You shall be holy, for I am holy.'"*

Memory verse

Leviticus 11:45 (ESV): "For I am the Lord who brought you up out of the land of Egypt to be your God. You shall therefore be holy, for I am holy."

1 Peter 1:15-16 (ESV): *"But as he who called you is holy, you also be holy in all your conduct, since it is written, 'You shall be holy, for I am holy.'"*

Recommended reading:

1. *The Attributes of God, Volume 1; A Journey Into the Father's Heart*, A. W. Tozer, Moody Bible Institute, Chicago, 1997.
2. *The Pursuit of Holiness*, Jerry Bridges, NavPress; Enlarged ed. edition (November 3, 2016)

3. *The Holiness of God*, R. C. Sproul, Ligonier Ministries; 25th Anniversary Edition (2010)

Action Plan: This is what I'm willing to give up to God so that he help me eliminate the unholy things in my life:

1)

2)

3)

Notes:

Chapter Ten

AND JUSTICE FOR ALL – GOD'S JUSTICE

Deuteronomy 32:4 *"He is the Rock, his works are perfect, and all his ways are just. A faithful God who does no wrong, upright and just is he."*

God's holy character, perfect in every way, naturally embodies a strong and unshakeable sense of justice. Strangely, though, the word *justice* is rarely attributed to anything having to do with God in today's world. Instead, justice is often derived from a subjective foundation of earthly laws that significantly varies between cultures, countries, religions, and histories. In this world justice is fluid; it is subject to precedent and as well as to consensus.

King Solomon, in Proverbs 21:15, offers his renowned wisdom on the subject of justice: *"When justice is done, it brings joy to the righteous but terror to evildoers."* When justice is dispensed, it should give the humble a sigh of relief and miscreants a pause and a disincentive to do—or not do--something. Justice gives what is earned: expected consequences for wrongdoing or exoneration from false accusation. It is righteous cause and effect, you might say.

When Moses wrote Deuteronomy 32:4, he was explaining God's very character when he wrote of God's justice: *"He is the Rock, his works are perfect, and all his ways are just. A faithful God who does no wrong, upright and just is he."* Simply put, because God is a rock of strength and unchanging perfection, his works are therefore perfect. Because his works are always perfect, all his ways are just. He is a faithful God who keeps his covenants with his people, even when they don't do so in return. He never does anything wrong or unjust. He is upright and he metes out justice when he must and because he must. Could Moses have said it any better?

In Deuteronomy 32:4, Moses uses the word מִשְׁפָּט (miš·pāṭ) for the word "just." Also, the word צַדִּיק (ṣad·dîq) is sometimes used in the Biblical record to denote the concept of justice, yet this word more specifically means "righteousness." The two words, righteousness and justice, are often intertwined. It is used to describe God, and it is sometimes even used to describe a very just, upright, and righteous person. For example, Noah is described in Genesis 6:9 as such: *"Noah was a just צַדִּיק (ṣad·dîq) man"* in the King James Version of the Bible. In the New International Version, it translates as, *"Noah was a righteous מִשְׁפָּט (miš·pāṭ) man."* Sometimes the words for righteousness and justice are synonymous.

Across various dictionaries, the word "just" means several things, such as being guided by truth, reason, and fairness according to what is right; something that is lawful; something in keeping with what is considered true. The very concept of being just is personified in God's personality, plans, and actions throughout history. God's justice is naturally a part of his righteous, holy, and loving character. He is true to himself and gives of what he is. He can do no less.

The righteous justice of God's character is complemented by his mercy. The perfect justice of God requires that he punish that which is not just, not good, not upright and not righteous. That would be you and me. Yet, working in tandem with his sense of perfect justice is his mercy, which spares his people from what they truly deserve. Bluntly speaking, heavenly justice should result in all of us being condemned to grovel in our sinful ways and die. We generally want to follow our momentary whims, selfish desires, and insatiable obsessions. God's mercy somehow tempers his perfect justice, leading him to mercifully satisfy it by paying the debt of our sin for us. By doing that, he willingly and mercifully chooses to save us from what our sin earns: condemnation, death, and destruction. This is an entirely different type of justice than we make meager attempts to practice in this world.

To reiterate a fundamental point, God's justice requires that we should all end in destruction and be condemned by a perfect and holy God. Amazingly, because of God's mercy, he doesn't give us what we deserve. And by his complementary justice and mercy, he chooses to offer forgiveness and to declare his people "just" and "righteous" and acceptable to him, when we are none of those things. How does he do this?

Through a promised Savior, Jesus Christ, God chose to transfer that justice--which needs to be meted out for sin and wanton disobedience--to someone who did not deserve it. Someone had to pay the debt of sin. Justice requires it. Once our debt was fully paid by Christ, God declared those of us who respond to him in faith and trust as "just" and as "*kaddash*," holy (remember that word in a previous chapter?) When God looks at the people who respond in faith and obedience to him, he sees the Savior, and he sees his perfection. That is a generous gift of sacrificial debt paying, and the Giver himself paid the debt.

When was the last time you were willing to be punished for another's crime and be tortured, ridiculed, and killed for it so that the guilty person could live, be forgiven, and declared good? Never. None of us would do it. Self-preservation, coupled with a sense of righteous indignation, dictates that we would be crazy to do this for anyone. Why? Because that criminal deserves what they've earned, we would say! It wouldn't seem fair, just, or even lawful for someone to be condemned in court, and then another perfectly law-abiding citizen is pulled from the audience and punished for that criminal's offenses. In today's courtrooms, such a meting out of justice to the perfect law-abiding citizen on behalf of the criminal would meet with a frenzy of new litigation and public backlash. One should always be punished for one's crimes. After all, isn't that fair in a civilized society? A just punishment should always fit the crime, whether large or small.

Each of us is tainted by a sinful will which simply cannot and will not choose to do the right thing every single time. Watch a toddler gaze around to see if anyone's looking, and instead of eating their allotted snack, or playing with their chosen toy, they'll reach out and grab it out of a younger child's hand. Ask the average person if they've ever told a little white lie on their mortgage application, or funneled a few questionable numbers to their accountant for processing their tax returns, and see if anyone will deny that they've just done this or that little thing maybe once or twice (and, hey, they didn't get caught, so what does it matter?) It matters. The propensity to do the wrong thing, at least some of the time, is in all of us. We would rather exercise our own will than obey another's if it is the path of least resistance. Mankind is not innately good; the sin seed is planted in all of us, whether one wishes to face it or not. Refusing to face that doesn't make the reality of it go away.

The irony is that each of us expects justice to be handed out to others, yet most of us will balk at it when it is meted out to us. When justice comes in our direction, we tend to raise the issue of "fairness," because our sinful state urges us to resist justice earned. We'd rather raise the fairness card and resist, deny, or weave grandiose excuses. The consequences are sometimes ugly. Each culture's sense of justice differs dramatically, and laws are based upon everything from tradition to a particular religion's definition of law and justice, to the whim of a dictator, and just about everything in between. It is subjective, fluid, and constantly evolving. Earthly justice is far from perfect, tainted by the very nature of those who define it.

Fortunately, the heart of God is gracious, good, merciful, and holy, and requires justice be given at all times and in all circumstances. Therefore, this broken world has to have

justice given on the issue of sin. The only way for God to deal
with our wayward hearts is to mete out justice. In his grace
and mercy, God chose from the beginning of time to provide
a promised person who would bear the punishment and
receive God's justice for an entire human history of infractions. A just God requires no less. And, remember, God does
not change, therefore his laws and his sense of justice do not
change, ever. From a perfect God comes perfect justice. The
necessary result of God's perfect justice is that from the very
beginning when sin entered this world through Adam and
Eve, God had to provide consequences.

Understanding God's Justice through Jesus Christ

God cannot be an author of sin; he only makes things
perfectly because he is holy. 1 John 1:5 tells us, "*God is light, and
in Him there is no darkness.*" Furthermore, James 1:13 declares:
"*Let no one say when he is tempted, 'I am being tempted by God, for
God cannot be tempted with evil, and he himself tempt*s no one.*"
Simply put, there is no sin in God; he is perfect. Adam and
Eve willfully chose sin, and that one fatal drop of poison
ruined the whole lot of us, much like the one bad grape I
always find in the refrigerator fruit drawer that quickly infects
the rest of the bunch, soon rotting and ruining the whole
bunch.

God requires consequences for bad behavior because he is a
God of justice always and forever. Someone had to pay the
price for exercising sin and ruining a perfect world. The first
consequences were that death entered the world. Beforehand,
God created a world where nothing died. Man did not even

eat meat, which would have required the slaying of an animal. Sin destroyed life that was meant to be eternal. Now, thanks to sin, our days are numbered. Entropy has set in, things break down and die, and nothing exists in a state of perfection any longer. Man's choices had grave consequences.

The key is that God chose to restore things, yet he must mete out justice because he is perfectly holy and just. Thus, there must be consequences commensurate with sin. But, because God is loving, gracious, forgiving, and patient, he desired to restore our relationship with him. That was wholly and completely his choice. Adam and Eve didn't desire restoration. Instead, they ran and hid like naughty kids who opened the forbidden cookie jar and ate as much as they could before getting caught. Their gut reaction was to take, run, hide, and play dumb. They weren't sorry; they were sorry they got caught.

Genesis 3:11-19 records for us the initial and eternal consequences of Adam and Eve's sin. God begins the dialogue after watching them run and hide in the garden after doing what they were told not to do (as if God couldn't see them!). God chats with them in parental fashion:

> (11) "....Have you eaten of the tree of which I commanded you not to eat?"
> (12) The man said, "The woman whom you gave to be with me, she gave me fruit of the tree, and I ate."
> (13) Then the Lord God said to the woman, "What is this that you have done?" The woman said, "The serpent deceived me, and I ate."
> (14) The Lord God said to the serpent, "Because you have done

this, cursed are you above all livestock and above all beasts of
the field; on your belly you shall go, and dust you shall eat all
the days of your life.
(15) I will put enmity between you and the woman, and
between your offspring and her offspring; he shall bruise your
head, and you shall bruise his heel."
(16) To the woman he said, I will surely multiply your pain in
childbearing; in pain you shall bring forth children. Your
desire shall be contrary to your husband, but he shall rule over
you."
(17) And to Adam he said, "Because you have listened to the
voice of your wife and have eaten of the tree of which I
commanded you, 'You shall not eat of it,' cursed is the ground
because of you; in pain you shall eat of it all the days of your
life;
(18) thorns and thistles it shall bring forth for you; and you
shall eat the plants of the field.
(19) By the sweat of your face you shall eat bread, till you
return to the ground, for out of it you were taken; for you are
dust, and to dust you shall return."

In Genesis 3:11-19 we see a holy and just God move into
action. A painless and perfect life given by God was poisoned
by people choosing to sin. This resulted in pain, humiliation,
back-breaking work, subjugation, and death. Why? Because
Adam and Eve broke a simple contract with a just and holy
God. Therefore, God had to respond accordingly. He had to
provide necessary consequences for the breaking of a
covenant. What loving parent wouldn't do that?

Genesis 3:15 provides a clue in human history that God's justice also works in tandem with other parts of his divine personality. Here is the verse: *I will put enmity between you (Satan/serpent) and the woman, and between your (Satan/serpent) offspring and her offspring; he (Satan) shall bruise your head, and you shall bruise his (Satan) heel.*" God proclaims at the inception of sin entering the world that he will be placing friction and conflict between mankind and Satan. God also says "*and you shall bruise his heel.*" Among Eve's offspring, far in the future, would arise one who would "*bruise the serpent's heel*" and conquer him. That person is Jesus Christ, God's promised Messiah. Only Jesus Christ, the future "*offspring*" of Eve and Adam, would be able to do that, but it would be many millennia in the future, at God's appointed time.

Sin entered the world through man's own heart and involved a specific, special tree. God would conquer sin in the world and restore and redeem man's heart, life, and soul via another tree, the cross, where the Messiah would ultimately be hung upon and crucified in first-century Rome, several millennia later. The Messiah, meaning "anointed one," would be God's own Son, born of a virgin (Mary), exactly as Scripture foretold in shockingly specific detail. From the Garden of Eden until the cross where Jesus Christ would be nailed to and crucified, God provided promise after promise and detail after detail of a specific person who would be a conqueror of sin and death.

God had to punish disobedience and sin. His justice requires it. I cannot emphasize this enough. Likewise, we must emphasize that God did not have to redeem and restore us. That was *his* choice. Why would he do this? He chose to do this because he is a loving, compassionate, patient, and gracious God who chooses to reconcile with us by providing the reconciler: The Messiah, Jesus Christ. God could have ended things right there in the Garden of Eden and proclaimed that mankind was a rotten idea. In his graciousness and love, he wanted to have a relationship with the only thing that he made in his image: people. He had to first provide earthly consequences for sin because his holiness and perfect justice required it. God sacrificially and selflessly chose to mete out justice for the sins of the entire world throughout all of human history upon his Son, Jesus Christ. God piled all of the rotten garbage of our sin on Christ's shoulders and stomped it out for good. Christ then declared in the last and final moments of his life, "*It is finished.*" *(John 19:30)*

I want to leave you with several verses in Old Testament Scripture, which God's people in the ancient world knew very well for several millennia. These verses of Scripture are God's promises of a Messiah would ultimately bring about justice for all, and conquer sin for good. Ponder over these, look them up, and read them in the context of the chapter in which they appear. These are reminders of God's justice:

- The Messiah would be the "*seed/offspring*" of a woman and would crush the head of Satan (Genesis 3:15).
- He would come from the "*seed/offspring*" of Abraham and would bless all the nations on earth (Genesis 12:3).
- He would be a "*prophet like Moses*" to whom God said we must listen (Deuteronomy 18:15).
- He would be born in "*Bethlehem of Judah*" (Micah 5:2).

- He would be *"born of a virgin"* (Isaiah 7:14).
- He would have a throne, a kingdom and a dynasty, or house, starting with King David, that *"shall be established forever"* (2 Samuel 7:16).
- He would be called *"Wonderful Counselor," "Mighty God," "Everlasting Father," "Prince of Peace,"* and would possess an everlasting kingdom (Isaiah 9:6-7).
- He would come *"to you; righteous and having salvation is he, humble and mounted on a donkey."* (Zechariah 9:9-10).
- He would be *"pierced for our transgression and crushed for our iniquities."* (Isaiah 53:5).
- He would *"die among the wicked ones but be buried with the rich"* (Isaiah 53:9).
- He would be *resurrected from the grave, "for God would not allow His Holy One to suffer decay"* (Psalm 16:10).
- He would *"come again from the clouds of heaven as the Son of Man"* (Daniel 7:13-14).
- He would be the *"Sun of Righteousness"* for all who revere Him and look for His coming again (Malachi 4:2).
- He is the One whom Israel will one day recognize as the *"One they pierced, causing bitter grief"* (Zechariah 12:10).

Though justice from God is perfect, planned, and carried out with precision, we do not always see this in manmade institutions or individuals in this life here on earth. Remember, this is a broken, sin-infused world. God will, at an appointed time, restore this world to its original perfection and make it even better. In the meantime, earthly institutions may not necessarily define, exercise, or bestow godly justice, as much as we'd like them to. When we find ourselves disappointed by a dearth of justice, it is imperative to remember that God the Just One is in charge. Remember, he is the "*Kaddash*," the Holy One, who is set apart and other than anything and anyone. His justice is perfectly timed and generously awarded to his children. When you see it, it sends shivers down your spine and makes you weep at the beauty of it, for it is a reflection of who God is.

We must be willing to receive his choice of justice when he gives it. Though we may have expectations of humble apologies from our adversaries, or generous restitution from those who have wronged us or robbed us of something, God may see justice differently and provide it accordingly. Awaiting it requires patience, trust, and peace in who he is. God gives us all justice now through Jesus Christ, who gave his life so that we can be declared just and acceptable by a perfect God and belong to him forever. This is mercy we have not earned; it is his choice to give it. Though people, organizations, governments, and even courts will not always dispense justice, we know that a justice-loving God will give it. If we know that God's perfection requires perfect justice, then we must do one thing only: wait patiently. He will give it, though his timing is quite different.

Moses understood God's justice, and he explains it this way in Deuteronomy 32:4, "*The Rock, his work is perfect, for all his ways are justice. A God of faithfulness and without iniquity, just and upright is he.*" God is a Rock, and he will stand firm and unshakeable and will give perfect justice to his people. If justice on this earth isn't offered, God will be faithful, and his perfect will and plans will obtain justice for us. Luke 18:7 adds some additional encouragement, "*And will not God give justice to his elect, who cry to him day and night? Will he delay long over them?"*

We must remember who is in charge of conquering our adversaries and meting out justice for us. Exodus 14:14 assures us that God will indeed wage battle and dispense justice on behalf of those who follow him, when he says:

"I will go out and fight for you. You have but to remain silent."

Study Questions:

1. What is the difference between God's justice and the world's idea of justice? Give specific examples.
2. Read through Genesis 3 and think about the interchange between the serpent and Eve. How is God's justice surprising? Specific? How does verse 15 encourage you that God immediately formulated a plan to crush Satan, the author of sin?
3. Read Isaiah 53. Where do you see God's justice will be meted out in the life of the foretold Messiah?
4. Explain in your own words why God had to carry out justice for mankind's sins upon His Messiah. Are you willing to share this with someone who does not yet know this good news?
5. Where in your life do you feel that God has—or hasn't—meted out justice for you? How can Exodus

14:14 and Deuteronomy 32:4 particularly encourage you in this?

6. How does God's attribute of holiness influence his justice? Give examples.

7. Do you remember a time when you did not wait for God's justice and you stepped ahead of him and tried to seize it yourself? Explain this and what the outcome was.

8. Review the list of God's Biblical promises of his Messiah, Jesus Christ. Which verse(s) impact you the most and why?

Additional Bible verses on God's justice

Do: *Discuss and ponder over these verses, and pray for God to illuminate each one. (For additional context, read the entire Biblical chapter in which each of these verses appears.)*

Isaiah 30:18 - *"Therefore the LORD longs to be gracious to you, and therefore He waits on high to have compassion on you For the LORD is a God of justice; How blessed are all those who long for Him."*

Psalm 89:13-14 - *"Powerful is your arm! Strong is your hand! Your right hand is lifted high in glorious strength. Righteousness and justice are the foundation of your throne."*

2 Thessalonians 1:6-8 - *"God is just: He will pay back trouble to those who trouble you and give relief to you who are troubled, and to us as well. This will happen when the Lord Jesus is revealed from heaven in blazing fire with his powerful angels. He will punish those who do not know God and do not obey the gospel of our Lord Jesus."*

Job 34:12 - *"Truly, God will not do wrong. The Almighty will not twist justice."*

Hebrews 6:10 - *"God is not unjust; he will not forget your work and the love you have shown him as you have helped his people and continue to help them."*

Psalm 146:7-9 - *"Who executes justice for the oppressed; Who gives food to the hungry The LORD sets the prisoners free. The LORD opens the eyes of the blind; The LORD raises up those who are bowed down; The LORD loves the righteous; The LORD protects the strangers; He supports the fatherless and the widow, But He thwarts the way of the wicked."*

Memory verses

1 John 1:9 - *If we confess our sins, he is faithful and just and will forgive us our sins and purify us from all unrighteousness.*

Deuteronomy 32:4 - *He is the Rock, his works are perfect, and all his ways are just. A faithful God who does no wrong, upright and just is he.*

Recommended reading:

Generous Justice; How God's Grace Makes Us Just, Timothy Keller, Penguin Random House LLC, New York, 2016

The Attributes of God, Volume 1, A. W. Tozer, Wing Spread Publishers, Camp Hill, PA, 2007

. . .

<u>Action Plan</u>: There are some areas where I need to pray for God's justice and to trust him:

1)

2)

3)

<u>Notes:</u>

Chapter Eleven

HE'S GOT THE POWER – GOD'S OMNIPOTENCE

Ephesians 3:20 *"Now all glory to God, who is able, through his mighty power at work within us, to accomplish infinitely more than we might ask or think."*

2 Corinthians 12:9a *"My grace is sufficient for you, for my power is made perfect in weakness."*

We have all heard the phrase, *"knowledge is power,"* yet few know who coined this phrase. It was an English philosopher, Sir Francis Bacon, who came up with this saying in the middle ages. Also, American President Thomas Jefferson used this phrase multiple times in various types of personal correspondence. We use this simplistic saying to explain why it appears that, for the most part, those who have "knowledge" have the power. That fuels our quest for as much education and knowledge as we can get—and give our children—and yet no one even thinks about what *knowledge* truly means, much less the concept of *power*.

King Solomon, in Proverbs 1:7, gives us an insight into what "knowledge" is. Let's start with that first. He says, *"The fear of the Lord is the beginning of knowledge."* So, we might deduce that, if we fear God, then we have begun to acquire knowledge, and that it starts with fearing and respecting someone who is infinitely more powerful, knowledgeable, and holy than ourselves. We frankly don't fear what or who we can easily understand and overpower. This is good because God *is* power and exercises a power that is so vast, limitless, and eternal, he is to be feared. That kind of power is called *omnipotence.*

The word, *omnipotent*, is the Latin word for *all-powerful* (*omni* means "all" and *potens* means "powerful"). This breadth and depth of power do not exist in man, beast, or within any physics professor's repertoire of various "forces" within the universe. You will never meet an omnipotent person, though you may find some who harbor delusional perceptions that they are all-powerful over someone or something. Omnipotence—all-powerfulness—is an attribute that only belongs to God. He is omnipotent, forever powerful, and in perfect tandem with this, he is all-knowledgeable (omniscient). His infinite and perfect knowledge is eternally and unchangeably in lock-step with his infinite and perfect power. That is innately who God is. He is the only all-powerful and almighty being who has and ever will exist. In comparison to God, no manmade idol, no person, and no force have any god-like power. Not even knowledge can empower the most brilliant of people to come nose-to-nose with God's omnipotence. Knowledge isn't power, I'm afraid. It's best to cast your lot in with King Solomon; he had it right.

God's power cannot be diminished to a puny concept of mere muscle. In this world, we often consider power and strength to be associated with human muscle and brute strength. It often works that way, though. The strongest arm wins the arm-wrestling match, the strongest general with the most powerful arsenal wins on the battlefield, and the physically strongest kid on the schoolyard usually wins the fight. God's omnipotence does not rely on flesh and blood or muscle and bone; his power is embodied in his very words. When God speaks, things get done, and he does it himself.

Finally, we often associate power with resources (currency, investments, real estate, and accumulations of inanimate objects such as art, rare vehicles, and pretty collections of things that have perceived value). While it is true that those who derive some type of power from knowledge and muscle can actually seize, purchase, or obtain resources, that is not omnipotence. It is merely expanded opportunity for choices and the ability to exercise those choices by trading or using those resources to satisfy one's motives. This will often enable someone to attribute power to themselves purely based upon accumulated resources and what one can do with them. This type of manmade power can also go further and extract resources from others, wielding an influence (positive or negative) by virtue of someone having more than someone else. But there is no innate force within the resource holder themself. It's simply a matter of *"He who has the most toys wins,"* as the saying goes. God's power has no basis in anything other than himself. He doesn't need anything to *be* powerful.

I began by addressing three things that we frequently associate with power: knowledge, muscle, and money. Now, let's throw all those things into the trash heap of earthly presumption, and we will move on to an unearthly power that deserves examination. Omnipotence is a whole other thing, and God is the only one who has it. Understanding omnipotence is getting to know God much, much better.

God's omnipotence in the creation of the universe (and everything within it)

God's omnipotence allows him the power to create a universe out of nothing, including everyone and everything within it, from the smallest sub-atomic particle to the furthest galaxy scientists have found so far. With his power to create anything and everything from nothing comes his absolute power to control everything. And, given that he is a good, loving, just, and merciful God, to name just a few of his attributes we've studied thus far, his omnipotence is only for good. His goodness fuels his loving control over every infinitesimal thing, including every person's mind, body, and soul. (We'll discuss this momentarily). This should be a relief to us, for a God with this kind of power would be utterly terrifying if he didn't temper his power with grace, goodness, love, mercy, and justice.

One need only read Genesis Chapter 1 to see what God does with his omnipotence: he creates everything by speaking, and his power brings it into existence:

> (1) In the beginning, God created the heavens and the earth.
> (2) The earth was without form and void, and darkness was over the face of the deep. And the Spirit of God was hovering over the face of the waters.
> (3) And God said, "Let there be light," and there was light.

(4) And God saw that the light was good. And God separated the light from the darkness.

(5) God called the light Day, and the darkness he called Night. And there was evening and there was morning, the first day.

(6) And God said, "Let there be an expanse in the midst of the waters, and let it separate the waters from the waters."

(7) And God made the expanse and separated the waters that were under the expanse from the waters that were above the expanse. And it was so.

(8) And God called the expanse Heaven. And there was evening and there was morning, the second day.

(9) And God said, "Let the waters under the heavens be gathered together into one place, and let the dry land appear." And it was so.

(10) God called the dry land Earth, and the waters that were gathered together he called Seas. And God saw that it was good.

(11) And God said, "Let the earth sprout vegetation, plants yielding seed, and fruit trees bearing fruit in which is their seed, each according to its kind, on the earth." And it was so.

(12) The earth brought forth vegetation, plants yielding seed according to their own kinds, and trees bearing fruit in which is their seed, each according to its kind. And God saw that it was good.

(13) And there was evening and there was morning, the third day.

(14) And God said, "Let there be lights in the expanse of the heavens to separate the day from the night. And let them be for signs and for seasons, and for days and years,

(15) and let them be lights in the expanse of the heavens to give light upon the earth." And it was so.

(16) And God made the two great lights—the greater light to rule the day and the lesser light to rule the night—and the stars.

(17) And God set them in the expanse of the heavens to give light on the earth,

18) to rule over the day and over the night, and to separate the light from the darkness. And God saw that it was good.

(19) And there was evening and there was morning, the fourth day.

(20) And God said, "Let the waters swarm with swarms of living creatures, and let birds fly above the earth across the expanse of the heavens."

(21) So God created the great sea creatures and every living creature that moves, with which the waters swarm, according to their kinds, and every winged bird according to its kind. And God saw that it was good.

(22) And God blessed them, saying, "Be fruitful and multiply and fill the waters in the seas, and let birds multiply on the earth."

(23) And there was evening and there was morning, the fifth day.

(24) And God said, "Let the earth bring forth living creatures according to their kinds—livestock and creeping things and beasts of the earth according to their kinds." And it was so.

(25) And God made the beasts of the earth according to their kinds and the livestock according to their kinds, and everything that creeps on the ground according to its kind. And God saw that it was good.

(26) Then God said, "Let us make man in our image, after our likeness. And let them have dominion over the fish of the sea and over the birds of the heavens and over the livestock and

over all the earth and over every creeping thing that creeps on the earth."

(27) So God created man in his own image, in the image of God he created him; male and female he created them.

(28) And God blessed them. And God said to them, "Be fruitful and multiply and fill the earth and subdue it, and have dominion over the fish of the sea and over the birds of the heavens and over every living thing that moves on the earth."

(29) And God said, "Behold, I have given you every plant yielding seed that is on the face of all the earth, and every tree with seed in its fruit. You shall have them for food.

(30) And to every beast of the earth and to every bird of the heavens and to everything that creeps on the earth, everything that has the breath of life, I have given every green plant for food." And it was so.

(31) And God saw everything that he had made, and behold, it was very good. And there was evening and there was morning, the sixth day.

What is the most repeated word you see from verse to verse? The word, *"said."* God's power is wielded by his very words; no muscle required. And what he says has such indescribable power, that he can form matter, forces—everything--out of nothing. That is omnipotence. What is the result of his power speaking creation into existence? God declares specifically and simply that it is *"good."* God's power is only used for good, every time, every day, and in everything he does. That is a type of power we don't possess. His omnipotence is not only supreme, but it is always good.

God's omnipotence as a Creator demonstrates a power that no one and nothing has, except God. Only he has control over the creation of life. Scientists may attempt to replicate a living cell in a Petrie dish within a lab somewhere deep in the bowels of a university or bio-research company, but God is the author of every atom, every molecule, and hence, every single thing in the universe. People merely take God's created matter and mold it and play with it, much like a child who pulls the play-dough out of a canister and tries to make something out of it, yet the dough has already been manufactured by someone else.

Even the nineteenth century-born inventor, Nikola Tesla, suspected that there was a common fundamental particle which all matter was formed out of. He wasn't far off with that suspicion; God has created the atom (proton, neutron, electron, boson, etc.), the basis of all matter. Though CERN, the European Council for Nuclear Research in Switzerland, spends day and night smashing atoms in its Large Hadron Collider to learn more about the sub-atomic particles within the atom, God has created those atoms and all of those particles. CERN merely plays a high-tech game of racquetball and smashes those atoms back and forth trying to break down what has already been made by God himself. Man, with his atomic colliders, only plays on the atomic ball court; he cannot create the atoms or particles himself.

Furthermore, words in the mouth of mankind may have the power to influence, cajole, and persuade, even to teach, yet they cannot create anything. God's very words create matter, space, and time, and a universe so vast that the strongest telescopes of the twenty-first century cannot find the end, the edge, or even any definite corner of the universe. A seemingly limitless expanse of creation filled with galaxies replete with billions of stars, planets, mysterious and little-understood black holes, pulsars, quasars, and other celestial matter, forces, and phenomena are beyond human comprehension. We like things neat and tidy in little boxes that we can understand. Vast distances of the space-time continuum are difficult to grasp, yet God has created them all. He does this using omnipotence that is outside of space and time. He created space and time itself, therefore he exists outside of that which he created.

God's power over the human soul

Let's examine things now in greater detail. We have discussed the power of God's spoken words bringing about creation in Genesis 1. Once he created these things, he did not simply declare it "*good*" and withdraw altogether with a hands-off disinterest. He chose his last and most important creation to be the one thing that was made in his "*image.*" He created man. All creation bears the divine imprint of God's hand, but Adam was special and was made to have dominion over all other created things. Next, in God's compassion and love, he chose to create a woman to complement Adam and be his helper, as well as procreate more people who were also made in God's image. We are their progeny, and what an amazingly complex creation of God we are!

David, in Psalm 139, muses over God's omnipotence, as well as God's omniscience and his omnipresence, all of which are intertwined. Psalm 139:13-16 provides us a glimpse into God's omnipotence in creation:

*(13) "For you formed my inward parts; you knitted me
together in my mother's womb.*
(14) I praise you, for I am fearfully and wonderfully made.
Wonderful are your works; my soul knows it very well.
*(15) My frame was not hidden from you, when I was being
made in secret, intricately woven in the depths of the earth.*
*(16) Your eyes saw my unformed substance; in your book were
written, every one of them, the days that were formed for me,
when as yet there was none of them."*

Also, in Zechariah 12:1 (Zechariah was one of the prophets of ancient Israel) God's creation of people's souls is addressed: *"Thus declares the Lord, who stretched out the heavens and founded the earth and formed the spirit of man within him..."* It is God alone who can create people and only God who can create and place a soul/spirit within each of us. No animal, plant, mountain, or river has a soul; they cannot make or discern moral issues. God chose to place a soul/spirit within the one thing that he created in his image: people. No branch of science, no philosopher, no king, no psychiatrist, and no machine can create a soul/spirit. God intentionally provided a soul within people so that we can have a relationship with him. No one can duplicate this kind of power.

God is loving and powerful, and he intentionally chose to create within people a soul that can discern moral issues in tandem with a mind that can think intellectually and creatively. God wanted people to have the capacity to discern his existence, to make moral choices of love and obedience, and to intelligently and spiritually respond back to him.

Matthew 22:37 states simply, *"...You shall love the Lord your God with all your heart and with all your soul and with all your mind."* It is as if God provided within each of us a unique keyhole, and God has the only key that will fit into that keyhole and open the door of our soul and our mind. No other thing can fit into that keyhole. Neither money, success, another deity, or the most beloved people in our lives can fit into that keyhole perfectly except the Creator.

Romans 1:20 describes God's power to create: *"For his invisible attributes, namely, his eternal power and divine nature, have been clearly perceived, ever since the creation of the world, in the things that have been made. So they are without excuse."* None of us have an excuse that we do not know there is one true god. He makes his presence and power in creation clear as a bell so that no one has any viable excuse for not sensing, seeing, and acknowledging his power behind all things. Our soul innately knows that he exists; our senses perceive that his hand is visible in creation. Our mind and intellect influence our will to choose whether we wish to acknowledge God or not.

God's power over the spiritual realm

The spiritual realm is as real as our three-dimensional world. It is a dimension or "principality" that hosts angels, demons, and Satan himself, yet those entities do sometimes appear in our dimension and can be seen, heard, and experienced. This is both good and bad. Some people are attracted to the spiritual realm as an arena within which they can wield power that they do not possess in this dimension. They open up windows of communication in the spiritual realm where there is a dark side—an abyss--that few truly understand.

Friedrich Nietzsche said, *"When you look into the abyss, it looks into you."* God has absolute power over that spiritual realm as much as he has absolute power over the visible creation that we live in. We must tread cautiously with things in this realm.

The historical Biblical record illustrates God's complete power over the spiritual realm. We can examine his power through the first-hand eye witness accounts of Jesus Christ conquering demons. Throughout the New Testament, where we see Jesus' power over demons and spirits that attempt to occupy and control people, we are seeing God's hand at work conquering the dark side of the spiritual realm. As an example, let's look at Matthew 8:28-34 and peer into God's hand wielding absolute power over demons:

(28) When He came to the other side into the country of the Gadarenes, two men who were demon-possessed met Him as they were coming out of the tombs. They were so extremely violent that no one could pass by that way.
(29) And they cried out, saying, "What business do we have with each other, Son of God? Have You come here to torment us before the time?"
(30) Now there was a herd of many swine feeding at a distance from them.
(31) The demons began to entreat Him, saying, "If You are going to cast us out, send us into the herd of swine."
(32) And He said to them, "Go!" And they came out and went into the swine, and the whole herd rushed down the steep bank into the sea and perished in the waters.
(33) The herdsmen ran away, and went to the city and

reported everything, including what had happened to
the demoniacs.
(34) And behold, the whole city came out to meet Jesus; and
when they saw Him, they implored Him to leave their region.

In this passage, God demonstrates complete authority and power over demons directly through his Son Jesus Christ by merely speaking to them. God exercises complete dominion over them and they know it; entities in the spiritual realm submit to him when he speaks. These demons know who God is and they fear him. Consequently, they bow to God's power and are relegated to occupying the bodies of a nearby herd of pigs, where God subsequently sends them over a cliff. Jesus openly and publicly intervenes in a spiritual battle and deals with it decisively. God's omnipotence wins every time over Satan's meager temporary power. It did then, and it does today.

I encourage you to explore further the multiple accounts of Jesus wielding God's absolute power over the dark side of the spiritual realm in these passages of the Bible:

- Matthew 12:22-32
- Mark 3:20-30
- Luke 11:14-26
- Mark 1:21-28
- Luke 4:31-37
- Matthew 4:1-11
- Mark 1:12-13
- Luke 4:1-13

It is vital to read these various historical Biblical accounts of the power that God wields over the spiritual realm through God the Son, Jesus Christ. They were witnessed by many, recorded, and remembered. These passages are instructive and demonstrate tangible and visible proof of God's omnipotence over the spiritual realm. These Biblical passages paint a clear picture of how God chooses to intervene in history and within the lives of individuals to demonstrate his power over sin, spiritual darkness, and evil.

God's omnipotence over events and history

God loves his people and will never let them be plucked from his hands. Jesus assures us in John 10:29, *"My Father, who has given them to me, is greater than all, and no one can snatch them out of the Father's hand."* God's power enables him to protect, provide for, and preserve his people against all odds, all enemies, and all circumstances. He is executing a particular plan from the foundation of the world, and no one and nothing can derail it. His omnipotence will not allow it.

We may make huge mistakes, miscalculations, and bad decisions, but these are overcome by God's perfect power and his will. Our choices are mere blips in the road to the full realization of God's perfect plans. No bad choice on our part can ever threaten God's power and ultimate plans for his people. God's omniscience and omnipresence work in perfect unison with his omnipotence. Man's selfish plans, the quest for power and significance, constant wielding of wars and conflicts, etc., cannot make even the smallest wave in the sea of God's vast power over history, events, and the lives of every individual.

In the Biblical record, God's power is compared to a solid and everlasting rock, a mighty hand and outstretched arm, a fortress, a strong shepherd, a healing power, a creating power, a providing power, just to name a few. Let's look at history and see how God's power in all of its facets displays itself in clear and definitive ways in his control of events, people, and outcomes. Throughout every single day of history, God's power is at work everywhere, in every circumstance, and within every person.

As an example, we will look at God's power in the life of Moses and the Exodus from Egypt.

God's power in the life of Moses and the Israelite Exodus from Egypt

The events surrounding the Biblical *exodus* (which means *departure*) of the enslaved ancient Israelites from Egypt began a decade or two earlier when a little three-month-old boy named Moses was placed in a basket and floated down the Nile. Soon thereafter, Pharaoh's daughter picked the basket up sometime between the twelfth and fifteenth century B.C. (scholars generally place this event within this 300-year time-frame based upon historical, archaeological, and Egyptological research). Chapters 1 – 4 of the Book of Exodus (written by Moses), records this.

During this timeframe of ancient Egyptian history, one of Egypt's pharaohs wasn't at all pleased that the Israelite population was growing quickly. He declared that any Israelite boy age three and under were to be slaughtered so that Egypt could maintain population control of this enslaved race. That is precisely why Moses' mother hid him at home for the initial three months of his life, and then she fashioned a nicely woven papyrus basket, covered it with tar and pitch to make it watertight, and laid her son into the basket. She placed the basket in the river with Moses' sister watching close by while it drifted down the Nile.

Pharaoh's daughter, upon finding the basket and the child, raised Moses in Pharaoh's house as her very own son. She inquired as to who the child's mother might be, found his birth mother, and she asked her to come to the palace and nurse the child until it was weaned. Moses was then raised among the ruling royalty of the most prosperous and advanced race at that time in the ancient world. Not bad for a kid who took a boat trip that not only saved his life, but it set the stage for his upbringing, and his unique future, all of which were in God's hands and part of God's specific plans.

The demonstration of God's power in this set of initial events of Moses' young life is in the form of protection, provision, and commissioning. God protected Moses from Pharaoh's edict that required slaying of Israelite boys under the age of three. Next, God ensured that Pharaoh's daughter would be standing at the Nile's shore at just the right time to pick up Moses out of the river. God intervened in the reign of Pharaoh and used it to further God's purposes at that time in history, which included using Moses' upbringing right in Pharaoh's palace. Also, God squelched any suspicions about who Moses truly was (an Israelite child, not an Egyptian). Naturally, it would have been of concern to Pharaoh and the members of his royal court that some unknown child was being raised, educated, and cared for right in the palace. They would have known that Pharaoh's daughter hadn't been pregnant nor delivered this child. This story shows that God is intensely specific in his orchestration of events. He is a distinct intervening force in cultural/economic/political circumstances, as well as individual human choices, so that he can weave the intricate tapestry of his perfect plans.

As Moses grows up in Pharaoh's palace, he begins to notice Egypt's abusive treatment of the enslaved Israelite population. He chooses to intervene in the mistreatment that an Egyptian perpetrates upon a Hebrew slave and reacts by killing the Egyptian. Acts 7:22-29 tells us that Moses was forty years old when he committed this murder. Pharaoh learns of this, and he seeks to have Moses killed for committing murder (it would appear that Moses, though raised in the palace, wasn't above the law). Moses fearfully flees the scene, and he embarks on a long, hot desert trip to the land of Midian (in the Sinai Peninsula). He is there for forty years. This is precisely what God had in mind; Moses had to grow up from being a brash, hot-headed young man to a much more mature man of eighty, who would be ready to listen, respond, and obey God. As we know, God had many significant plans for Moses.

While Moses remains in the land of Midian, he begins to visibly see God's powerful hand intervening in events in his life. Moses marries a Midianite woman, and as he tends his father-in-law's sheep, shocking things begin the happen. Look with me at Exodus 3, which is a detailed record of Moses' encounter with God:

(1) Now Moses was tending the flock of Jethro his father-in-

law, the priest of Midian, and he led the flock to the far side of the wilderness and came to Horeb, the mountain of God.

(2) There the angel of the Lord appeared to him in flames of fire from within a bush. Moses saw that though the bush was on fire it did not burn up.

(3) So Moses thought, "I will go over and see this strange sight —why the bush does not burn up."

(4) When the Lord saw that he had gone over to look, God called to him from within the bush, "Moses! Moses!" And Moses said, "Here I am."

(5) "Do not come any closer," God said. "Take off your sandals, for the place where you are standing is holy ground."

(6) Then he said, "I am the God of your father, the God of Abraham, the God of Isaac and the God of Jacob." At this, Moses hid his face, because he was afraid to look at God.

(7) The Lord said, "I have indeed seen the misery of my people in Egypt. I have heard them crying out because of their slave drivers, and I am concerned about their suffering.

(8) So I have come down to rescue them from the hand of the Egyptians and to bring them up out of that land into a good and spacious land, a land flowing with milk and honey—the home of the Canaanites, Hittites, Amorites, Perizzites, Hivites and Jebusites.

(9) And now the cry of the Israelites has reached me, and I have seen the way the Egyptians are oppressing them.

(10) So now, go. I am sending you to Pharaoh to bring my people the Israelites out of Egypt."

(11) But Moses said to God, "Who am I that I should go to Pharaoh and bring the Israelites out of Egypt?"

(12) And God said, "I will be with you. And this will be the sign to you that it is I who have sent you: When you have

brought the people out of Egypt, you will worship God on this mountain."

(13) Moses said to God, "Suppose I go to the Israelites and say to them, 'The God of your fathers has sent me to you,' and they ask me, 'What is his name?' Then what shall I tell them?"

(14) God said to Moses, "I am who I am. This is what you are to say to the Israelites: 'I am has sent me to you.'"

(15) God also said to Moses, "Say to the Israelites, 'The Lord, the God of your fathers—the God of Abraham, the God of Isaac and the God of Jacob—has sent me to you.' "This is my name forever, the name you shall call me from generation to generation.

(16) "Go, assemble the elders of Israel and say to them, 'The Lord, the God of your fathers—the God of Abraham, Isaac and Jacob—appeared to me and said: I have watched over you and have seen what has been done to you in Egypt.

(17) And I have promised to bring you up out of your misery in Egypt into the land of the Canaanites, Hittites, Amorites, Perizzites, Hivites and Jebusites—a land flowing with milk and honey.'

(18) "The elders of Israel will listen to you. Then you and the elders are to go to the king of Egypt and say to him, 'The Lord, the God of the Hebrews, has met with us. Let us take a three-day journey into the wilderness to offer sacrifices to the Lord our God.'

(19) But I know that the king of Egypt will not let you go unless a mighty hand compels him.

(20) So I will stretch out my hand and strike the Egyptians with all the wonders that I will perform among them. After that, he will let you go.

(21) "And I will make the Egyptians favorably disposed to-

ward this people, so that when you leave you will not go
empty-handed.
(22) Every woman is to ask her neighbor and any woman
living in her house for articles of silver and gold and for cloth-
ing, which you will put on your sons and daughters. And so
you will plunder the Egyptians."

In this highly detailed historical record, God is personally introducing himself to Moses for the very first time. Each verse bears reading several times, as you watch the conversation unfold. God intervenes in nature and sets afire a bush that continuously burns, yet does not burn up into ashes. This gets Moses' attention, which is precisely what God intended to do. Next, God calls Moses' name twice; he wants to be sure Moses hears him and stops in his tracks. Moses hears the voice and responds, *"Here I am."* They've mutually introduced themselves to each other now.

Next, God stipulates one rule before proceeding further (vs. 5 – 6):

(5) "'Do not come any closer,' God said. 'Take off your sandals,
for the place where you stand is holy ground.
(6) I am the God of your father, the God of Abraham, the God
of Isaac and the God of Jacob.' At this, Moses hides his face,
because he is afraid to look at God."

God's power and holiness infuse the ground with holiness so profound that Moses is asked to go shoeless in reverence and humility. And, God reminds Moses that he is the same God who Moses' ancestors followed, listened to, and obeyed. This is a gentle reminder of God's intervention in Moses' people's history and a foreshadow of more of this powerful intervention to come in Moses' own life.

Verses 7-9 record God's concern for the Israelites. He declares that he's watching, listening, and is ready for action, which will include Moses' help (though God certainly doesn't need it):

> (7) "The Lord said, 'I have indeed seen the misery of my people in Egypt. I have heard them crying out because of their slave drivers, and I am concerned about their suffering.
> (8) So I have come down to rescue them from the hand of the Egyptians and to bring them up out of that land into a good and spacious land, a land flowing with milk and honey—the home of the Canaanites, Hittites, Amorites, Perizzites, Hivites and Jebusites.
> (9) And now the cry of the Israelites has reached me, and I have seen the way the Egyptians are oppressing them."

God demonstrates that he is caring and compassionate, and he is ready to intervene after seeing his people's circumstances becoming difficult, oppressive, and miserable. He declares that he has a specific plan to rescue them and reveals where he is going to send them next. God finishes with a commissioning statement to Moses to get up and go, and that he is being sent to Pharaoh for a purpose (Exodus 3:10): "So now, go. I am sending you to Pharaoh to bring my people the Israelites out of Egypt."

In God's omniscience, he already knows what his plans are and how they'll unfold, and he begins the task—with Moses being asked to join him—of executing those plans for his people. Given God's power, he can easily make everything come to fruition in history simply by speaking (remember the creation, when God simply speaks things into existence?). At the same time, he is a relational God who wishes to include others in his plans and give them the satisfaction of being a part of them. He withholds his power which can make all things happen; instead, he tempers his power by including others in the execution of his plans.

What do we sometimes do when asked to tackle a difficult challenge? We step back, decline the opportunity, and let our inadequacies reign. This is precisely what Moses does in response to hearing what challenging plans God has for him to take part in. Exodus 3:11 records Moses' weak re*sponse: 'Who am I that I should go to Pharaoh and bring the Israelites out of Egypt?'"* We can see here that God includes Moses in his plans and Moses graciously declines and doesn't think he's up to the challenge. God is patient and compassionate and he knows people often lack confidence, especially when they are up against daunting odds. "God's response" in verse 12 is tender and encouraging: *"I will be with you. And this will be the sign to you that it is I who have sent you: When you have brought the people out of Egypt, you will worship God on this mountain."*

Still unconfident, Moses retorts weakly in Exodus 3:13: *"'Suppose I go to the Israelites and say to them, 'The God of your fathers has sent me to you,' and they ask me, 'What is his name?' Then who shall I tell them?"* God responds to Moses' unrelenting lack of confidence and reminds Moses who God is in Exodus *3:14 by saying, "I am who I am. This is what you are to say to the Israelites: I am has sent me to you."* In Exodus 3:15 God adds further clarification: *"Say to the Israelites, 'The Lord, the God of your fathers—the God of Abraham, the God of Isaac and the God of Jacob—has sent me to you. This is my name forever, the name you shall call me from generation to generation.'"* God doesn't give up on Moses's weakness. He patiently and gently reminds him that he *"will be with you,"* and that *"I am who I am."* This close and personal conversation between God and Moses is a portrait of who God eternally is: powerful, omniscient, loving, compassionate, and patient. Like Moses, we are often unsure, unbelieving, lacking initiative, and generally lazy to tackle intimidating challenges. Essentially, we mistrust God's omnipotence.

Next, God shares more of his plans and tells Moses to assemble Israelite elders and tell them God appeared to him and is aware of how badly Egypt has been treating the Israelites. Moses relates that God has promised to save them and take them somewhere to a very particular place of his choosing. God assures Moses that the elders will indeed listen to him. Moses is told that he needs to go see Pharaoh and announce that God has appeared and that the Israelites need to go and worship the Lord and offer sacrifices. In God's foreknowledge, he shares that he knows that Pharaoh will say *"no"* and won't ever say *"yes"* unless *"a mighty hand compels him*

(vs. 19)." Finally, God says that he will be exercising his power in intervening directly in Pharaoh's decisions: (20) *"So I will stretch out my hand and strike the Egyptians with all the wonders that I will perform among them. After that, he will let you go.*
(21) *And I will make the Egyptians favorably disposed*

toward this people so that when you leave you will not go
empty-handed."

After this initial commissioning of Moses' involvement in
God's plan for the Israelite's rescue from Egypt, Exodus 4 – 12
records and describes in detail the power of God's intervention in sending plagues upon Egypt. It also describes God
continuing to *"harden Pharaoh's heart"* until the final plague
that will kill all "first-born" in Egypt. Also, the Biblical record
details God changing Pharaoh's heart into submission, which
results in Pharaoh's final plea for the Israelites to please,
please leave and never come back. Each plague was symbolic
of God's power over the pantheon of Egyptian gods who were
believed to have power over various aspects of nature. This is
crucial for us to understand. Only the one true and real God,
the *"I am,"* has the power to control events, and peoples'
hearts, motives, and decisions, and bend them to his perfect
will. The historical Biblical records details that, after 430
years of enslavement in Egypt, God freed the Israelites and
led them into a new future.

As Egyptian soldiers pursued the fleeing Israelites across the
desert to the Red Sea (it is called *"Yam Suph,"* which means the
Red Sea or Reed Sea), the mighty outstretched arm of God,
working through Moses, literally parted the waters and
allowed a pathway for the fleeing Israelites to cross. And, as
the soldiers approached, God's hand wielded its power against
them. Moses' outstretched arm, filled with God's presence
and power, closed the Red Sea over the heads of the pursuing
Egyptian soldiers, horses, and chariots. The terrified Israelites
huddled together in at an encampment nearby where God
told them to wait silently. Exodus 14:14 records God's words

to Moses and his people: *"I will go out and fight for you; you have but to remain silent."* Namely, God has the power to handle the situation, so sit down, be still, and shut up!

Consider carefully this historical account of Moses and his close and communicative relationship with God, for he illustrates for all of us how very, very close and personal we can be with God, the powerful *"Yahweh/Jehovah," the great "I am."* Though incredibly powerful, God is amazingly gentle and personal, compassionate, and understanding, even when Moses demonstrates little trust and minimal confidence. God chooses to exercise his power through people just like Moses, you, and me. He prefers to engage with us, temper his power by working through us, and thereby connect with us. By doing so God openly demonstrates his character and draws us to himself.

God's power in the life of Jesus Christ

Let's move forward on the historical timeline now to the period of 1st century Rome. It was a powerful empire that began as a tiny village on the Tibor River in central Italy in the eighth century B.C. and became the greatest and most powerful empire of its time. At the apex of Rome's powerful empire a tiny baby was born to a humble Jewish couple, who we know as Mary and Joseph. This couple were the parents of *Yeshua* (ישוע) or Jesus.

There is no better place to begin seeing the power of God's hand in Jesus' life than during the events surrounding Jesus' conception and birth. We begin with a humble teenage Jewish woman, Mary (a descendent of King David, of the tribe of

Judah), who is visited by an angel by the name of Gabriel. We will explore Luke 1:26-56 and Matthew 1:18-25, as these passages descriptively and accurately record the story of Jesus' conception being initiated by God himself. Note that Matthew was an eyewitness of Jesus' life and his information is a primary source. Luke was not only a physician at the time of Christ in the 1st century A.D., but was a keen aggregator of eyewitness (primary source) information about Jesus, including that of Mary, Jesus' mother.

Luke 1:26-38 is our starting point:

> (26) "In the sixth month the angel Gabriel was sent from God to a city of Galilee named Nazareth,
> (27) to a virgin betrothed to a man whose name was Joseph, of the house of David. And the virgin's name was Mary.
> (28) And he came to her and said, 'Greetings, O favored one, the Lord is with you!'
> (29) But she was greatly troubled at the saying, and tried to discern what sort of greeting this might be.
> (30) And the angel said to her, 'Do not be afraid, Mary, for you have found favor with God.
> (31) And behold, you will conceive in your womb and bear a son, and you shall call his name Jesus.
> (32) He will be great and will be called the Son of the Most High. And the Lord God will give to him the throne of his father David,
> (33) and he will reign over the house of Jacob forever, and of his kingdom there will be no end.'
> (34) And Mary said to the angel, 'How will this be, since I am a virgin?'
> (35) And the angel answered her, 'The Holy Spirit will come

upon you, and the power of the Most High will overshadow you; therefore the child to be born will be called holy—the Son of God.

(36) And behold, your relative Elizabeth in her old age has also conceived a son, and this is the sixth month with her who was called barren.

(37) For nothing will be impossible with God.'

(38) And Mary said, 'Behold, I am the servant of the Lord; let it be to me according to your word.' And the angel departed from her."

Dissecting this detailed historical record, we see that God has the plan and the power to create a child within Mary, and he sends a messenger to Mary to tell her to expect this to occur. God even asserts his parental power and authority and names the child (vs. 31), as well as deems the child to be his own son (vs. 32). Jesus will be sitting on the throne of his ancestor, King David, and he will have a kingdom that will be eternal (vs. 33). This is no normal child. God's method, however, for bringing this all to fruition was a specific fulfillment of prophecy in the ancient historical records of Israel. Mary is a virgin (she is merely betrothed to marry Joseph at that time). The angel tells her that God will send his Holy Spirit, and he will (verse 35): *"come upon you, and the power of the Most High will overshadow you."* Much like God's imparting of holiness to the very bush and ground where Moses first met him, God imparts his innate holiness to his child. Why can God do all of this? Because, verse 37 tells us, *"For nothing will be impossible with God."*

God essentially intervenes in the upcoming marriage of Mary and Joseph and lays out his plans which will alter the couple's betrothal relationship greatly, as well as alter the course of their marriage, their child-raising, and the trajectory of Jesus' life forever. Mary will later bear the child in the town of Bethlehem (during the year of the Roman census) and that is where God's plans further unfold to fulfill very specific prophecy. The book of Micah (chapter 5, verse 2) foretells of the savior son of God being born in Bethlehem: *"But you, Bethlehem Ephrathah, though you are small among the clans of Judah, out of you will come for me one who will be ruler over Israel, whose origins are from of old, from ancient times."* (Micah was a prophet of ancient Israel who prophesied from approximately 737 to 696 B.C. and wrote the Book of Micah.) When Jesus was born in Bethlehem, this specifically fulfilled that prophecy of Micah from seven centuries prior.

On a personal note, I have mentioned in a previous chapter that God had intervened personally and tangibly in my own life and enabled me to have children against all medical odds and statistics. I know how life-changing such a circumstance can be. No one could have done this but God. And only he could have conceived his son within Mary's virgin womb. Omnipotence just works like that. It defies the odds, confounds logic, and supersedes human explanation. Amazingly, this virgin birth was foretold eight hundred years prior by the Prophet of ancient Israel, Isaiah, in Isaiah 7:14, *"Therefore the Lord himself will give you a sign: The virgin will be with child and will give birth to a son, and will call him Immanuel."* (The name *"Immanuel"* means "God with us.")

God has the power to control and fulfill prophecy; he is in control of space and time, events, choices, and circumstances. He orchestrates details in the lives of everyday people to fulfill prophecies at extremely specific times of his choosing. That is why the Bible warns severely against "false" prophecy, i.e. prophecies that do not happen. This is why it is imperative to get to know God. He has made it quite easy to know him through recorded history because he has stepped into history face to face to be sure we know him. When false leaders and false prophets appear throughout the millennia, including today, those who know the one true God will notice that other false "gods" tend to come and go and that their prophets portend events that never occur.

Throughout the life of Jesus, God's own Son, who is the promised *Messiah* (the word *Messiah* means savior/liberator) God intervenes in events, circumstances, and within people's individual lives to further his plans for his Son. The ultimate plan is God's fulfillment of his promises of a Savior who will reconcile people once and for all with God. And, as I have stated, God's plans—and his prophets' prophecies—always happen. Thus, to fulfill promises, God ensures that things do not happen until an *"appointed time,"* so that his plans can come to fruition when and how he wishes. This term, *appointed time,* appears over and over throughout the Old Testament and in the New Testament books of the Bible.

Read each of the following Bible verses; they illustrate God's omnipotent control of time, circumstances, and events:

- Genesis 18:14 – *"Is anything too hard for the Lord? At the appointed time I will return to you, about this time next year, and Sarah shall have a son."*
- Genesis 21:2 – *"So Sarah conceived and bore a son to*

Abraham in his old age, at the appointed time of which God had spoken of him."

- 2 Samuel 24:15 – *"So the Lord sent a pestilence on Israel from the morning until the appointed time. And there died of the people from Dan to Beersheba 70,000 men."*
- *Habakkuk 2:3 – "For still the vision awaits its appointed time; it hastens to the end—it will not lie. If it seems slow, wait for it; it will surely come; it will not delay."*
- Psalm 75:2 – *"When I select an appointed time, it is I who judge with equity."*
- *Psalm 102:13 – "You will arise and have pity on Zion; it is the time to favor her; the appointed time has come."*
- 1 Corinthians 7:29 – *"This is what I mean, brothers: the appointed time has grown very short. From now on, let those who have wives live as though they had none"*
- Mark 1:14-15 – *"Now after John was arrested, Jesus came into Galilee, proclaiming the gospel of God, and saying, 'the time is fulfilled, and the kingdom of God is at hand, repent and believe in the gospel.'"*

Throughout recorded history, God exercises his omnipotent governance of time by orchestrating events, circumstances, and people to adhere to the *appointed time* for his son Jesus' final fulfillment of God's promises. Beginning at age thirty, Jesus engaged in a poignant and powerful ministry of teaching, healing, the performance of miracles, and of sharing of God's plan, which we call "The Gospel" (the good news), of God's redeeming, reconciling, and saving of mankind from sin. We have already established the fact that sin separates us from God. He planned to offer up to the world a savior/liberator, a Messiah, who would be a once-and-for-all propitiation (offering) for people's sin. Mankind was promised this from the very beginning. This promise, described in specific detail, is throughout the Old Testament books, from Genesis to Malachi, spanning several millennia. Every Jew of the ancient world knew the Messiah was coming and why. The question was always when he would come.

In 30 A.D Jesus traveled throughout the region of Jerusalem, including parts of Samaria, Jordan, Perea, and Capernaum, along with his disciples, and shared the good news about God's plan of saving people from their sin. Jesus shocked both the Jewish priests and the general public by stating that he was the foretold Messiah. Even more controversial was Jesus' declaration that "*I and the Father are one.*" *(John 10:30)* This infuriated the Jewish priests, for they considered such a proclamation to be blasphemous and untrue. This could not have been further from the truth.

John 10:24-39 sheds light on this interplay between well-educated priests (who knew ancient scripture's prophecies of a Messiah) and Jesus:

> (24) "The Jews who were there gathered around him, saying, 'How long will you keep us in suspense? If you are the Messiah, tell us plainly.'
> (25) Jesus answered, 'I did tell you, but you do not believe. The works I do in my Father's name testify about me,
> (26) but you do not believe because you are not my sheep.
> (27) My sheep listen to my voice; I know them, and they follow me.
> (28) I give them eternal life, and they shall never perish; no one will snatch them out of my hand.

(29) My Father, who has given them to me, is greater than all; no one can snatch them out of my Father's hand.

(30) I and the Father are one.'

(31) Again his Jewish opponents picked up stones to stone him,

(32) but Jesus said to them, 'I have shown you many good works from the Father. For which of these do you stone me?'

(33) 'We are not stoning you for any good work,' they replied, 'but for blasphemy, because you, a mere man, claim to be God.'

(34) Jesus answered them, 'Is it not written in your Law, 'I have said you are 'gods'?

(35) If he called them 'gods,' to whom the word of God came—and Scripture cannot be set aside—

(36) what about the one whom the Father set apart as his very own and sent into the world? Why then do you accuse me of blasphemy because I said, 'I am God's Son'?

(37) Do not believe me unless I do the works of my Father.

(38) But if I do them, even though you do not believe me, believe the works, that you may know and understand that the Father is in me, and I in the Father.'

(39) Again they tried to seize him, but he escaped their grasp."

The book of John records Jesus' conversation with his disciples. He encourages them—and us—with the truth of who he is: He is God the Son. Jesus wields God's power, fulfills his plans, and works in perfect unison with him:

(1) "Do not let your hearts be troubled. You believe in God; believe also in me.

(2) My Father's house has many rooms; if that were not so, would I have told you that I am going there to prepare a place for you?

(3) And if I go and prepare a place for you, I will come back and take you to be with me that you also may be where I am.

(4) You know the way to the place where I am going.'

(5) Thomas said to him, 'Lord, we don't know where you are going, so how can we know the way?'

(6) Jesus answered, 'I am the way and the truth and the life. No one comes to the Father except through me.

(7) If you really know me, you will know my Father as well. From now on, you do know him and have seen him.'

(8) Philip said, 'Lord, show us the Father and that will be enough for us.'

(9) Jesus answered: 'Don't you know me, Philip, even after I have been among you such a long time? Anyone who has seen me has seen the Father. How can you say, 'Show us the Father'?

(10) Don't you believe that I am in the Father, and that the Father is in me? The words I say to you I do not speak on my own authority. Rather, it is the Father, living in me, who is doing his work.

(11) Believe me when I say that I am in the Father and the Father is in me; or at least believe on the evidence of the works themselves.

(12) Very truly I tell you, whoever believes in me will do the

works I have been doing, and they will do even greater things
than these, because I am going to the Father.
(13) And I will do whatever you ask in my name, so that the
Father may be glorified in the Son.
(14) You may ask me for anything in my name, and I will do
it.'"

My purpose in taking you through this significant Biblical overview of Christ's entry into history's stage is that a Messiah was foretold and promised for several millennia. This is a recorded fact. When he arrived on the scene and declared, taught, and proved who he was, the result was resistance, outrage, and fear on the part of the Romans and of the Jewish priests. This stirred up a firestorm of doubt, fear, and indignation. God's power in directing human circumstances and events infused Christ's life and ministry and simultaneously held at bey the enraged motives of those with the power and influence in society to indict and condemn Jesus to death much earlier.

The Book of John, particularly in chapters 16-18, descriptively records a sequence of events that lead to Jesus' indictment, condemnation, and execution, via the Roman cross. These events could easily have occurred much earlier, within the previous three years of Jesus' public ministry, for he was incessantly followed by angry religious leaders who were livid at Jesus' proclamation that he was the Messiah. They did not want to believe it, despite irrefutable miracles, demonstrated dominion over demons, illness, and disease, and Jesus' indisputable teaching. They desired to indict and condemn Jesus many times, yet God thwarted their plans until the pre-appointed time, *"the hour,"* which Jesus and God both knew. God's omnipotence, as always, brings all of his plans to fruition in his way and in his timing.

Questions to Ponder

Why do we want to know, trust, and have a relationship with such a powerful God? Doesn't he, by his own power, take things into his own hands? He doesn't really need people at all, does he? No. This is a god who desires people to know him and trust his power and plans. This is a god who, though not needing a relationship with us, wants it anyway. He wants heaven to be full of people who love him, who desire a relationship with him, who obey him, and who trust him. God's house will not be filled with strangers who do not know him, do not love him, and do not trust him. Would you want people like that in your own home?

Residing in God's presence in heaven is an eternal gift. This life on earth is surprisingly short; it is important to ponder what happens afterward. In our hearts and minds we all sense —and know--that there is indeed something "next." God wants you to respond to him and gives an open invitation for everyone to do so. But he isn't surprised when some choose to reject him and go their own way. His omniscience informs him beforehand of who will and won't want a relationship with him. He doesn't use muscle to coerce his beloved sheep to come into his sheepfold.

You may ask, *"Why did he need a son? Couldn't he get everything done, as an omnipotent God can, all by himself?"* Some struggle with this and resist the idea that Jesus is God's son, the fore-told Messiah, and a savior promised. God's power is infused in his triune (three-part) being: God the Father, God the Son, and God the Holy Spirit. All are a part of him; he is all. He works out his perfect plans through all three parts of himself. God the Son humbled himself to enter human history in a flesh and bone body so that he could conquer sin and death, which plagues us all. He executed the planned role of a servant savior who would liberate people from sin. God the Father promised him, appointed his time to enter the world's stage to teach and prove who he was, and then God the Son completed and fulfilled the mission of dying in our place as a perfect sacrifice in our stead. What God promises he delivers.

God the Father, God the Son, and God the Holy Spirit all work in perfect and powerful unison, yet all are distinct. They work in perfect synergy and absolute agreement to create, to plan, and to execute their perfect will with omnipotence, wisdom, and righteousness. God the Father, Jesus (God the Son), and God the Holy Spirit all work together as a perfect symphony of omnipotence and harmony. That's why the job gets done once and for all of conquering man's sin on the cross. Someone had to do it; God decided it would be him.

John 15:13 sums things up perfectly: *"Greater love has no one than this, that someone lay down his life for his friends."* That *"someone"* is God.

Making it Real

The omnipotence of God is a profound subject. No other manmade god has any power, for they are all part of human imagination and manufacturing, much like a stone idol or an idealized higher being that only exists within our mind. Yet, if we have a relationship with God, how can we share this with others? We have his power within us if we belong to him, and it ought to be obvious and visible to others. We start by knowing who he is, what he has done, what promises he keeps, and what he has done and is currently doing in our lives. People are going to want you to show them, tell them, and describe to them what experiences you have had with God's power in your life if you profess to belong to him.

I have provided a great deal of Scripture for you in this chapter, for the omnipotence of God is a massive character attribute to describe. His power works in perfect synergy with all other character traits that he has. The entire Biblical record is a synergetic, holy and God-inspired compilation and record of experiences, conversations, narratives, histories, poetry, wisdom, prophecies (100% of which come true), gospels, and epistles (letters) that shed consistent light on God's power and how it is wielded for good. Helping others to understand a God who is this powerful requires pointing people to Biblical Scripture. Simply put, the Bible is a record of who God is.

Compile your own experiences where you have seen God's power working in your life. What you have experienced of his power is an irrefutable testimony to others. It is your story of him working directly and visibly in your own life. Your story is uniquely yours, for God's plans for you are uniquely part of his overall plans. Be open, willing, and prepared to explain how his power, purpose, and work in your life has changed you. Build something like *"stones of remembrance"* as many did in ancient times to remind themselves and declare publicly what

God had done for them. This can be in the form of a prayer journal, a poem, a memoir, a picture or painting, even a "shadow box," which is filled with various small items that are reminders of times, circumstances, and things that reflect God's hand personally working in your life. As an example, over thirty years ago, I kept a detailed prayer journal, and as prayers were answered I checked them off as a reminder that God had chosen to answer that prayer. I pulled out that journal recently, thirty years later, and I was shocked to see how many prayers had been answered. It was sobering and awe-inspiring.

People are hungry for the one true God; being one's own god has grown wearisome and disappointing for many. When speaking to those of other faiths, be confident in proclaiming to them that God keeps his promises—always. Point them to the Bible, using some of the passages which I have provided throughout this book. The God of the Bible leads his people to a very different destination than other manmade gods. This must be made very clear. God's way is to heaven; heaven is his home and the road there is narrow with few who walk upon it. There are no other gods who live there except Jehovah. Other *gods'* ways are the wide road to eternal separation from the one true God. It is a risky business to travel the wide road. Matthew 7:13-14 states it plainly: *"Enter by the narrow gate. For the gate is wide and the way is easy that leads to destructions, and those who enter by it are many. For the gate is narrow and the way is hard that leads to life, and those who find it are few."*

Share the truth even if it elicits other's indignation, resistance, or disinterest. The truth is plainly stated in John 14:6-7, *"Jesus answered, 'I am the way and the truth and the life. No one comes to the Father except through me. If you really know me, you will know my Father as well. From now on, you do know him and have seen him.'"* A life that rests upon this profound knowledge that there is only one door through which we pass to enter into a relationship with God is a life that should look very different than the world. That door is Jesus Christ, God's promised Savior. There is no other, I'm afraid. Choosing another door to God is choosing another God altogether.

Given the gravity of knowing God and the consequences of rejecting him, it is important to get to know God and to share him with others in all spheres of our life. The implications of someone not knowing God are extremely serious. We can play an integral part in sharing God's plan of redemption, reconciliation, and salvation from sin and death by sharing what we know of God to others. He commissions us to "*Go out and make disciples of all nations,*" (Matthew 28:19, ESV), and be an active part of his plans. This involves sharing our story of God's power, how he is working in our own lives, as well as the lives of many who have preceded us. Going out into our everyday lives, modeling God's character attributes to others, telling those around us about who he is, what he has done, and what his plan of redemption is, should be the foundation of our daily lives, like the very air that we breathe.

But, the first issue at hand is to know just how powerful God is. He is the Creator who has the power to speak and a universe is created. He is a God to be feared, yet a God who desires your love. He is a God who creates, then offers life as a personal gift to you, so that you can get to know him. He is a God who is deeply involved in the large-scale issues as well as the minutia of life. He is a God who wants a close and personal relationship.

1 Corinthians 1:18 says, *"The message of the cross is foolish to those who are headed for destruction! But we who are being saved know it is the very power of God."*

* * *

Study Questions

1. Read *2 Corinthians 12:9a*. What does this tell you about God's power? Does it make you feel uncomfortable being weak, and letting someone else be strong for you?

2. How do earthly concepts of power differ from God's omnipotence?

3. How does Psalm 139:13-16 give you an insight into God's personal and creative power? How does this passage encourage you as you see God's hand weaving life one person at a time?

4. God's power exhibited in the life of Moses has many facets. Describe areas of God's power in Moses' life that are awe-inspiring to you and why.

5. How is God's power visibly manifested through Jesus Christ, His Son? (There are many answers to this question. Read Luke 1:26-56 and Matthew 1:18-25 for insight.) Does this help you to see that Jesus is God?

6. What ways does God's omnipotence manifest itself in Genesis 1?

7. What have you learned about God's power over the human soul?

8. What new things have you learned about God's power over the spiritual realm (look up some—or all —of these verses below)?

Matthew 12:22-32

Mark 3:20-30

Luke 11:14-26

Mark 1:21-28

Luke 4:31-37

Matthew 4:1-11

Mark 1:12-13

Luke 4:1-13

9. God has power over time itself. What new things have you learned about this? How does his power over time encourage you in being patient and trusting in him?

Additional Bible verses on God's omnipotence

Do: *Discuss and ponder over these verses, and pray for God to illuminate each one. (For additional context, read the entire Biblical chapter in which each of these verses appear.)*

2 Peter 1:3 - *"By his divine power, God has given us everything we need for living a godly life. We have received all of this by coming to know him, the one who called us to himself by means of his marvelous glory and excellence."*

Colossians 1:16 - *"For by him all things were created, in heaven and on earth, visible and invisible, whether thrones or dominions or rulers or authorities—all things were created through him and for him."*

Psalm 147:5 - *"Great is our Lord, and of great power: his understanding is infinite."*

Hebrews 1:3 - *"The Son radiates God's own glory and expresses the very character of God, and he sustains everything by the mighty power of his command."*

1 Corinthians 1:18 - *"The message of the cross is foolish to those who are headed for destructions! But we who are being saved know it is the very power of God."*

Ephesians 4:6 - *"...one God and Father of all, who is over all and through all and in all"*

Jeremiah 10:12-13 - *"But God made the earth by his power, and he preserves it by his wisdom. With his own understanding, he stretched out the heavens. When he speaks in the thunder, the heavens roar with rain. He causes the clouds to rise over the earth. He sends the lightning with the rain and releases the wind from his storehouses."*

Memory verses

2 Corinthians 12:9a - *"My grace is sufficient for you, for my power is made perfect in weakness."*

Ephesians 4:6 - *"...one God and Father of all, who is over all and through all and in all."*

Recommended reading:

As Kingfishers Catch Fire: A Conversation on the Ways of God, Eugene H. Peterson, 2017, Alive Literary Agency, Colorado Springs.

The Power of Knowing God: A 6-Week, No-Homework Bible Study, Kay Arthur, 2012, WaterBrook Press, Colorado Springs.

. . .

<u>Action Plan</u> - These are some areas where I need to lean more on God's power, not my own:

1)

2)

3)

Notes:

Chapter Twelve

GIFTS FROM THE HEART – GOD'S GENEROSITY AND GOODNESS

1 Timothy 6:17 *"Instruct those who are rich in this present world not to be conceited or to fix their hope on the uncertainty of riches, but on God, who richly supplies us with all things to enjoy."*

Ephesians 1:3 *"Blessed be the God and Father of our Lord Jesus Christ, who has blessed us with every spiritual blessing in the heavenly places in Christ."*

In our journey thus far, we have identified in history, within the lives of real people, and in the historical Biblical record that God has a rich and multi-faceted character. We have learned unequivocally that he is a loving Shepherd, a gracious Creator, and an omnipotent champion for his people. In light of this, it is no surprise that he is a generous and good God. This shouldn't surprise us. I merge these two traits, generosity and goodness, for they are inextricably interrelated. His goodness fuels his generous heart, and his desire to give to the world forgiveness, reconciliation, and a relationship, things that none of us deserves, belies his profoundly unconditional goodness.

In this world, we admire generosity, philanthropy, and gift-giving. We have expectations of others' generosity on certain occasions and holidays; it is an assumption and an expectation that we somehow deserve it, or at very least the occasion warrants it. Generosity and goodness warm the heart of both the giver and the receiver. Yet, goodness and generosity are not innate to mankind. Though we may feel a surge of goodness and generosity on a given day, it is fleeting at best. It is selfish and expectant of something in return at its worst.

This is not the type of generosity and goodness that emanates from God. Let's explore this further.

God's selfless and self-sacrificing generosity

Let's now examine some elements of God's unique kind of generosity as it is revealed in the Biblical record. First, God reveals much about his selfless and big-hearted generosity in John 3:16: *"For God so loved the world, that he gave his only Son, that whoever believes in him should not perish but have everlasting life."* There are few in this world who have not heard of this defining verse about God's love, sacrificial generosity, and promise. Because God loves this world full of sinful people, he literally sacrificed his own Son, an integral part of his triune (three-part) being, to pay the price for our sin. Additionally, God provided several millennia of promises and assurances that he would send this Savior at an appointed time, and he has completely fulfilled that promise. It is a historical fact; it happened. To sacrifice oneself for another and pay the penalty for their bad behavior is the ultimate gift. John 15:3 describes God's sacrificial generosity this way: *"Greater love has no one than this, that someone lay down his life for his friends."*

God's generosity is marked by who he is: good, compassionate, patient, forgiving, loving, faithful, merciful, etc. It is not based upon the recipient's merit, for no one has earned his generous sacrifice nor his provision of forgiveness, reconciliation, and an eternal togetherness with him after this short life on earth is over. It is indeed a gift that is freely offered to mankind, and one does not and cannot earn it. I cannot emphasize this enough. You see, what we, unfortunately, earn via our sinful state is a limited life on this earth, death, and separation from God.

Romans 6:23 promises us: *For the wages of sin is death, but the free gift of God is eternal life in Jesus Christ, our Lord."* Tough as it may seem, our sinful selves are unable to earn anything but separation from God and ultimately a limited life ending in death. This shouldn't come as a surprise. You cannot earn what is a gift; the gift is forgiveness, reconciliation, and eternal life that is bought and paid for by the sacrifice of Jesus Christ, God's own Son. God's generous heart offers it freely because God has paid for the gift himself.

Other gods--false gods--are never generous. They simply cannot be. They extract work, endless obligation, and crippling resources from their followers. A false god offers no self-sacrifice; they require things to be done by their followers for the selfish benefit of that false god, whatever and whomever it may be. The God of the Bible, the one true God, is the only

God of love, self-sacrifice, creation, omnipotence, omniscience, and generosity. Fabricated gods can only provide false hopes; they cannot give anything else other than what they are: false.

God's generosity is also profound when contrasted against our sinful state. His grace and love provide a fertile ground for the selfless generosity he gives us when we are deep in the mire of depravity, misbehavior, and selfishness. Romans 5:6-11 explains this:

> *(6) "For while we were still weak, at the right time Christ died for the ungodly.*
> *(7) For one will scarcely die for a righteous person—though perhaps for a good person one would dare even to die—*
> *(8) but God shows his love for us in that while we were still sinners, Christ died for us.*
> *(9) Since, therefore, we have now been justified by his blood, much more shall we be saved by him from the wrath of God.*
> *(10) For if while we were enemies we were reconciled to God by the death of his Son, much more, now that we are reconciled, shall we be saved by his life.*
> *(11) More than that, we also rejoice in God through our Lord Jesus Christ, through whom we have now received reconciliation."*

Let's break down this overview of God's generosity step by step. Verse 6 says, *"For while we were still weak, at the right time Christ died for the ungodly."* In our sinful state, weak and unable to rectify our separation from God, he bridged that gap for us by providing his promised Savior for *"the ungodly,"* at *"the right time,"* (i.e. a very particular time God had already specifically chosen). We did nothing to initiate or deserve this. Nothing.

Next, verse 7 and 8 says, *"For one will scarcely die for a righteous person—though perhaps for a good person one would dare even to die--but God shows his love for us in that while we were still sinners, Christ died for us."* This is a gentle reminder by the Apostle Paul that we rarely feel the desire to sacrifice ourselves for another, even if they're righteous or good. It's against our very nature to desire to do this, though some will choose to do this for a loved one.

Because of his goodness, God sacrificed the promised Savior for a sinful world. He did this because he is a God who desires to love the unlovable, to be generous to wayward children who deserve nothing, and he desires a relationship with us. Ultimately, God wishes to pay our debts for our sins, so that his heavenly home can be opened to those who receive his free gift of forgiveness, reconciliation, and salvation from sin. As if that weren't enough, God opens the front door of his heavenly home and welcomes us inside and gives us a new status. We become his sons and daughters. God is generous and hospitable; he wants people who love him to be with him, to belong to him, and to receive his inheritance.

Romans 5:9 explains what happens when we desire to respond to God (which is wholly through the power of his utterly irresistible grace) and willingly accept his free gift of eternal life: *"Since, therefore, we have now been justified by his blood, much more shall we be saved by him from the wrath of God."* By the sacrificially shed blood of Jesus Christ, God's Son, we have been declared righteous by Jesus' atoning death in our place. Because Christ was perfect (he is perfect because he is God), his self-sacrificing death for us is acceptable to himself. The debt of sin has been paid, and death and sin have been conquered. We who respond to God and accept his free gift of eternal life through Christ's sacrifice are spared God's judgment and wrath. Therefore, God generously declares those who accept Christ's sacrifice to be righteous and holy because they are clothed with Jesus' holiness and God sees us as such. Can any of us accomplish this on our own? No.

Finally, in Romans 5:10-11, we are assured that *"For if while we were enemies we were reconciled to God by the death of his Son, much more, now that we are reconciled, shall we be saved by his life. More than that, we also rejoice in God through our Lord Jesus Christ, through whom we have now received reconciliation."* While we were sinful and separated from God, he reached out first. He promised and provided a savior to conquer our sin and death. By doing this he reconciled us with himself. This is a generous act of shocking grace that is undergirded with love and forgiveness that is based upon nothing that we have done. God, in his goodness and generosity, has intentionally reached out into depraved, sinful human history his hand of reconciliation and selfless sacrifice. He does this out of innate goodness.

As we have established repeatedly in this study, we broke the bridge between us and God. He, the bridge-builder, has reconstructed it with blood and suffering of his own Son, and then beckoned us to walk across that bridge and simply receive his outstretched hand in faith and trust. He sends his Holy Spirit to do the work of pulling us to him; we in our sin can't even muster the desire to reach back. God says bluntly—

but kindly: *"You did not choose Me, but I chose you and appointed you that you should go and bear fruit, and that your fruit should remain, that whatever you ask the Father in My name He may give you."* (John 15:16)

What other "god" do you know of who would do this?

God's bountiful and plentiful generosity

All of us strive for as many resources as we can obtain, as much health as we can have, as much leisure as we can squeeze into our lives, and as much happiness as we can imagine. None of this defines bounty or plentiful generosity; it is our self-woven basket of expectations. Unfortunately, in our present culture, we admire those who have more stuff than they really need, have earned more than they did last year, have vacationed as often as time permits, and have retirement accounts bulging with exponentially growing numbers. These are merely our gifts to ourselves, a culture of independent and insatiable children who strive for the fountain of youth at great expense, endlessly desire closets full of toys, and can never, ever have enough. Like the bumper sticker says, *"He who has the most toys wins!"*

This doesn't sound like God's idea of generosity or bounty because it isn't. That is *our* sinful definition of generosity. Earthly generosity, deep down, is ultimately based upon pleasing the self. The god of the self is insatiable. When, in a given moment, we desire to do good or be generous, we inadvertently desire this in order to earn that warm and fuzzy feeling of personal joy in doing a generous act for another. At other times, we will do "good" out of obligation, temporary inclination, or guilt. This seems like an accusatory, judgmental, and harsh definition of our motives to be generous or good at any given time. Truth is often unpleasant and very, very hard to discern in ourselves. Without knowing God's type of unconditional goodness and generosity, which is based upon who he innately is, we can only practice a counterfeit version it.

Let's examine this against the backdrop of God's idea of bountiful, plentiful, and life-altering blessings. Luke 15:11-32 shows us a perfect example of God's undeserved bounty and plentiful generosity in things that are much more important than the everyday stuff of life. God's heart is a bottomless sea of infinite forgiveness, love, and provision, and we see this in the Biblical account of the prodigal son:

(11) "And he said, 'There was a man who had two sons.
(12) And the younger of them said to his father, 'Father, give me the share of property that is coming to me.' And he divided his property between them.'
(13) Not many days later, the younger son gathered all he had and took a journey into a far country, and there he squandered his property in reckless living.
(14) And when he had spent everything, a severe famine arose in that country, and he began to be in need.
(15) So he went and hired himself out to one of the citizens of that country, who sent him into his fields to feed pigs.
(16) And he was longing to be fed with the pods that the pigs ate, and no one gave him anything.
(17) But when he came to himself, he said, 'How many of my father's hired servants have more than enough bread, but I perish here with hunger!

(18) I will arise and go to my father, and I will say to him,
"Father, I have sinned against heaven and before you.
(19) I am no longer worthy to be called your son. Treat me as
one of your hired servants.'
(20) And he arose and came to his father. But while he was
still a long way off, his father saw him and felt compassion,
and ran and embraced him and kissed him.
(21) And the son said to him, 'Father, I have sinned against
heaven and before you. I am no longer worthy to be called
your son.'
(22) But the father said to his servants, 'Bring quickly the best
robe, and put it on him, and put a ring on his hand, and shoes
on his feet.
(23) And bring the fattened calf and kill it, and let us eat and
celebrate.
(24) For this my son was dead, and is alive again; he was lost,
and is found.' And they began to celebrate.'
(25) Now his older son was in the field, and as he came and
drew near to the house, he heard music and dancing.
(26) And he called one of the servants and asked what these
things meant.
(27) And he said to him, 'Your brother has come, and your
father has killed the fattened calf, because he has received him
back safe and sound.'
(28) But he was angry and refused to go in. His father came
out and entreated him,
(29) but he answered his father, 'Look, these many years I
have served you, and I never disobeyed your command, yet
you never gave me a young goat, that I might celebrate with
my friends.
(30) But when this son of yours came, who has devoured your
property with prostitutes, you killed the fattened calf for him!'

(31) And he said to him, 'Son, you are always with me, and all that is mine is yours.

(32) It was fitting to celebrate and be glad, for this your brother was dead, and is alive; he was lost, and is found.'"

In polite conversation, folks often refer to the "prodigal son" as a cliché' rather than a powerful illustrative story that Jesus Christ used to describe God's bountiful generosity in providing undeserved forgiveness. Jesus directed this *parable* (a story about a common subject that teaches a moral lesson) at the Pharisees (Jewish high priests), who were outraged at Jesus fraternizing with tax collectors and prostitutes, the lowest echelon of sinners in polite 1st-century society. Many, many millennia of law-based righteousness coupled with a pagan world with a pantheon of gods to serve, please, and endlessly work for, had stratified society. One's public "goodness" and adherence to religious laws had established many echelons of those who were "good" and acceptable and those who were not. Jesus tore through that manmade veil of who is acceptable and who isn't. On a larger scale, the story is directed at all of us then and now, and it is as an analogy of people's sin and God's incredible goodness, love, and grace that is freely offered and wholly undeserved.[1]

In this parable, Jesus wants each of us to know that we are all prodigal sons, whether we realize it or not. Strangely, we tend to relate to the other self-righteous brother who thinks he has done everything right. The reality is, we are all lost and wayward sons and daughters, and our loving heavenly Father is a generous god in extending boundless forgiveness, love, and reconciliation to us. Moreover, he is a father who finds us in our lost state and provides us the things we truly need, not the things we necessarily want. What we need is to be found, saved, and freed from deadness in sin and to be made alive in Christ, so that we can have a relationship with God and spend an eternity with him.

God does all the seeking and finding of his people, and then offers the reconciliation and forgiveness, because he is a good Father who wishes to demonstrate his profound generosity. He does this irrespective of who we are, what family we were born into, what we do for a living, or what socio-economic level we are in. He seeks out those who he knows are his sons and daughters (because he is omniscient, and he knows who will respond to him), and he finds each and every one of them. When he finds us, it is a life-altering relief.

* * *

Lost and Found

I know what it feels like to be lost, and then to be found. Almost fifty years ago, while I was in second grade, my school took us to a very large park for a field trip. After several hours, I noticed that the park was strangely empty and none of my schoolmates were anywhere to be found. I ran from one end of that park to the other and then began shaking with fear and realization that I had been forgotten and left behind. I ran outside the boundaries of the play equipment and onto the adjacent street, because, to my horror, I saw the school bus taking off without me. I screamed at the top of my lungs and ran after that bus like an Olympic sprinter, but to no avail. A mother and her daughter on bicycles were approaching me and saw what was happening, grabbed me lovingly and gently, and kept me from running any further in the middle of the street. They calmed me and asked me what school the bus was from, which, thankfully, I knew. They looked up where the school was in the Yellow Pages and proceeded to get me back to the campus within the hour. Once back on the familiar school grounds, a teacher leaned over a nearby walkway rail and said, "I'm so glad you were found. Bless your heart!"

The feeling of utter relief, gratefulness, and joy at being found and brought back to the loving arms of my little school and to my parents was something that has remained deep within my heart for decades. I often feel that same deep level of unspeakable gratitude and joy that my God found me once long ago in a lost and sinful state, rescued me, and saved me from separation from him. Better yet, I am astounded and grateful that he declared me to be his adopted daughter forever. It is with repentance, remorse, and sadness that I sometimes catch myself taking this for granted. The elation at being lost and then found by God himself can sometimes be muddied by a life filled with too many things, too much busyness, and lists of self-made goals that I keep swimming upstream to reach.

Recognizing the type of generosity and goodness that God exercises toward me makes my inadvertent pursuit of earthly stuff appear absurd. We can choose to swim in a shallow pond of our own making, or we can dive deep into God's bottomless ocean of bountiful love and grace already pre-prepared for us, and bask in reconciliation, self-sacrifice, forgiveness, and an eternal relationship with him. His bountiful basket of blessings is comprised of things we can never manufacture, earn, or find ourselves on this earth. Those are gifts that are solely his to give. As Ephesians 1:3 reminds us: *'Blessed be the God and Father of our Lord Jesus Christ, who has blessed us with every spiritual blessing in the heavenly places in Christ."*

God is Jehovah Jireh: "The Lord Will Provide"

We all like our needs to be met, especially basic needs like food, water, and shelter. When we don't see that being satisfied, it is human nature to step up and do something, as well as whine, worry, and be resentful of those who we perceive are supposed to be providing for our needs. Worse, we look at others and tend to see what they have that we do not. The road of comparison often leads to frustration, resentment, discontentment, and envy. All of this becomes a vicious circle that is nearly impossible to extricate oneself from.[2]

But what if we were to let God define our needs? Philippians 4:19 assures us that, *"My God will supply every need of yours according to his riches in glory in Christ Jesus."* The key is that God supplies what he perceives and knows are our true needs. We get into trouble when we turn our wants into must-haves. God has riches to give us through the sacrificial work of Jesus Christ that rescues our very souls from eternal separation from him. He knows that our most pressing needs are to be freed from the sin, to be forgiven, and to be declared righteous by the atoning work of Jesus Christ. It is a need that God knows each of us has, and he has done the work of fulfilling it. All we are expected to do is to respond to God the Holy Spirit opening up our heart to him so that he can breathe his will into us and we can respond in faith. That spiritual gift of faith, given to us by God, enables us to be made cognizant of our sin, induced to repent of it, and to lean solely and completely upon one thing: the finished one-time atoning and saving work of Jesus Christ upon the cross.

Sadly, though, we often prefer to be our own problem-solver, our own giver, and our own savior, and we are perfectly happy with that little arrangement. It's easier that way, we tell ourselves. We are fairly certain that we don't have to be accountable to anyone. Whatever we deem are our own personal needs, wants, and desires should be fulfilled, we secretly feel. As a result, we are eagerly ready to take things into our own hands. If we tend to be on the lazy side, then we simply designate someone else or some government or organizational entity to fulfill those needs we decide must be fulfilled. The result is that we desire closets full of inanimate things, mindless ease, endless entertainment, raving success, others' admiration, and limitless abundance because fairness requires that, if others have it and pursue it, then we should too. Yet, it has been declared to all humanity that God has eternal blessings so profound, we can scarcely imagine the implications. Sadly, we choose to turn our eyes to things other than God's riches.

In C. S. Lewis' book, *Weight of Glory*, he describes this battle between our own puny perceived needs and wants and what God generously desires for us:

> *"Our Lord finds our desires not too strong, but too weak. We are half-hearted creatures, fooling about with drink and sex and ambition when infinite joy is offered us, like an ignorant child who wants to go on making mud pies in a slum because he cannot imagine what is meant by the offer of a holiday at the sea. We are far too easily pleased."* [3]

What examples can we find of this strange conflict between the boundless and eternal provision of God and our own selfish focus on our perceived earthly needs? We can learn from others who have relentlessly chosen messy, worthless mud pies rather than waiting for God to provide them with things they couldn't possibly imagine.

Let's examine God's provision for the Israelites in the wilderness after being extricated from 400 years of enslavement in ancient Egypt. We will delve into the historical account of Exodus 15:22-25, a record of events which occurred after Moses initially liberated the Israelites from Egyptian slavery:

> *(22) "Then Moses made Israel set out from the Red Sea, and they went into the wilderness of Shur. They went three days in the wilderness and found no water.*
> *(23) When they came to Marah, they could not drink the water of Marah because it was bitter; therefore it was named Marah.*
> *(24) And the people grumbled against Moses, saying, 'What shall we drink?'*
> *(25) And he cried to the Lord, and the Lord showed him a log, and he threw it into the water, and the water became sweet."*

This portion of the historical record of God sending Moses to bring the Israelites out of Egypt focuses on the people's encounter with a very basic need: water. Previously, God had put numerous plagues upon Egypt before the Israelites very eyes, he rescued them from an oppressive and obstinate Pharaoh, he miraculously parted the Red Sea letting the Israelites safely cross it, and then he closed the water over the heads of the pursuing Egyptians. Now, at the first sign of one basic need not being met, i.e. water that is too bitter to consume, they *"grumble against Moses, saying, 'What shall we drink?'"* This is a mud pie moment. There are more to come in this Biblical passage.

Moving forward in the Book of Exodus to Chapter 16, we will see a mud pie moment regarding food, another basic need. This record is descriptive of what many of us do when faced with a perception that our needs are not being met. I will comment intermittently:

> *(1) "They set out from Elim, and all the congregation of the people of Israel came to the wilderness of Sin, which is between Elim and Sinai, on the fifteenth day of the second month after they had departed from the land of Egypt.*
> *(2) And the whole congregation of the people of Israel grumbled against Moses and Aaron in the wilderness,*
> *(3) and the people of Israel said to them, 'Would that we had died by the hand of the Lord in the land of Egypt, when we sat by the meat pots and ate bread to the full, for you have brought us out into this wilderness to kill this whole assembly with hunger.'"*

As we can see, two months and fifteen days after being rescued from Egyptian slavery, the people began to grumble again and were dreaming of "mud pies," a foolish desire to go back to Egypt where at least they could have Pharaoh provide food. Needless to say, God had a plan all along to provide food for the Israelites. Now, let's continue:

> *(4) "Then the Lord said to Moses, 'Behold, I am about to rain bread from heaven for you, and the people shall go out and gather a day's portion every day, that I may test them, whether they will walk in my law or not.*
>
> *(5) On the sixth day, when they prepare what they bring in, it will be twice as much as they gather daily.'*
>
> *(6) So Moses and Aaron said to all the people of Israel, 'At evening you shall know that it was the Lord who brought you out of the land of Egypt,*
>
> *(7) and in the morning you shall see the glory of the Lord because he has heard your grumbling against the Lord. For what are we, that you grumble against us?'*
>
> *(8) And Moses said, 'When the Lord gives you in the evening meat to eat and in the morning bread to the full, because the Lord has heard your grumbling that you grumble against him—what are we? Your grumbling is not against us but against the Lord.'"*

In this record, it is clear that God sees the needs, hears the concerns, and has had a plan all along to provide *"manna"* a sweet flake-like substance that God calls *"bread from heaven."* Moses sees past the difficult circumstances and knows God is a good giver and that he will provide for the Israelites. However, Moses warns about grumbling and whining that it is directly *"against the Lord."* He implies that grumbling against God belies mistrust, disbelief, and discontentment and that desiring to go back into slavery just to fill their bellies is grossly disrespectful, selfish, and worldly.

> *(9) "Then Moses said to Aaron, 'Say to the whole congregation of the people of Israel, 'Come near before the Lord, for he has heard your grumbling.'*
> *(10) And as soon as Aaron spoke to the whole congregation of the people of Israel, they looked toward the wilderness, and behold, the glory of the Lord appeared in the cloud.*
> *(11) And the Lord said to Moses,*
> *(12) 'I have heard the grumbling of the people of Israel. Say to them, at twilight you shall eat meat, and in the morning you shall be filled with bread. Then you shall know that I am the Lord your God.'"*

In verses 9 – 11, God responds to petulance, discontentment, and mistrust by reminding the Israelites that his own plans are for their good and that he has ears and can hear their ungrateful grumbling. This is followed by God choosing to appear "*in the cloud*" where he speaks to Moses specifically about the fact that he (God) sees, hears, and knows peoples' needs, and that he fills them day and night. He does this so that they will see and experience that he is "*the Lord your God,*" and trust that his plans and good gifts are better than Egyptian slavery.

Now, let's watch God deliver on what he promises.

> *(13) "In the evening quail came up and covered the camp, and in the morning dew lay around the camp.*

(14) And when the dew had gone up, there was on the face of the wilderness a fine, flake-like thing, fine as frost on the ground.
(15) When the people of Israel saw it, they said to one another, 'What is it?' For they did not know what it was. And Moses said to them, 'It is the bread that the Lord has given you to eat.
(16) This is what the Lord has commanded: 'Gather of it, each one of you, as much as he can eat. You shall each take an omer, according to the number of the persons that each of you has in his tent.'
(17) And the people of Israel did so. They gathered, some more, some less.
(18) But when they measured it with an omer, whoever gathered much had nothing left over, and whoever gathered little had no lack. Each of them gathered as much as he could eat.
(19) And Moses said to them, 'Let no one leave any of it over till the morning.'
(20) But they did not listen to Moses. Some left part of it till the morning, and it bred worms and stank. And Moses was angry with them.
(21) Morning by morning they gathered it, each as much as he could eat; but when the sun grew hot, it melted."

What we have here is God demonstrating that he knows their needs and that he has personally planned and visibly provided a daily provision for their sustenance: manna. However, the first thing the Israelites do is look at the manna and question what it is. Moses has to remind them that it is what God said he would be providing and to go forth from their tents and begin gathering it to eat (because it won't last overnight). Many still did not trust God's provision and gathered too much, such that they left it till morning uneaten. We can call this hoarding. This was a sign that they still did not trust God's provision. (Note: an "*omer*" is approximately 9.3 Cups or between 1.560 kg. to 1.770 kg.)

> *(22) "On the sixth day they gathered twice as much bread, two omers each. And when all the leaders of the congregation came and told Moses,*
> *(23) he said to them, 'This is what the Lord has commanded: 'Tomorrow is a day of solemn rest, a holy Sabbath to the Lord; bake what you will bake and boil what you will boil, and all that is left over lay aside to be kept till the morning.'*
> *(24) So they laid it aside till the morning, as Moses commanded them, and it did not stink, and there were no worms in it.*
> *(25) Moses said, 'Eat it today, for today is a Sabbath to the Lord; today you will not find it in the field.*
> *(26) Six days you shall gather it, but on the seventh day, which is a Sabbath, there will be none.'"*

In this set of verses, we see that God provides according to Sabbath law (no work on the seventh day) and allows his people to gather twice as much, so they don't have to gather the manna on the Sabbath and break their law which prohibited work on the Sabbath day. He did not allow the gatherings of manna on the sixth day of the week to spoil overnight. Also, he did not send from heaven any manna on the Sabbath day at all. This should have proven to the Israelites that they could trust God and that they should do as he asked. Well, not quite:

> (27) "On the seventh day some of the people went out to gather, but they found none.
> (28} And the Lord said to Moses, 'How long will you refuse to keep my commandments and my laws?
> (29) See! The Lord has given you the Sabbath; therefore on the sixth day he gives you bread for two days. Remain each of you in his place; let no one go out of his place on the seventh day.'
> (30) So the people rested on the seventh day.
> (31) Now the house of Israel called its name manna. It was like coriander seed, white, and the taste of it was like wafers made with honey.
> (32) Moses said, 'This is what the Lord has commanded: Let an omer of it be kept throughout your generations, so that they may see the bread with which I fed you in the wilderness, when I brought you out of the land of Egypt.'
> (33) And Moses said to Aaron, 'Take a jar, and put an omer of manna in it, and place it before the Lord to be kept throughout your generations.'
> (34) As the Lord commanded Moses, so Aaron placed it before the testimony to be kept.
> (35) The people of Israel ate the manna forty years, till they came to a habitable land. They ate the manna till they came to the border of the land of Canaan.
> (36) (An omer is the tenth part of an ephah.)"

Going through this highly descriptive historical narrative, you can see that it is human nature to be discontented, mistrusting, unsatisfied, and disbelieving that God is a good and generous provider. Like the ancient Israelites, we also can be reticent to believe that God's plans are always good. We define his goodness by circumstances and our expectations, not by who God is. It is our innate tendency to exercise impatience and set forth to provide for our own perceived wants and needs when God isn't performing up to our expectations and timing. This is, time and time again, what the Israelites did. That is why we, like the Israelites, are satisfied far more with the puny mud pies of our own plans, than the heavenly omnipotence and generosity of our good, generous, and perfect god.

It all really boils down to one thing: who God is. That issue is pivotal to the meaning of our day-to-day lives. It is the common thread throughout all twelve chapters of this book. It is the foundational truth linking all sixty-six books of the Bible. There is no other ancient writing that is a record of God and his creation, his introduction of himself into the lives of mankind, a record of his promises, his prophetic communications through chosen people, and his 100% guaranteed fulfillment of every single one of those promises and prophecies thus far.

There may be a wide variety of ancient writings that you have come across. Ancient cultures have produced some quite colorful and profound literary, historical, and poetic pieces of writing depicting highly descriptive esoteric, mythical, and legendary stories of some god (or gods), none of whom have ever existed. Mythology is the stuff of the human imagination and the need for the mind to make sense out of a complex world and fashion an answer of where we all came from, and why we are here.

The god of the Bible, *Yahweh*, is the only god there is, and the only entity who created this universe, you and me, and every living thing. He is the only God who visibly changes the human heart, mind, and soul. Throughout the millennia, God has made himself known, and he made sure that his people recorded what he said and did, what promises he made and subsequently fulfilled, and told them to pass it on to their progeny.

I have endeavored to introduce you to the God who is holy, omniscient, unchanging, omnipotent, just, merciful, gracious, forgiving, loving, faithful, patient, compassionate, and gener-ous. There is no other god like this. This is the only God who has personally introduced himself to mankind from the very beginning and began his creation as a once-perfect place for our enjoyment and a stage where we can forge a close and personal relationship with him.

This is a God who desires a relationship with people, for people are the only thing he chose to create in his image. This is a god who will not force himself upon us and demand a rela-tionship. He fixed what we have ruined, allowed his Son to pay the price for our sins, and he offers a free gift of eternal life with him when this short life is over. What he patiently expects is for some of us to respond.

Let us examine today the "mud pies" in our lives which we have created for ourselves and are satisfied with for now. Look intently at the journey you have made through the Biblical narrative we have covered in this book and the twelve distinct attributes of God's character that he has demonstrated to the world. Make an honest assessment of whether you truly see more clearly now who God is and what he has done for you personally. Ask yourself whether you prefer the mud pies or desire the life-changing generous gifts that God has reached out and extended to you. Remember, you cannot earn God's gifts of generous forgiveness and reconciliation nor his open door to eternal life with him forever. He has done all the leg work; he desires for you to respond to him and reach back with an open heart and accept his free gifts.

If you have already responded to and willingly accepted God's generous gift of forgiveness and reconciliation, it is a sure sign that he began the regenerative process of changes within your heart, your soul, your mind, and your life. If he had not done this, you could not have reached back in response. In the deadness of human depravity, none of us can reach back to him until he regenerates the heart. If he has done this in your own heart, embrace his goodness and model it to others. It is what God expects of us.

Making it real

If we know God, how do we model his generosity and his goodness? I have emphasized throughout this book that the perfect model for God's attributes is Jesus Christ. Why? Because he was God's own Son. Once we know God and his Son, and we respond to them in complete faith, God spends the rest of our lives making us like his Son, who radiates and reflects God's glory. All of God's attributes are embodied in Jesus; God wants us to be like him. This shouldn't surprise us, for any parent wishes for their child to be the very best they can become. God wants us to belong to him so that he can wash us up, fix the mess that we are, clothe us in new garments of righteousness that Jesus gives us (and which we can never manufacture or earn ourselves), and prepare us over our lifetimes to be with him in his heavenly home forever.

Let's see how we can begin to internalize, reflect, and practice that kind of godly generosity. Summarizing what we've covered in this chapter about God's profound generosity to a fallen world, we have seen how God's generosity is marked by patience, forgiveness, and self-sacrifice. Reflecting that in our own lives is difficult at best and impossible for most of us. God's Holy Spirit has to swoop into our hearts and regenerate us, otherwise, we will rarely desire to unconditionally and selflessly be good or generous others.

We are a culture of the self. The self is a demanding god to follow, for it requires constant feeding, incessant attention, and is jealous of any other gods that threaten it. In this state of being, there is no left-over generosity for anyone else. Thus, the first issue we all have to face is that God needs us to take our gaze off of ourselves and focus upon him, accept his free gift of eternal life, repent of what we are, and follow him. We have to deny our self, that sinful, petulant, and demanding child that wants love, attention, and a constant stream of earthly things to entertain and affirm it. God wants you and me to give that up and focus fully on him alone. He'll take care of the rest. Galatians 2:20 encourages us to see things this way: *"I have been crucified with Christ. It is no longer I who live, but Christ who lives in me. And the life I now live in the flesh I live by faith in the Son of God, who loved me and gave himself for me."*

Once we have given our faith, hope, and trust to him alone, then the generosity spigot will begin to be opened by God's Holy Spirit within our hearts. We will undergo a lifelong regeneration process, and we will begin to notice that changes are continuously taking place in our thoughts, desires, goals, and relationships and that they are changes not of our own making. We will begin to have eyes to see the needs of others and focus less on the self. Seeing those needs in others, the Holy Spirit knits within the hearts of God's followers new threads of generosity toward others and genuine concern for their struggles and needs. Old broken threads of self-absorption will be gently removed from the tapestry of our lives. As an assurance, 2 Corinthians 5:17 declares, *"Therefore, if anyone is in Christ, he is a new creation. The old has passed away; behold, the new has come."*

Patience, forgiveness, and self-sacrifice, all of which God has generously shown us and which Jesus equally modeled in his life, will begin being woven into the fabric of our new hearts. People will begin to see this, as our regenerated hearts put into practice the fresh new attributes that God breathes into our new selves. We literally become *"a new creation,"* with the old dying, because it must; it is unacceptable to God. As we retreat from focusing on the self and place our eyes on God, we will begin to see in ourselves a God-given desire to share our resources with others, rather than hoard them for ourselves. We will begin to develop a deeper level of generosity in all aspects of life. God desires us to exercise all of his spiritual gifts generously to others. He will instill in us a desire to be bountiful, openhearted, bighearted, and liberal in what we give to and do for others.

* * *

I'd like to share with you a young woman who illustrated generous self-sacrifice, patience, faith, and love, all at the expense of her safety, convenience, and comfort. Her name is Dee. She spent nine months in a local community-based Bible study which I have enjoyed attending in recent years. Dee was quiet, patiently listening to others' participation during our small group time. One day, all of us began to know who Dee really was, as she suddenly divulged that she had just returned from eleven years in the mission field, where she had lived a twelve-hour drive from the closest market, right smack in the middle of the "bush" in Zambia (and also Botswana). We all went home that day and looked on the map to see where Zambia and Botswana were located.

She had left the U.S. for Zambia eleven years prior with her husband and her three young children in tow, one of them who was a mere infant. Dee and her husband gave their lives to God and felt a strong calling to give up their lives in the United States and share God and his Son Jesus Christ with a small group of folks in the middle of the African bush. Upon their arrival, Dee's husband was immediately hit by a severe unexpected illness. Rather than turning around and just going home, they endured, they trusted God, and they stayed until her husband recovered. Next, they took their family on a long ride into the interior of Zambia in an isolated area far from any modern conveniences (and, as I mentioned, a twelve-hour drive from the nearest market).

There in the African "bush" Dee pulled together some hard-to-find ingredients and baked her mother's cinnamon bread recipe. Those ingredients came at a steep price. She fervently baked that cinnamon bread, cut it into pieces, and she shared it with the people in the village under a grass-topped hut-like structure with no walls called a "*chimbusu.*" Her husband talked candidly with the curious people there about a loving, generous, and gracious God who sacrificed his own Son for them, so they could be reconciled with God and know him personally, and have an opportunity to spend an eternity with him.

As people munched exuberantly on the strange-but-delicious cinnamon bread, Dee's family spent eleven years repeating this scenario over and over again. People were hungry for this God of the Bible and his savior Son, and they responded wholeheartedly. This missionary family's enormously generous self-sacrifice of comfort, health, safety, convenience, and sustenance modeled God so clearly to these isolated people--coupled with a generous helping of delicious cinnamon bread--that they brought many people to God's outstretched hand in faith and salvation.

I use Dee and her family as an example of God-honoring generosity, goodness, and self-sacrifice in obscurity, for their story is not known by many. They work under the radar, they have written no books logging their experiences, and they seek no reward or recognition. That is precisely why I wished to introduce you to Dee and her family, for they are a perfect example of living out the type of inconvenient, self-sacrific-ing, and god-like generosity that is life-changing to others. They radiated God's character to others; they displayed day in and day out a type of goodness and generosity that portrayed the very heart of God. They modeled Jesus in dusty obscurity, seeking no recognition and no self-aggrandizement. The people of Zambia were hungry for God—and often another piece of cinnamon bread! The local people embraced God's generous love when they were introduced to him through Dee's family.

Giving to others what is not convenient, what is costly to us personally, and offering it continuously to all, is the type of generosity that God exhibits to each and every one of us. His gift cost him everything; the gifts of reconciliation, salvation from sin, and eternal life were paid for by Jesus Christ. We are asked to simply respond in grateful acceptance and embrace God, much like these isolated people in the Zambian bush country did when Dee and her family sacrificed all they had to bring God to them and model him in their own lives.

Godly generosity is the gift that keeps on giving. God's gift of forgiveness, reconciliation, and eternal life with him is freely offered to us now. If you have not reached out to his outstretched hand, consider all you have learned about him. God wants you to reach back; he has opened his gift and placed it squarely on the table of history—and in the heart of every person--for you to see. All you need to do is reach out a hand in gratitude and faith in him and take the gift he has paid for dearly.

Psalm 34:8 encourages us to reach back to partake of God's good gifts:

"Oh, taste and see that the Lord is good! Blessed is the man who takes refuge in him!"

* * *

Study Questions

1. How is God's generosity inextricably tied to his goodness? Define his type of generosity and goodness and how it is often different from our own idea of what generosity and goodness look like.

2. Read John 3:16 and Romans 5:6-11. How has God demonstrated generosity to each of us in giving up his Son for us? How God's supreme self-sacrifice changed your life? How is his sacrifice different from the types of sacrifices that we make?

3. Luke 15:11-32 is a perfect example of God's undeserved bounty and plentiful generosity. Read this passage and explain why you think the father was more generous to the wayward/prodigal son than the one who appeared to have it all together? How is this story an analogy of God's generosity and forgiveness to us?

4. Read through this quote again from C. S. Lewis (from his book *Weight of Glory*):

> *"Our Lord finds our desires not too strong, but too weak. We are half-hearted creatures, fooling about with drink and sex and ambition when infinite joy is offered us, like an ignorant child who wants to go on making mud pies in a slum because he cannot imagine what is meant by the offer of a holiday at the sea. We are far too easily pleased."*

What do you see as some of the "mud pies" in your life which you occupy yourself with instead of focusing more upon God? (There is no right answer to this. Search your heart.)

5. Philippians 4:19 assures us that, *"My God will supply every need of yours according to his riches in glory in Christ Jesus."* We often think our needs are not being met by God and fall into discontentment, impatience, and unbelief. Why do you think this is the case? (Provide an example of this in your own life).

6. Review Exodus 16, the narrative of God's provision for the Israelites in the wilderness. How do you see the Israelites' behavior in your own life, i.e. discontentment, unbelief, whining, etc.?

7. How do you struggle with generosity to others? Do you equate this with not understanding God's own generosity in your own life?

8. David, in Psalm 34:8, says, *"Oh, taste and see that the Lord is good! Blessed is the man who takes refuge in him!"* What do you think it means to *"taste"* and to *"see"* that the Lord is *"good"*? Why do you think his goodness in this verse is tied to being *"blessed"* by taking *"refuge"* in God? In what areas of your life do need to take refuge in God?

Additional Bible verses on God's generosity and goodness

Do: Discuss and ponder over these verses, and pray for God to illuminate each one. (For additional context, read the entire Biblical chapter in which each of these verses appears.)

Jeremiah 29:11-12 - *"For I know the plans I have for you," declares the LORD, "plans to prosper you and not to harm you, plans to give you hope and a future. 12 Then you will call on me and come and pray to me, and I will listen to you."*

Romans 8:28 - *"And we know that in all things God works for the good of those who love him, who have been called according to his purpose."*

John 3:16 - *"For God so loved the world, that he gave his only Son, that whoever believes in him should not perish but have everlasting life."*

Psalm 145:7 - *"They shall eagerly utter the memory of Your abundant goodness and will shout joyfully of your righteousness."*

Nahum 1:7 - *"The Lord is good, a refuge in times of trouble. He cares for those who trust in him."*

Memory verses

Psalm 145:7 *"They shall eagerly utter the memory of Your abundant goodness and will shout joyfully of your righteousness."*

1 Timothy 6:17 *"Instruct those who are rich in this present world not to be conceited or to fix their hope on the uncertainty of riches, but on God, who richly supplies us with all things to enjoy."*

Recommended reading:

Weight of Glory, C. S. Lewis, HarperCollins, New York, 1976

A Thousand Gifts: A Dare to Live Fully Right Where You Are, Ann Vos Kamp, Zondervan, Grand Rapids, Michigan, 2010

. . .

<u>Action Plan</u> - These are some areas where I need to learn to see and taste God's generosity in my life and also exercise it with others.

1)

2)

3)

Notes:

EPILOGUE

In the twelve chapters of this book, you have engaged in a journey of getting to know the only God that there is. It is an awe-inspiring walk, and yet we have taken together a mere twelve steps in learning of his declared and demonstrated character attributes that have been revealed to us throughout history and within the lives of everyday people.

The Biblical record has descriptively and accurately recorded for us that God is gracious, compassionate, omniscient, loving, faithful, patient, forgiving, unchanging, holy, just, omnipotent, generous, and good. Because he is a loving and forgiving God, he chooses to initiate a relationship with us. He knocks on the door of our heart, and if we respond, he boldly comes in to clean house and prepare us to walk with him. When we come to love him, he initiates within us an insatiable desire to know him in a deeper way. And, knowing him in a deeper and more comprehensive way will make us love him all the more.

As we've seen in this study, he keeps his promises and is a God to be trusted. He is generous and loving and offers us a priceless gift that we can never earn: forgiveness, cleansing from sin and depravity, complete reconciliation, and eternal life with him after this short jaunt through our earthly life is over. How did he do this? He accomplished this through the finished work of Jesus Christ, his Son. God's promise was signed, sealed, and delivered. No other savior, false god, or person has done this for us. None will, and none can. Jesus declared: "*I am the way the truth and the life. No one comes to the Father except through me. If you really know me, you will know my Father as well.*" (John 14:6-7a)

We need to be reminded daily that God is sufficient for us in all things and in all circumstances. There is nothing and no one who can satisfy but him. Charles Spurgeon, in his sermon, "You are my portion, O Lord, Psalm 119:57," leaves us with a challenge to remember moment by moment who God is and to stand firmly with him:

"Look at your possessions, O believer, and compare your portion with the lot of your neighbors. Some of them have their portion in the field; they are rich, and their harvests yield them a golden increase; but what are the harvests compared with your God, who is the God of harvests?

What are the bursting granaries compared with Him, who is the Farmer, and feeds you with the bread of heaven? Some have their portion in the city; their wealth is abundant, and flows to them in constant streams, until they become a very reservoir of gold; but what is gold compared with your God?

You could not live on it; your spiritual life could not be sustained by it. Put it on a troubled conscience, and could it allay its pangs? Apply it to a hopeless heart, and see if it could stop a solitary groan, or give one grief the less?

But you have God, and in Him you have more than gold or riches ever could buy. Some have their portion in that which most men love—applause and fame; but ask yourself, isn't your God more to you than that?

What if a myriad of trumpets should sound your praise, would this prepare you to pass the Jordan, or cheer you in prospect of judgment? No, there are griefs in life which wealth cannot alleviate; and there is the deep need of a dying hour, for which no riches can provide.

But when you have God for your portion, you have more than all else put together. In Him every want is met, whether in life or in death. With God for your portion you are rich indeed, for He will supply your need, comfort your heart, assuage your grief, guide your steps, be with you in the dark valley, and then take you home, to enjoy Him as your portion forever..."[1]

"The Lord is my portion; I promise to keep your words." (Psalm 119:57)

Nicole Ann Mardian

NOTES

1. AN UNEXPECTED GIFT – GOD'S GRACE

1. "The Apostle Paul and His Times: Christian History Timeline." *Christian History | Learn the History of Christianity &*
   the Church, 1 July 1995, www.christianitytoday.com/history/issues/issue-47/apostle-paul-and-his-times-christian-history-timeline.html.
2. Tozer, A. and Fessenden, D. (1997). *The Attributes of God: A Journey into the Father's Heart.* Chicago, IL: Moody
   Bible Institute.
3. Fitzpatrick, E. and Thompson, J. (2011). *Give them Grace: Dazzling Your Kids with the Love of Jesus.* Wheaton, Ill.,
   Crossway.
4. Bonhoeffer, Dietrich. (1995). *The Cost of Discipleship*, Simon & Schuster Inc., New York, NY.
5. Spurgeon, C. (2017). *Morning & Evening.* Hendrickson Publishers, Inc.

2. SUNSETS AND SONGS – GOD'S COMPASSION

1. Craig, v. (2018). *The Revival that Changed a Century.* [online] CBN.com - The Christian Broadcasting Network.
   Available at: http://www1.cbn.com/churchandministry/the-revival-that-changed-a-century.
2. Bridges, J. (2010). *Respectable Sins.* Navpress Pub Group.
3. Ruffin, B. (2013). *Fanny Crosby.* Uhrichsville, Ohio: Barbour Pub.
4. "Strong's #07355 - Old Testament Hebrew Lexicon." *StudyLight.org*, www.studylight.org/lexicons/hebrew/07355.html.
5. Van Pelt, M. (2019). *The Old Testament God of Compassion and Mercy, Miles Van Pelt.* [online] Ligonier Ministries.

3. FORESIGHT IS 20-20 VISION – GOD'S OMNISCIENCE

1. Spurgeon, C. (2017). *Morning & Evening.* Hendrickson Publishers, Inc.

4. THE GREATEST GIFT OF ALL – GOD'S LOVE

1. Spurgeon, C. (2017). *Morning & Evening*. Hendrickson Publishers, Inc.
2. Lewis, C. S. (2017). *The Four Loves*. HarperCollins.

5. GREAT IS THY FAITHFULNESS – GOD'S FAITHFULNESS

1. ten Boom, C. (2006). *The Hiding Place,* Chosen Books, Grand Rapids, MI.

6. PATIENCE IS A VIRTUE – GOD'S PATIENCE

1. "Patience Definition and Meaning - Bible Dictionary." *Bible Study Tools,* www.biblestudytools.com/dictionary/patience/.
2. Spurgeon, C. (2017). *Morning & Evening*. Hendrickson Publishers, Inc.
3. (1987) Hudson Taylor, Men of Faith Series, Bethany House Publishers.
4. Bridges, J. (2010). *Respectable Sins*. Navpress Pub Group.

7. FORGIVE AND FORGET – GOD'S FORGIVENESS

1. Morris, H. (1989). *Twice Pardoned: An Ex-Con Talks to Parents and Teens.* Focus on the Family Publishing,
2. John Lane Testimony, April 19, 2018, https://www.youtube.com/watch?v=Khwo4BsWBF8
3. Elliot, E. (2015). *Through Gates of Splendor*. [United States]: Tyndale House Publishers, Inc.

9. BE HOLY, FOR I AM HOLY – GOD'S HOLINESS

1. Tozer, A. and Fessenden, D. (1997). *The Attributes of God: A Journey into the Father's Heart*. Chicago, IL: Moody Bible Institute.
2. Outline of Otto's concept of the numinous (based on The Idea of the Holy). Trans. John W. Harvey. Oxford: Oxford University Press, 1923; 2nd ed., 1950 [Das Heilige, 1

12. GIFTS FROM THE HEART – GOD'S GENEROSITY AND GOODNESS

1. "The Parable of the Prodigal Son." *Ligonier Ministries*, Sept. 2019, www.ligonier.org/learn/devotionals/parable-prodigal-son/.
2. Kruger, Melissa B. (2012) *The Envy of Eve: Finding Contentment in a Covetous World.* Christian Focus.
3. Lewis, C. S. (2013) *The Weight of Glory: A Collection of Lewis' Most Moving Addresses.* HarperCollins UK.

EPILOGUE

1. Spurgeon, C. (2017). *Morning & Evening.* Hendrickson Publishers, Inc.

Made in the USA
Coppell, TX
04 May 2023

16408277R00203